A SOCIAL HISTORY OF THE SEA ISLANDS

THE UNIVERSITY OF NORTH CAROLINA SOCIAL STUDY SERIES

UNDER THE GENERAL EDITORSHIP OF HOWARD W. ODUM. BOOKS MARKED WITH *
PUBLISHED IN COÖPERATION WITH THE INSTITUTE FOR RESEARCH IN SOCIAL SCIENCE

BECKWITH: *Black Roadways: A study of Folk Life in Jamaica* 3.00
BRANSON: *Country Life in America* 2.50
BRANSON: *Farm Life Abroad* 2.00
*BREARLEY: *Homicide in South Carolina* .... *In preparation*
*BROWN: *Public Poor Relief in North Carolina* 2.00
*BROWN: *State Highway System of North Carolina* .... *In preparation*
*BROWN: *State Movement in Railroad Development* 5.00
CARTER: *Social Theories of L. T. Hobhouse* 1.50
CROOK: *General Strike, The* 6.50
FLEMING: *Freedmen's Savings Bank, The* 2.00
*GREEN: *Constitutional Development in the South Atlantic States, 1776-1860* ..$4.00
GREEN: *Negro in Contemporary American Literature, The* 1.00
*GRISSOM: *Negro Sings a New Heaven, The* 3.00
HAR: *Social Laws* 4.00
*HEER: *Income and Wages in the South* 1.00
*HERRING: *History of the Textile Industry in the South* .... *In preparation*
*HERRING: *Welfare Work in Mill Villages* 5.00
HOBBS: *North Carolina: Economic and Social* 3.50
*JOHNSON: *Folk Culture on Saint Helena Island* 3.00
*JOHNSON: *John Henry: Tracking Down a Negro Legend* 2.00
*JOHNSON: *Social History of the Sea Islands* 3.00
JORDAN: *Children's Interest in Reading* 1.50
KNIGHT: *Among the Danes* 2.50
LOU: *Juvenile Courts in the United States* 3.00
*METFESSEL: *Phonophotography in Folk Music* 3.00
MILLER: *Town and Country* 2.00
*MITCHELL: *William Gregg: Factory Master of the Old South* 3.00
*MURCHISON: *King Cotton is Sick* 2.00
NORTH: *Social Differentiation* 2.50
ODUM: *Approach to Public Welfare and Social Work, An* 1.50
*ODUM (Ed.): *Southern Pioneers* 2.00
*ODUM and WILLARD: *Systems of Public Welfare* 2.00
*ODUM and JOHNSON: *Negro and His Songs, The* 3.00
*ODUM and JOHNSON: *Negro Workaday Songs* 3.00
POUND: *Law and Morals* 2.00
*PUCKETT: *Folk Beliefs of the Southern Negro* 5.00
*RHYNE: *Some Southern Cotton Mill Workers and Their Villages* 2.50
ROSS: *Roads to Social Peace* 1.50
SALE: *Tree Named John, The* 2.00
SCHWENNING (Ed.): *Management Problems* 2.00
SHERRILL: *Criminal Appeals in North Carolina* 3.00
*STEINER and BROWN: *North Carolina Chain Gang, The* 2.00
*VANCE: *Human Factors in Cotton Culture* 3.00
*WAGER: *County Government and Administration in North Carolina* 5.00
WALKER: *Social Work and Training of Social Workers* 2.00
WHITE: *Some Cycles of Cathay* 1.50
WILLEY: *Country Newspaper, The* 1.50
WINSTON: *Illiteracy in the United States* 3.50

The University of North Carolina Press, Chapel Hill, N. C.; The Baker and Taylor Co., New York; Oxford University Press, London; The Maruzen Company, Tokyo; Edward Evans & Sons, Ltd., Shanghai.

SPRING PLOWING

A SOCIAL HISTORY OF THE SEA ISLANDS

WITH SPECIAL REFERENCE TO ST. HELENA ISLAND,
SOUTH CAROLINA

BY

GUION GRIFFIS JOHNSON, Ph.D.
Research Associate
Institute for Research in Social Science
University of North Carolina

CHAPEL HILL
THE UNIVERSITY OF NORTH CAROLINA PRESS
1930

COPYRIGHT, 1930, BY
THE UNIVERSITY OF NORTH CAROLINA PRESS

FOR

ELIZABETH STEPHENS GRIFFIS

PREFACE

THIS STUDY of the social history of the Sea Islands of South Carolina and Georgia, and more particularly of St. Helena Island, South Carolina, is one of three volumes resulting from the coöperative research project concerning Negro culture on St. Helena Island made under the joint auspices of the Institute for Research in Social Science of the University of North Carolina and the Social Science Research Council. It was originally planned as a brief background study, but, in the search for data, so many valuable manuscript pieces were unearthed from dusty attics, strong-boxes, and long-forgotten chests that it was deemed advisable to lengthen the study into many pages. Later, the archives of the United States Treasury Department were opened for purposes of this research, and for the first time a complete picture of the Sea Islands during the Federal occupation throughout the Civil War has been made possible.

I have attempted to trace the history of one of the largest of the Sea Islands in its relation to the larger history of the coastal area of which it is inextricably a part. I have been concerned chiefly with cultural developments rather than with men and with politics, and I have always sought to discover the historical antecedents of life on St. Helena as it is today. I have brought this history to the close of the Reconstruction Period. The subsequent history of the Island—the struggle of the people to keep their land in the face of poverty, the destruction of their money crop by the coming of the boll weevil and the consequent economic re-adjustment, the prosperity of a few despite these handicaps, the broadening influence of Penn School on the lives of the people—is told in *Black Yeo-*

manry by T. J. Woofter, Jr. Other special aspects of the island culture, such as the Gullah dialect, folk songs, and folklore, are presented in the third volume, *Folk Culture on St. Helena Island*, by Guy B. Johnson.

In the preparation of this manuscript I have become greatly indebted to many persons. To name all of those who have assisted me in obtaining data or in putting me on the trail of old plantation records would make a long list. I am grateful to each of them. I am especially indebted to Mr. William Elliott, of Columbia, South Carolina, who has generously lent me all of his family papers bearing on the study and who has carefully gone over my manuscript; to Mr. A. S. Salley, Jr., secretary of the Historical Commission of South Carolina, who very kindly made the records in his office accessible for purposes of this study and who has made many valuable notations on my manuscript; to Miss Rossa B. Cooley and Miss Grace B. House, principals of Penn Normal, Industrial, and Agricultural School, of St. Helena Island, who have graciously facilitated the collection of data; to Professor J. G. de R. Hamilton and Professor R. D. W. Connor, of the History Department of the University of North Carolina, and Dr. Katharine Jocher, assistant director of the Institute for Research in Social Science, who have carefully read the manuscript; and to Dr. T. J. Woofter, Jr., director of the St. Helena project, who has sympathetically guided this study to its completion. I am also indebted to Mr. George Foster Peabody and the Corporation of Yaddo for a delightful summer at Triuna Island, on Lake George, where much of this manuscript was written.

June, 1930.   G. G. J.
Chapel Hill, North Carolina.

CONTENTS

PAGE

CHAPTER I
THE PRIZE OF THREE NATIONS............. 3
The Sea Islands—The Franco-Spanish contest—The Anglo-Spanish contest—The coming of the home-seeker—Types of settlers.

CHAPTER II
THE STAPLE CROPS 17
Naval stores and provision crops—Indigo culture—Introduction of sea-island cotton—Early method of cultivation.

CHAPTER III
THE LABORERS AND THE LAND............. 31
Pre-revolutionary slave trade—The slave market for St. Helena Island—Extent of slaveholding—Size of St. Helena plantations.

CHAPTER IV
SEA-ISLAND COTTON CULTURE............. 46
The planting routine—Beginning of experimental agriculture—Marsh mud and sea-island cotton—Rotation of crops—The agricultural lottery—The planter and his factor.

CHAPTER V
PLANTATION MANAGEMENT 74
The overseer—Organization of slave labor—The task system—Slave rations—Medical care of the slave—Infant welfare—Plantation profits and losses.

CHAPTER VI
THE PLANTERS 103
The home-seekers—Social classes—The "big house"—Early interest in education—Religion—Recreation.

CHAPTER VII

THE SLAVE COMMUNITY 124

The slave and the lash—Cultural development—Social classes—Slave marriages—Family life—Leisure time—Religion and education.

CHAPTER VIII

"CONTRABAND OF WAR" 154

The capture of Port Royal—The problem of the conquering army—The social experiment—Training for citizenship—The land sales—The Negro as a landowner.

CHAPTER IX

THE AFTERMATH 191

A St. Helena picture in 1865—Was freedom too easy?—The starving time—The Negro as a citizen.

BIBLIOGRAPHY 216

INDEX 229

ILLUSTRATIONS

SPRING PLOWING		*Frontispiece*
A TIDAL CREEK ON ST. HELENA ISLAND	*facing page*	24
HOPETON PLANTATION ON THE ALTAMAHA	*page*	63
BRINGING IN MARSH GRASS	*facing page*	84
THE "BIG HOUSE" ON COFFIN'S POINT PLANTATION, ST. HELENA ISLAND	*facing page*	108
A ST. HELENA ISLAND PRAISE HOUSE	*facing page*	148

A SOCIAL HISTORY OF
THE SEA ISLANDS

CHAPTER I

THE PRIZE OF THREE NATIONS

SAILING NORTHWARD in 1525 a hundred leagues from La Florida, Pedro de Quexos, pilot of Ayllon's two caravels, suddenly came upon a neck of land protruding abruptly seaward between two magnificent sounds. A closer examination showed the headland to be beautifully wooded with pines, cedars, and mighty live oaks gracefully festooned with funereal moss. Quexos thought that his saint, Elena, had certainly brought him good fortune in leading him to this garden spot on her day, and so in her honor he christened the projecting land in the name of Spain *Punta de Santa Elena,* and the broad river which bordered it Santa Elena. Today the point is the eastern projection of St. Helena Island, and Santa Elena River is now Port Royal Sound, but Ayllon's pilot gave the name which the English later applied to a sound, an island, and a parish.

THE SEA ISLANDS

St. Helena Island is one of the largest of the Sea Islands fringing the coast of South Carolina. It is fifteen miles in length and varies from three to five miles in width. Located practically midway by water between Charleston and Savannah, it is in the immediate vicinity of a natural harbor which was described by early explorers as one of the best on the entire Atlantic coast. Indeed, Jean Ribaut, commander of the first French expedition to Florida, pronounced it "one of the greatest and fayrest havens of the worlde" where "without danger all the shippes in the worlde myght be harbored."[1]

The coastal region of which St. Helena Island forms a part is, as Ribaut described it, "a country full of havens, rivers and islandes." Deep tidal rivers cut and divide the land into numerous islands of varying sizes, and the islands themselves are interlaced by broad tidal creeks. These facts recommended the region to the Spanish, French, and English as an ideal place for settlement, for as Robert Sandford, "Secretary and Chief Register for the Lords Proprietors of their County of Clarendon" in Carolina, said in 1666:

the whole Country is nothing else but severall Islands made by the various intervenings of Rivers and Creeks, yett are they firme good Lands (excepting what is Marsh) nor of soe smale a seize, but to continne many of them thousands of acres of rich habitable wood land, whose very bankes are washed by River or Creek, which besides the fertility adde such a comodiousnesse for portage as few Countryes are equally happy in.[2]

These geographic conditions have also made for the isolation of the region. The soil is a light sand which makes road building difficult. The numerous marshes have to be crossed by causeways and the rivers by long bridges. It requires, therefore, a considerable outlay of capital to provide modern transportation facilities for the Sea Islands. As a result, most of them are still without bridges and good roads; they have been left to develop as they might. Today, in going to St. Helena Island, one must cross three rivers and two islands before one at last

---

[1] Jeannette T. Connor (ed.), *Jean Ribaut, The Whole & True Discouerye of Terra Florida*, pp. 90-91.
[2] A. S. Salley, Jr. (ed.), *Narratives of Early Carolina*, p. 101.

arrives at his destination, for St. Helena is the buffer between two other islands and the Atlantic. Long bridges span these rivers now so that one may go all the way by automobile, but until 1927 one could cross Beaufort River, the largest of the three, only by means of a bateau which operated as a casual ferry between Beaufort and Ladies Island. But in the days when transportation was chiefly by water, these very rivers, which are now so difficult to span, were one of the chief assets of the region.

THE FRANCO-SPANISH CONTEST

The Spanish were the first to claim the St. Helena region both by exploration and by occupation. Spain, indeed, shows a record of one hundred and forty-two years of activity in this territory[3] before 1663 when King Charles II of England by letters patent included it in a grant to eight Lords Proprietors and delivered it to one hundred years of protested ownership before England finally gained a clear title to the region by the Treaty of 1763. In 1521 Francisco Gordillo and Pedro de Quexos, Spaniards, reconnoitered the South Atlantic seaboard, and after Quexos' expedition for Lucas Vasques de Ayllon in 1525, Santa Elena, as the Spanish came to call this section, was the most northern frontier of their Atlantic coastal region.

When Jean Ribaut explored this same region for Admiral de Coligny in 1562 and built Charlesfort on what is now Parris Island,[4] he called the vicinity Port Royal, the name which the English later adopted. Ribaut's fort

---
[3] Mary Ross, "The Spanish Settlement of Santa Elena (Port Royal) in 1578," *Georgia Historical Quarterly*, IX, 352.
[4] Parris Island lies across Beaufort River from St. Helena Island.

was the first Protestant settlement in North America and the first white settlement near St. Helena Island.[5]

In 1566 Pedro Menendez de Avilés, adelantado and captain-general of Florida and its provinces, erected the presidio San Filipe near the site of Charlesfort, which had been destroyed by Hernando Maurique de Rojas in 1564. Here Spain maintained a garrison for ten years, when the Indians burned the fort after having forced the Spanish to evacuate it.[6] In 1577, however, the Spanish erected Fort San Marcos, a larger and more substantial building, and about it there grew a town of more than sixty houses, for here Spain maintained a garrison and a mission until 1587 when Santa Elena was again abandoned.[7] The activities of the Spanish after the abandonment are not clear, but by 1655 missions had been reopened.

These missionary efforts were carried on first by Jesuits and later by Franciscans. Spain's frontier policy, unlike that of England, was based upon the mission.[8] At Santa Elena, just as at every other Spanish frontier in North and South America, missionaries, under the protection of a guard and a fort, sought to instruct the Indians in religion, agriculture, and the arts. They settled the barbarous tribes in a village adjacent to the mission-fort, instructed them in the faith, and attempted to teach them the ways of civilized life.

[5] For an account of Ribaut's activities at Port Royal see Connor, *Jean Ribaut*.
[6] For a description of the three forts built on Parris Island in the sixteenth century see A. S. Salley, Jr., "The Site of Charlesfort," in Connor, *Jean Ribaut*, pp. 113-124.
[7] For a comprehensive account of Spanish activities in Georgia and South Carolina, see Herbert E. Bolton, *Arredondo's Historical Proof of Spain's Title to Georgia: A Contribution to the History of One of the Spanish Borderlands*.
[8] H. E. Bolton, "The Mission as a Frontier Institution in the Spanish-American Colonies," *American Historical Review*, XXIII, 42-61.

THE ANGLO-SPANISH CONFLICT

When Captain William Hilton in 1663 explored the Carolina coast southward from Cape Fear under the auspices of a group of Barbadians, the Anglo-Spanish contest for Santa Elena began. Upon his arrival at Parris Island, Hilton found there a Spanish garrison from San Augustín, and he immediately withdrew to avoid capture.[9] Three years later when Robert Sandford explored this region he found signs of preparations for new buildings on Parris Island and "a faire wooden Crosse of the Spaniards erecčon" in the Plaza of the town. Sandford considered Santa Elena, or Port Royal, as he called the territory, the most favorable site for the settlement of a colony and recommended it highly to the Lords Proprietors of Carolina who sent him on the expedition.

Dr. Henry Woodward who went with Sandford remained with the cassique of Santa Elena who gave him "formall possession of the whole Country to hold as Tennant at Will of the right Hono^{ble} Lords Proprietors." But the English had to face twenty years of conflict before they could claim the possession of Santa Elena.[10] In this conflict Dr. Woodward played an important role, for his sojourn with the Indians and his subsequent capture by the Spaniards taught him not only the tongues of the natives, but the methods of the Spanish as well.[11]

---

[9] For the accounts of Hilton, Sandford, and Woodward in the Santa Elena, or Port Royal, territory, see Salley, *Narratives of Early Carolina*, pp. 31-57, 75-107; "Shaftesbury Papers," *South Carolina Historical Society Collections*, V, 18-28, 57-82.

[10] Bolton, *Arredondo's Historical Proof of Spain's Title to Georgia*, pp. 28-44.

[11] For a biography of Woodward see Joseph W. Barnwell, "Dr. Henry Woodward, The First English Settler in South Carolina and Some of His Descendants," *South Carolina Historical and Genealogical Magazine*, VIII, 29-41.

The impetus for the settlement of Carolina came from Barbados where there was a clamor for more and cheaper lands. Sir John Colleton, a Barbadian planter, interested seven other English noblemen[12] in the Carolina country, and they joined him in a petition to King Charles II for a grant of the region. In 1663 the King issued a charter to these eight Lords Proprietors for all the region from 36° to 31° north latitude and two years later he extended the boundaries north to 36° 30' and south to 29°.

Following Sandford's recommendation of Port Royal, the Proprietors chose this place as the site for the first settlement of their province.[13] In August, 1669, they sent from England three vessels under the command of Joseph West with about one hundred and fifty settlers. After many hardships and misfortunes, including the wreck of one ship at Barbados and of another at Nevis, the adventurers finally reached Port Royal in March, 1670. Here they learned that the Westoes, a war-like tribe of Indians, had scourged Santa Elena and the northward country as far as Kiawah (Ashley River). Fearful of planting in a region under such conditions, they examined the land and found on St. Helena Island "that the land was good land supplyed with many Peach trees and a competence of timber, a few figg trees and some cedar here and there and

[12] The Earl of Clarendon; the Duke of Albemarle; William, Lord Craven; John, Lord Berkeley; Anthony, Lord Ashley (later Earl of Shaftesbury); Sir George Carteret; Sir William Berkeley.

[13] An earlier settlement had been attempted in 1665 when a company "of adventurers for Carolina," organized at Barbados, located on the Cape Fear River, calling their settlement Charles Town. The settlers abandoned this region in 1667, some going to Albemarle settlement, some to Nansemond County, and some to Boston. See Edward McCrady, *The History of South Carolina Under the Proprietary Government, 1670-1719*, pp. 75-93; and *Colonial Records of North Carolina*, I, 148-151, 157-159, 177-208.

that there was a mile and a half of cleare land fitt and ready to plant."[14] The governor, William Sayle, sent, however, one of the vessels to Kiawah "to viewe that land soe much commended by the Caseeka" of that region. Those waiting at St. Helena soon received word that the land on the Ashley River was "more fit to plant in," and they at once took up anchor for that place, landing at "Albemarle Point," which was soon renamed Charles Town, the first high point on the western bank of the Ashley, where they settled.[15] A few weeks later Spain made this settlement legal by recognizing in the treaty of 1670 all English occupations then actually established.[16]

While Spain conceded Charles Town to England, she did not admit that Santa Elena was English territory. Accordingly, in 1686, the Spanish wiped out the colony of Scots which Lord Cardross had established at Port Royal two years earlier.[17] Coming in three galleys, the Spaniards, aided by a force of Indians, assaulted the Scotch colony of Stuart's Town "where there was not above 25 men in health to oppose them."[18] They burned the settlers' houses and "destroyed and carried away all that they had because (as the Span^{ds} pretended) they were settled

[14] Salley, *Narratives of Early Carolina*, p. 119.
[15] In 1672 another Charles Town (Charleston) was laid out on the east side of the Ashley and soon became the heart of the settlement.
[16] For the treaty see Chalmers, *A Collection of Treaties*, II, 35.
[17] Verner W. Crane, *The Southern Frontier, 1670-1732*, pp. 28-30; McCrady, *South Carolina Under the Proprietary Government*, pp. 195-196.
[18] "Edward Randolph to the Board of Trade," in Salley, *Narratives of Early Carolina*, p. 205. For a list of settlers see *ibid.*, p. 292. For an account of the attack see Bolton, *Arredondo's Historical Proof*, pp. 41-43; A. S. Salley, Jr., *Records in the British Public Record Office Relating to South Carolina, 1685-1690*; Crane, *The Southern Frontier*, p. 31; McCrady, *South Carolina Under the Proprietary Government*, pp. 216-217; "Introduction to the Report on General Oglethorpe's Expedition," in B. R. Carroll, *Historical Collections of South Carolina*, II, 350-351.

upon their land." The settlers, except several who were killed in action, escaped to Charles Town. Then the Spaniards proceeded to Edisto Island where they sacked the plantations of Governor Morton and Paul Grimball, secretary of the province.

THE COMING OF THE HOME-SEEKER

The Spanish threat was effective in preventing the establishment of a colony at Port Royal, but it was not sufficient to frighten away the lone settler in search of land and timber. The provincial officials and others settled at Charles Town encouraged the movement southward. Governor John Archdale, in his *Description of Carolina*, expressed himself as being eager to see "the principal place in Carolina, call'd Port-Royal . . . seated with English and Scots in a considerable Body, because 't is a bold Port, and also a Frontier upon the Spaniard at Augustine."[19]

The first person daring enough to take out land on St. Helena Island seems to have been Thomas Nairne who was "imployed by the Generall Assembly of this Province [Carolina] in the quality of an Agent, and itenerary Justice Among the Indians, subject to our Government,"[20] but the warrant for his tract does not appear among the records of this period. The first warrant on record was issued in 1698 and ordered that the surveyor lay out "unto M.ʳ John Steuart a Plantation Containing One Thous.ᵈ Acres of Land on y.ᵉ Island of St. Helena, being a

---

[19] Salley, *Narratives of Early Carolina*, p. 292.
[20] *Calendar of State Papers, Colonial Series, America and West Indies*, XXIV, 632; A. S. Salley, Jr., *Journal of the Commissioners of the Indian Trade, 1710-1715*. For the subsequent history of Thomas Nairne and his death at the hands of the Yamasees, see Crane, *Southern Frontier, passim*.

Neck of Land formerly Inhabited by the Pocatalagoes, Lying North West of y.ᵉ Lands Settled by M.ʳ Thomas Niern[e]."[21]

Other warrants[22] were issued from time to time, one in 1699, two in 1700, four in 1701, until by 1711 twenty-five warrants for 11,085 acres of land on the Island had been issued.[23] The acreage authorized by these warrants varied in size from 70 to 1,018 acres with half of the settlers taking out from 200 to 500 acres.[24] In a few instances one person obtained several warrants over a period of two or three years. For example, John Stewart, after having received a warrant for 1,000 acres in 1698, obtained in 1701 three other warrants for a total of 2,590 additional acres. In the meantime land was being taken up slowly on the adjoining islands, and in 1700 the birth of the first white child was recorded.[25] In this year it was reported "that the River of Port Royal becomes every Day better known and more inhabited."[26]

As early as 1706 the settlement around Port Royal was important enough for the provincial officials to recommend the establishment of a garrison there.[27] The earliest mention of the town of Beaufort seems to have been in

---

[21] A. S. Salley, Jr., *Warrants for Lands in South Carolina, 1692-1711*, p. 152.

[22] The issuance of a warrant for land was the preliminary step in obtaining the land. It did not necessarily follow that a person who obtained a warrant for a given tract of land also obtained the grant, or legal title, for it; nor did it mean that he actually settled there.

[23] Those who had obtained warrants by 1711 were John Stewart, John Watt, Thomas Nairne, John Cowan, John Norton, William Meggett, James Cockran, William Kimball, Daniel Dicks, Arthur Dicks, Randolph Evans, Richard Capers, William Capers, Sarah Norton, John Cowan, Jr., and Edward and Hugh Hext.

[24] Salley, *op. cit., passim.*

[25] Robert Mills, *Statistics of South Carolina*, p. 366.

[26] Crane, *Southern Frontier*, p. 61n.

[27] *Calendar of State Papers, Colonial Series*, XXIII, 286.

1710 when the Lords Proprietors in a meeting on December 20 agreed that a seaport town should be erected at Port Royal in Granville County to be called Beaufort Town.[28] The charter was issued January 17, 1710/11. In 1712 St. Helena's Parish was established by an act of the General Assembly. This act states that "several persons are settled to the southward of Colleton County on Port Royal Island, St. Helena Island, and several adjacent islands in Granville County.[29]

The Yamasee War suddenly interrupted the growth of settlement.[30] The Yamasees, once the friends of the English and Carolina's chief means of destroying Spanish Guale, having been ill treated by some of the traders among them, without warning opened war upon the English in May, 1715, at the Yamasee town of Pocotaligo. The inhabitants of Port Royal and adjoining islands, with a few exceptions, received word of the attack in time to escape to Charles Town in a ship which had been seized for smuggling and lay in Port Royal River. But two hundred Carolinians were slain in the revolt.

The war, however, opened the Yamasee lands to settlement, for the Indians were forced across the Savannah to San Augustín. The following spring, the General Assembly of the province, at the suggestion of the Proprietors, passed an act granting certain privileges and exemp-

---

[28] *Collections of the South Carolina Historical Society*, I, 181. For the early history of Beaufort see Henry A. M. Smith, "Beaufort—The Original Plan and the Earliest Settlers," *South Carolina Historical and Genealogical Magazine*, IX, 141-160.

[29] Public Records of South Carolina, VI, 1-3.

[30] See Crane, *Southern Frontier*, pp. 162-186; McCrady, *South Carolina Under the Proprietary Government*, pp. 531-536; "Introduction to the Report of General Oglethorpe's Expedition," in Carroll, *Historical Collections of South Carolina*, II, 354-355.

tions to those taking up land in the region which in 1707 had been set aside for the sole use of the Yamasees. The land, however, was to be opened only to actual settlers, "New Comers," from Great Britain, Ireland, or any of His Majesty's plantations in America, who were not to be permitted to convey their tracts for seven years. Each person was to be allowed 300 acres of river land and 400 acres of back land at a quit-rent of 12 pence a hundred acres and £3 purchase money for every hundred acres, to be paid within four and a half years.[31]

The settlement around Port Royal grew more rapidly after the opening of the Yamasee lands, but at best the increase in population was slow. The date of the earliest grant to a lot in Beaufort found on record is July 25, 1717, but before the middle of August more than seventy lots had been granted. Yet in 1722 the General Assembly of the province was found passing an act stating that "the fort at Beaufort is so much out of repair and the great gun carriages so rotten that the same is defenceless and of no service, whereby the inhabitants have no place of security for their families in time of alarm, which so much dispirits them that it may occasion a desertion of those frontiers."[32] In 1728/29 Thomas Lowndes of Charles Town, in a letter to the Secretary of the Board of Trade, stressed the necessity of their encouraging "a good settlement" at Port Royal for the purpose of "obstructing . . . the Spanish navigation" from that port.[33] About 1730 the population

---

[31] The quit-rent at which lands had been taken up previous to this act was one shilling per hundred acres. See Grant Books in the office of Secretary of State, Columbia, S. C., and Memorial Books in the office of the Historical Commission of South Carolina, Columbia.
[32] *Statutes at Large of South Carolina*, III, 180.
[33] *Colonial Records of North Carolina*, III, 11.

of St. Helena's Parish was estimated at seventy families,[34] and the parish at that time included the large territory bounded on the east by St. Helena Sound and Combahee River, on the north by a line from the head of Combahee River to the Savannah River, and on the south by the ocean.

The growth of Beaufort may be taken as an index to the growth of St. Helena Island. Various acts passed by the General Assembly in behalf of Beaufort indicate that the town was small and had but little commercial business even to the time of the American Revolution.[35] An act of 1740 sought "to encourage the better settling and improvement of Beaufort Town," and one of 1748 mentions that "the small number of vessels trading to Beaufort Port Royal are not sufficient to encourage a pilot or pilots to furnish themselves with boats for the use of the harbour." Acts of 1752 and 1762 indicate that the town was still small and its commerce unimportant.

TYPES OF SETTLERS

The inhabitants of St. Helena's Parish, like those of Charles Town, were "persons of all sorts" coming "from the more Northern English Collonys, and the Sugar Islands, England, and Ireland."[36] They came, seasoned planters from Barbados with a knowledge of the slave regime which was well established there as early as 1643,[37]

---

[34] David Humphreys, "An Account of Missionaries Sent to South Carolina," in Carroll, *Historical Collections of South Carolina*, II, 551.

[35] For a review of these acts see Henry A. M. Smith, "Beaufort," *South Carolina Historical and Genealogical Magazine*, IX, 142-150. For the acts see *Statutes at Large of South Carolina*, III, IV, *passim*.

[36] Samuel Wilson's statement concerning Charles Town in his "Account of Carolina" found in Salley, *Narratives of Early Carolina*, p. 167.

[37] Ulrich Bonnell Phillips, *American Negro Slavery*, pp. 46-47.

merchants from England with white indentured servants, adventuresome tradesmen who had scarcely more than enough to pay their passage money, indigent persons who sold themselves into servitude for seven years that they might have the opportunity of making their fortunes in the new world. The Proprietors at first encouraged only those to settle in Carolina who had capital with which to begin planting. The reason for this attitude is indicated in one of Lord Ashley's letters to Sir John Yeamans, written when the Ashley River colony was only a year old:

> I am glad to heare soe many considerable men come from ye Barbados for wee finde by deare experience y^t noe other are able to make a Plantacon but such as are in condition to stock & furnish themselves ye rest serve only to fill up numbers & live upon us & therefor now we have a competent number untill we are better stocked with provisions I am not very fond of more company unless they be substantial men.[38]

Soon, however, the Proprietors were not so choice in regard to the type of person settling in Carolina and advertised the new country to rich and poor alike.

The register of St. Helena's Parish, which was begun in 1752 but which gives information of the inhabitants as early as 1710, indicates the various places from which came the settlers of St. Helena Island as well as of the entire parish. The places mentioned as the former homes of inhabitants are Bridgenorth and Ludlow in Shropshire, Bristol, Canterbury in Kent, Dorchester, Liverpool, London, and Ireland, Scotland, Wales, France, Switzerland, the Netherlands, Barbados, and Bermuda.[39]

---

[38] *Colonial Records of North Carolina*, I, 210.

[39] Joseph W. Barnwell and Mabel L. Webber (eds.), "St. Helena's Parish Register," *South Carolina Historical and Genealogical Magazine*, XXIII, 8-25, 47-71, 102-151, 171-204, *passim*.

The register also gives some information as to the life of the settlers, for in some instances a person's occupation is recorded after his name. The register indicates that the following types of settlers were to be found among the inhabitants from 1752 to 1785: barber, boatman, carpenter, cooper, cordwainer, Indian trader, leather dresser and breeches maker, labourer, mariner, master of a piragua, merchant, overseer,[40] painter, planter,[41] pump maker, sailor, schoolmaster, ship carpenter, shipwright, shoemaker, soldier, surgeon, tailor, and weaver.

These early invaders of the southern frontier were adventurers from many sections and from many stations in life. Very few had any previous experience in wresting a livelihood from virgin land or building a home in the wilderness. Yet they were the men who laid the foundation for the prosperity which made possible one of the highest types of ante-bellum culture.

[40] "Overseer of Ireland" is also mentioned.
[41] "Planter of England" is also mentioned.

CHAPTER II

THE STAPLE CROPS

ALTHOUGH the Lords Proprietors of Carolina encouraged the settlers of their province to grow tropical and semi-tropical plants, such as indigo, cotton, and ginger,[1] these were not the products to which the people turned their chief attention. Thomas Ashe, in mentioning the occupations of the settlers in 1682, described conditions which prevailed in the province for the first half century. Of the planters he wrote:

> Their Provision which grows in the Field is chiefly Indian Corn ... they do not much regard or encourage its [tobacco] planting, having already before them better and more profitable Designs in Action. Tarr made of the resinous Juice of the Pine (which boyl'd to a thicker Consistence is Pitch) they make great quantities yearly, transporting several Tuns to Barbadoes, Jamaica, and the Caribbe Islands.[2]

NAVAL STORES AND PROVISION CROPS

The settlers on St. Helena Island followed the example of those about Charles Town and turned their attention to the manufacture of naval stores. They converted their fine live oaks into ships beams and masts; the pines, into pitch and tar. In 1712 the charter of Beaufort points to the chief occupation of the inhabitants, stating that "a port upon the River called Port Royal in Granville County" would be "the most proper place in that part of the province for ships of Great Britain to take in masts, pitch, Tar, Turpentine, & other naval stores."[3]

---

[1] McCrady, *South Carolina Under the Proprietary Government*, pp. 115-116.
[2] "Thomas Ashe's Carolina," in Salley, *Narratives of Early Carolina*, p. 174.
[3] Public Records of South Carolina, VI, 1-3.

While thus exploiting the natural resources of the Island, the settlers raised only provision crops and hogs.

Although rice culture[4] was begun in South Carolina before 1690 and had become one of the staple commodities by 1724, rice was never raised to any extent on St. Helena Island. Rice culture during the colonial period was confined for the most part to the inland swamps which could be flooded from fresh-water ponds and rivers, as, for example, Combahee River. Salt water is poisonous to the rice plant,[5] and St. Helena Island has only a few small fresh-water ponds. In these few ponds some rice was raised of a different variety from the famous Madagascar rice, but the amount was necessarily small.

INDIGO CULTURE

Almost from the first settlement of South Carolina, indigo was grown in the province and at intervals a bounty was allowed for its production, but it was not until near the middle of the eighteenth century that it became an important article for exportation.[6] In it St. Helena Island found a staple which supplemented and to some extent supplanted the provision crops and the export of naval stores. As early as 1748 the dye was exported to Eng-

---

[4] See A. S. Salley, Jr., "The Introduction of Rice Culture into South Carolina," *Bulletins of the Historical Commission of South Carolina*, no. 6. For a discussion of rice culture during the ante-bellum period see Edmund Ruffin, *Report of the Commencement and Progress of the Agricultural Survey of South Carolina for 1843*, and R. F. W. Allston, *Essay on Sea Coast Crops*, which appears also in *DeBow's Review*, XVI, 589-615.

[5] Frederick Law Olmsted, *A Journey in the Seaboard Slave States*, p. 469.

[6] In a letter written by Elizabeth (usually abbreviated to Eliza:) Lucas in 1739 she refers to her efforts to produce indigo on her father's plantation in South Carolina. This has led some writers to assert that she first planted indigo in South Carolina and that from her experiments the great indigo industry in the province developed. The records of the province show that some indigo was produced in South Carolina before Miss Lucas was born.

land and attracted immediate attention, for Great Britain was at that time importing annually 600,000 pounds of indigo from France at the rate of about £150,000 sterling. The following year Parliament allowed a bounty of 6 pence a pound on indigo from the British colonies, and indigo culture at once grew in the favor of South Carolina planters. By 1754 the export from Charles Town had reached 216,924 pounds, and on the eve of the Revolution it had mounted to more than a million and a half pounds.[7]

Indigo had become, next to rice, the most important source of wealth in the province. Moses Lindo, a London Jew and expert indigo sorter, had done more to stimulate the growth and the excellence of the dye than any other man in South Carolina.[8] As surveyor and inspector-general of indigo for South Carolina, he taught the planters to distinguish the grades and to improve the cultivation of the plant and the manufacture of the dye. The prices were usually excellent, ranging generally from 4 to 6 shillings a pound.

A light, dry soil was best suited to indigo culture; hence it was cultivated in considerable quantities on the Sea Islands. During the colonial period both the annual and perennial plants were grown. About 1760 Governor Glen wrote that the plant most frequently used in South Carolina was the annual, the sort generally cultivated in the West Indies.[9] The perennial, however, was less trouble

[7] *Year Book*, City of Charleston, 1883, pp. 402-403.
[8] B. A. Elzas, *The Jews of South Carolina*, chap. III.
[9] "A Description of South Carolina," in Carroll, *Historical Collections*, II, 203. George Milligan, writing in 1763, quotes "an ingenious planter" as saying that there was in the province a great variety of seed, "and from every sort good indigo may be made but none answers so well in this colony as the true Guatimala." Carroll, *op. cit.*, II, 533.

to grow and thrived on poorer land, provided the soil was dry and loose.

Planting began about the first of April. The soil, after having been well prepared, was furrowed with a drill-plough, or more often with a hoe, two inches deep, and the seed sown thinly in these trenches. A South Carolina planter estimated in 1763 that a bushel of seed would sow four acres.[10] In ten or fifteen days the young plants appeared and were immediately hoed to loosen the earth about them. When the plant was in full bloom, in June or July,[11] it was cut regardless of its height, for at that time the leaves were thick and full of juice.

With the cutting of the weed, the planter was ready to begin the process of manufacturing the dye. The plants were cut off near the ground and placed under water to ferment in a shallow vat, or steeper, as it was called. This process, which usually required some twelve hours, took the dye stuff out of the leaves. The fermenting solution was then drawn from the steeper into another vat, known as the battery, where it was violently agitated with paddles for fifteen or twenty minutes to complete the fermentation and to collect the particles of dye.

As soon as the solution acquired a blue tinge, lime water from the lime vat was carefully stirred into it until a cloudy hue appeared. The indigo water was then beaten again until granulation began and the dye stuff left to precipitate to the bottom of the vat for four or five hours. The water was drawn off and the paste which had settled in the bottom carefully strained through a horse-hair sieve

[10] *Ibid.*, p. 533.
[11] Milligan's authority states that the blooms usually appeared four months from the time of planting.

to clean it and then hung up in bags for several hours to drain out the water. Afterwards the bags were put through a press to free the indigo from any remaining water and the stiff paste spread on a plank, cut into small pieces about two inches square, and placed in a drying-house so that it might have a free circulation of air without being exposed to the sun which might burn it to a cinder in a few hours. While in the drying-house, the indigo had to be turned carefully three or four times a day until it was sufficiently dried to prevent its being spoiled, and it had to be kept as much as possible from flies. When thoroughly dry, the dye was packed in barrels for market.

The indigo raised in Beaufort District commanded the top price in market,[12] and it was still grown in large quantities even after the Revolution. In 1791, Mrs. Charles Capers, the wife of a St. Helena planter, stated that the planters of the Island were "wholly attentive to the Cultivation of Indigo."[13]

In some sections of the coastal region, especially in Orangeburgh District, indigo was grown throughout the ante-bellum period, and small quantities even after the Civil War. In 1828 William Elliott, of Beaufort District, wrote to the *Southern Agriculturist*, of Charleston, to encourage a more widespread growth of the plant.[14] In defense of his position, he cited the case of Donald B. Jones, of Orangeburgh, a member of the House of Representatives, who, in 1827, employed five hands in the production of cotton and five hands in the production of

[12] Mills, *Statistics of South Carolina*, p. 368.
[13] Mrs. Capers to Mrs. Russell, March 25, 1791. Copy of original in possession of Penn School, St. Helena Island, S. C.
[14] *Southern Agriculturist*, Feb., 1828, pp. 64-66.

indigo. The five who raised indigo made a net profit of $225 more than the five who cultivated cotton. In 1845 Thomas W. Glover, of Orangeburgh, wrote for the *Report on the Geology of South Carolina* a detailed statement concerning the cultivation and manufacture of indigo.[15] South Carolina indigo was then selling from 40 to 80 cents a pound, and the average production varied from twenty-nine to sixty pounds an acre.

The cultivation of indigo, however, was a precarious undertaking. The soil had to be well prepared before planting; the furrows weeded thoroughly; the caterpillars kept off the plants; the stalks cut with a special kind of hook and handled cautiously in being carried to the vats to prevent the bluish bloom from being rubbed off the leaves; the fermentation closely watched; and the introduction of lime water carefully regulated to produce the best quality of dye. After one had painstakingly watched over his crop from the preparation of the soil to the daily turning of the squares of paste in the drying house, he might even then lose his entire output by its sweating and rotting in the barrels.

Nevertheless, sea-island planters were willing to take the risk as long as Great Britain was paying a bounty, for an acre of virgin land often produced about eighty pounds of good indigo. "One slave may manage Two Acres and upwards," wrote Governor Glen, "and raise Provisions besides, and have all the Winter Months to saw Lumber and be otherwise employed in."[16] Thus the production of

---

[15] M. Tuomey, *Report on the Geology of South Carolina*, pp. xxiii-xxiv. A writer in *DeBow's Review* for 1850, (VIII, 495), also urges the cultivation of indigo.

[16] Carroll, *Historical Collections*, II, 204-205.

indigo on St. Helena Island did not interrupt the manufacture of naval stores which was the first occupation of the settlers. After the indigo crop had been laid by, the slaves were employed in "sawing Lumber and making Hogsheads and other Staves, to supply the Sugar Colonies." Indigo culture fitted in so well with the accustomed regime of the settlers that they continued to raise it despite the uncertain returns.

INTRODUCTION OF SEA-ISLAND COTTON

The Revolution virtually cut off the market for indigo and, of course, put an end to the British bounty. The steeping vats had for a long time been considered an additional menace to health in this already unhealthy region.[17] At the same time a new staple, sea-island cotton, which offered fabulous profits, began to be raised in the tidewater region. The seed known in Georgia and South Carolina as sea-island cotton came from the Bahama Islands where it had been introduced by the Board of Trade from Anguilla, an island of the Caribbean Sea.

Several Georgia planters experimented with the seed in 1786, among whom were Thomas Spalding and Alexander Bisset whose plants although sturdy did not ripen pods. Two years later, however, Alexander Bisset exported the first bag of sea-island cotton grown in the United States.[18] To the gratified surprise of the Georgia planters, the fruit yielded a finer fiber than that grown in

---

[17] *Southern Agriculturist*, Feb., 1828. William Elliott, in his article on indigo, states that he will not admit that the steeping vats "impair the health of the country until I can find that our country has become healthier since the Indigo culture has been superseded by that of Cotton. But I readily admit, that the steeping vats must be unpleasant in those sections where the settlements are thick."

[18] Whitemarsh B. Seabrook, *Memoir on the Origin, Cultivation and Uses of Cotton*, pp. 18, 19; *DeBow's Review*, I, 304.

the Bahamas. The plant was tall; the seed black; and the fiber, long, strong, and silky. Richard Leake, one of those who had first received the seed, at once began production on a large scale. In 1788 he wrote, "I shall raise about 5,000 pounds in the seed from about eighty acres of land and the next year I expect to plant from fifty to one hundred acres."[19]

Seed of the new product was soon obtained in South Carolina, where William Elliott, of Hilton Head Island, near Beaufort and St. Helena, seems in 1790 to have been the first to raise a successful crop.[20] He had bought five and a half bushels of seed at 14 shillings a bushel in Charleston, and he sold his crop at 10½ pence a pound. The following year John Screven, of St. Luke's Parish, planted thirty or forty acres on his plantation on May River and sold the cotton in Georgia at from 1 shilling, 2 pence to 1 shilling, 6 pence sterling a pound. The next year John Rose planted a small field on Oakatee Creek and sold the 600 pounds which he raised at 2 shillings a pound. By this time many other planters on the Sea Islands and the mainland were experimenting with the long staple cotton, and in 1793 such prominent planters as James King, of St. Paul's Parish, Colonel Edward Barnwell and Captain John Joyner, of St. Helena's Parish, and General William Moultrie, of St. John's Parish, Berkeley,

---

[19] E. J. Donnell, *Chronological and Statistical History of Cotton*, p. 45; Phillips, *American Negro Slavery*, p. 152.

[20] The best account of the history of the introduction of sea-island cotton and its culture is to be found in Seabrook, *Memoir on the Origin, Cultivation and Uses of Cotton*. The account in *DeBow's Review*, I, 304-315, is based upon Seabrook's history. J. A. Turner (ed.), *The Cotton Planter's Manual*, pp. 280-286, also contains some information concerning the development of the culture of sea-island cotton.

A TIDAL CREEK ON ST. HELENA ISLAND

were growing the cotton. The struggle between indigo and sea-island cotton had already begun. By 1798 the latter had clearly won.

The spread of sea-island cotton planting was largely hastened by the excellent prices which the long-staple brought. The English market welcomed the new staple. In 1799 the cotton sold readily in Liverpool at 5 shillings a pound. In South Carolina, the price ranged from 9 pence to 1 shilling during the early days of the production; then it rose to 2 shillings and upwards and there remained until 1806 when the Franco-English hostilities caused the price to slump. But large fortunes had already been made. Captain James Sinkler received 3 shillings a pound for a crop of 300 acres which produced 216 pounds to the acre. Peter Gaillard, of St. John's, Berkeley, made an average of $340 a hand, and William Brisbane, of St. Paul's, was so wealthy after two years of growing sea-island cotton that he retired and sold his plantation to William Seabrook at an exorbitant price, but Seabrook paid for it in two years.

Not all, however, who planted sea-island cotton realized so great profits as these planters. The longest and silkiest fibers commanded the highest prices. For many years Kinsey Burden, Sr., of St. John's Parish, Colleton, occupied first place in the production of a fine staple, and for many years he carefully guarded the secret of his success. In 1805 he produced cotton worth 25 cents a pound more than that of his neighbors. William Elliott was among the first to guess that the secret of Burden's success lay in the quality of the seed used, and soon sea-island cotton planters everywhere were experimenting with seed in the attempt to obtain a silky staple. In 1828 Hugh Wilson sold two bags of extra fine cotton at $2 a pound, probably the highest price ever obtained for sea-island cotton.

The growth of sea-island cotton was limited to a small area along the coast of South Carolina and Georgia, for the plant would prosper only in a light, sandy soil, known as the salt-water lands. The sea-island cotton area in the ante-bellum period was a belt of coastal land from twenty to thirty miles wide, extending from Santee River, including St. John's Parish, Berkeley, to the everglades of Florida.[21] Eutaw Springs in St. John's, Berkeley, was the extreme northern point at which the plant was cultivated.

EARLY METHOD OF CULTIVATION

The planters of the crop quickly systematized the method of cultivation so that, by 1802, the general routine in South Carolina and Georgia was about the same. The seed was planted in early spring as soon as the weather would permit. At first it was planted in separate holes, but soon came to be drilled and the plants grown at intervals of two or three feet on ridges five or six feet apart. Instead of being hoed only four times with the last hoeing about the middle of July, the crop was now hoed at more frequent intervals, all work ceasing when the plant began freely to put out fruit, which was usually early in July. The crop was harvested from September until December. The fiber was quickly damaged by bad weather and the fields, accordingly, had to be picked frequently to save the staple. The bolls opened but slightly and picking was dif-

---

[21] R. F. W. Allston, *Essay on Sea Coast Crops*, reprinted in *DeBow's Review*, XVI, 593; Seabrook, *op. cit.*, pp. 18, 19.

ficult so that a hand seldom averaged more than seventy-five or a hundred pounds a day, whereas on the upland cotton fields a hand often picked two hundred pounds or more in a day.

The method of culture in practice in St. Helena's Parish in 1828 has been described by William Elliott, the son of the first planter to raise a successful crop of sea-island cotton in South Carolina:

The judicious Planter, whose plantation affords him the opportunity of choice, will select for his Cotton field, such high lands of a light brown or yellow complexion, as were covered by an original growth of hickory, laurel, red bay, interspersed with the live and white oaks, and the towering palmetto. He lays out his field into squares, of one-fourth of an acre, (105 feet,) and in the winter months, proceeds to list in the sward, with its cover of fennel or grass. On this *list*, the *bed* is subsequently raised; and, if the ground has lain fallow for some years, or if the soil be naturally close, the plough is sometimes run through the intervals, to pulverize it, and facilitate the process of bedding which is always performed by the hoe and usually commences about the middle of March. The beds are commonly five feet apart from centre to centre. The planting begins about the 20th of March, and extends to the 20th of April, and is thus performed:—A number of holes, four inches deep and twelve inches long, are cut by the hoe on the top of the bed, leaving the space of one foot between each hole. The seed which is changed every second year, is . . . carefully cleansed of such as are *coated* or *tufted with green* (that being considered *an indication of degeneracy*,) and then plentifully dropped and carefully covered. When the plant has attained its fourth or sixth leaf, if no grass should threaten it sooner, it is *hoed down*, which is effected by cutting the bed nicely down, and drawing the earth into the centre of the alley, in the shape of a small list. A fortnight before, or sooner, if the plants show the want of it, the earth is drawn to their roots, and they are slightly thinned.

At every subsequent working, which after the first, is invariably a hauling or drawing up the earth to the plants, they are gradually thinned until June, when careful hands are selected to give the final thinning. This is a nice point, on which nothing like uniformity of practice prevails. In high lands, whose fertility has been impaired by frequent cropping, as many as one hundred and twenty stalks may be left in a task row, (105 feet). In newer, stronger or lower lands, where the growth of the plants is increased, the number must be proportionably diminished.

The plants are hauled, whenever the growth is checked by drought or threatened by grass, *until the middle of July,* beyond which period, it is unsafe to haul the earth to any fields but such as have been planted late in the season. . . .

We gather it as soon as possible after it has burst the pods, that it may avoid injury as well from dirt, as from too much exposure to the sun. Women and boys prove the most efficient pickers. The greatest care is used by them to separate the Cotton, all dried leaves or other substances may impair or discolour the staple. It is then spread, if wet, on a scaffold and exposed to the sun; but, if gathered in dry weather, *on the floor in the house,* to suffer whatever moisture it has imbibed to escape, before it is stowed away in bulk. It is then passed once through a patent whipper, (M'Birnie's,) and sorted in the seed, at the rate of one to two hundred pounds to the hand. It is now ready for the gin. Eave's was formerly in successful use; but that, as well as the barrel gin, has been superseded by the common foot or crank gin, whose extreme simplicity of structure has given it an advantage over others more efficient, but more complicated . . . thirty pounds of clean Cotton as a day's labour, are easily turned out to each gin. It is then moted, often, but not always, on frames of wire or latticed wood, at a rate varying from fifteen to thirty pounds to the hand, and is then packed and ready for market.[22]

The preparation of the staple for market was the most tedious part of the growth of sea-island cotton. Before 1820, however, this was not considered to be the case.

[22] William Elliott, "On the Cultivation and High Prices of Sea-Island Cotton," *Southern Agriculturist,* I, 152-154.

The pickers made no effort to remove the dead leaves from the lint; the ginners allowed stained and unstained cotton to go alike into the gin; moting was accomplished by women who sat upon the floor and beat the cotton with twigs; many planters ginned, moted, and packed the cotton in the same room; and the spinner frequently on opening a bag of cotton would find, in addition to the staple, crushed seeds, potato skins, and parts of old clothing.

Sea-island cotton prepared in this manner was suited only for coarse fabrics. As the demand for the long staple became greater for making fine laces and muslins and as the high prices went to those who carefully handled their cotton, planters were forced to use more painstaking methods. The gin house, although only a simple barn, had separate rooms for the different processes. The cotton on being gathered was never exposed to the sun as formerly, but dried on a scaffold inside. Upon being dried, it was taken to the whipper which extracted the sand and imperfect fibers, and then sent to the assorters each of whom, provided with boxes for clean cotton, worked before a long table covered with wire or wooden slats, sorting the cotton according to color and fineness. From the sorters the staple went to the gins, and from there to the moting tables where women picked out the broken seeds and stained fibres. The lint was then packed into round bags of about three hundred pounds each, 1,500 pounds of seed cotton being required for a bale of this size.

Whitemarsh B. Seabrook, of Edisto Island, estimated in 1844 that fifty-four laborers[23] were required to prepare

[23] This estimate was based upon the use of the foot-gin which was ordinarily employed in 1860 as well as in 1844. When a steam gin was used the number of ginners was reduced to six; when an Eave's improved steam gin, to three.

the seed cotton for market as follows: one dryer; one turner and one feeder of the whipper; thirty assorters, grading fifty pounds each a day; twelve ginners, preparing twenty-five pounds of lint each a day; seven moters at forty-three pounds each; a packer and a re-inspector. Estimating the services of each slave at 50 cents a day, Seabrook concluded that it cost a planter $27 to gin a bale of sea-island cotton.[24] On the average plantation it required from fifty to sixty days of labor to cultivate and gin a bale of fine cotton.[25]

In the production of naval stores, the cultivation of indigo, and the growth of the long staple cotton, planters soon learned that their most urgent need was a larger labor supply than the sparsely settled province could afford. They turned for this supply to the African slave market.

---

[24] Seabrook, *Memoir on the Origin, Cultivation and Uses of Cotton*, p. 31.
[25] Allston, *Essay on Sea Coast Crops*, p. 15.

CHAPTER III

THE LABORERS AND THE LAND

PLANTERS coming to South Carolina from Barbados, Jamaica, Antigua, and St. Kitts brought with them the idea of the plantation regime with slavery as the basis of the labor system. In 1682 Samuel Wilson, writing an account of Carolina for the Lords Proprietors as an advertisement designed to attract settlers, spoke of the necessity of slaves in the province, "without which a Planter can never do any great matter."[1]

PRE-REVOLUTIONARY SLAVE TRADE

Prior to 1730 the accessible data concerning the slave trade in South Carolina are scanty, but the enactment of numerous laws laying a duty on the importation of slaves indicates that the slave population was rapidly increasing.[2] In the years after 1730, the importation of slaves into South Carolina ranged, when the import duty was not prohibitive, from as low as 72 in 1749 to as high as 11,641 in 1773.[3] The trade was carried on by British and South Carolina merchants, and the slave vessels, largely from New England, usually came consigned to a merchant who conducted a general importing trade in Charles Town. The arrival of a cargo brought planters to the sale in great numbers. Henry Laurens, one of the leading slave importers in the province, mentioned a sale in 1755 attended

---

[1] "Account of Carolina," in Salley, *Narratives of Early Carolina*, p. 174.
[2] Elizabeth Donnan, "The Slave Trade Into South Carolina Before the Revolution," *American Historical Review*, XXXIII, 804-828.
[3] Based upon estimates made by Elizabeth Donnan, *op. cit.*, pp. 807-809.

by forty or fifty planters from so great a distance as seventy miles from Charles Town.[4]

The price of slaves depended in general upon the economic conditions of the province, although other factors contributed to the general fluctuation of prices which characterized the pre-revolutionary slave market. In 1756 Laurens wrote: "The price of Slaves here while they are imported in moderate numbers is wholly influenced by the values of our Staples, Rice and Indigo, and these have been depreciated much below the prices of last Year, so have the Planters slacked in the purchase of Slaves, lowered the prices and lengthened out the Credit."[5] The price of slaves was so unstable that it seldom remained the same for many months during the year. For instance, in the spring of 1755, Negro men were bringing £260 to £270; in the fall, as high as £330. From 1751 to 1773 the price of prime men varied from £245 to £350. During a frenzied purchase in 1764, *The South-Carolina Gazette* estimated that planters had spent for new Negroes £177,870 sterling, or £1,250,090 currency.[6]

Many planters bought their slaves with cash or with produce but many more bought on credit. The terms of purchase varied as widely as the purchase price. In 1755 Laurens suggested to a correspondent that he ignore "the measure lately adopted in Charles Town, for the sale of Negroes . . . three Months Credit, to Purchasers with Interest from the Date," but instead to "deal with each

---

[4] Donnan, *op. cit.*, p. 816, citing Laurens Letter Book, July 31, 1755. In possession of South Carolina Historical Society, Charleston.

[5] *Ibid.*, p. 819 n, citing Laurens to Capt. Samuel Linnecar, May 8, 1756.

[6] *Ibid.*, p. 822, citing *The South-Carolina Gazette*, June 29, 1765.

Man who shall require Credit" separately.[7] Merchants encouraged payment in cash or in produce by offering a discount, sometimes as much as 5 per cent, "on all Sums paid down," although to induce a ready sale they advertised occasionally that they would give as much as twelve months credit without interest.

The favorite Negroes of the South Carolina planters were those from Gambia and the Gold Coast, although Negroes from other parts of the African coast were imported and, to encourage their acceptance, were sold at lower prices than the Gambia Negroes. Into the Charles Town market there came cargoes advertised as being from the "winward Coast of Guiney," "the Masse-Congo country," "Cape Mount on the Grain Coast"; there came Negroes from Bassa on the Winward Coast, from Bance Island, from Angola, and "Calabars from Bight," Coromantines, and "healthy young Fantees."

Although merchants, in selling new Negroes, invariably advertised the tribe or the geographic section from which the Negroes came, it is interesting to note that none of these facts was mentioned in selling seasoned slaves. It would seem that tribal differences tended to disappear as the slave became seasoned.[8]

By 1708 the number of slaves almost equalled the number of the whites in the province of South Carolina;[9]

---

[7] *Ibid.*, p. 814, citing Laurens to Smith and Clifton, May 26, 1755; to Satterthwaite, Inman, and Company, Nov. 22, 1755; to John Lewis Gervais, Feb. 28, 1772.

[8] In this connection see *ibid.*, p. 817n. The writer has noticed the same tendency in advertisements of seasoned slaves in North Carolina and Virginia as well as in South Carolina.

[9] "Sir Nathaniel Johnson's Report to the Council of Trade and Plantations," *Calendar of State Papers, Colonial Series*, XXIV, 739; also in McCrady, *South Carolina under the Proprietary Government*, pp. 477-481, 723. The estimates of

by the close of the colonial period the proportion of blacks to whites was almost two to one.[10] The closing of the African slave trade[11] in 1808 by provision of the Constitution in 1787 shut off the supply of new Negroes, but before that time most of the sea-island plantations had become well stocked with slaves. In most cases the internal slave trade and the natural increase of the plantation stock were sufficient to take care of the demand for more laborers in instances of expansion on the sea-island plantations.

THE SLAVE MARKET FOR ST. HELENA ISLAND

The planters on St. Helena Island bought their slaves at the Charleston market in common with other planters in that vicinity, for it was at Charleston that they transacted most of their business. Like other planters, too, they undoubtedly stocked their plantations with slaves from various tribes and various African localities,[12] pre-

Rev. Samuel Thomas, made in 1706 and based on the number of families connected with the Church of England and the Dissenter meetings in each of the six existing parishes outside of Charles Town, show 3,000 whites and 1,000 Negro Slaves. *The South Carolina Historical and Genealogical Magazine*, V, 1131-34.

[10] Edward McCrady, *The History of South Carolina under the Royal Government, 1719-1776*, p. 807.

[11] In 1787 South Carolina, following the example of other states, passed an act to close the African slave trade in her ports, and by similar acts kept her ports closed for sixteen years, although it was hinted that the inhabitants on the coast and the border smuggled in slaves occasionally. In 1803 the State Legislature reopened the African slave trade, but continued to exclude West Indian Negroes and required that slaves brought in from other states have official certificates of good character.

[12] Frank Moore, (ed.), *Rebellion Record*, III, 309. The reporter for the *New York World* who accompanied the Union troops in the capture of Port Royal, November 7, 1861, said of the slaves on Hilton Head, "Every variety of negro and slave was represented. . . . Darkies of genuine congo physiques, and darkies of the genuine Uncle Tom pattern, darkies young and jubilant, darkies middle-aged, and eager, and gray-haired, solemn-looking fellows. Some appeared mystified and some intelligent."

ferring, perhaps, as did other South Carolina planters, the Gambia and Guiney Negroes. In 1791 a St. Helena planter's wife thought that the consuming interest of the Islanders was to raise more indigo to buy more slaves. The profits of the crop, she said, are "mostly expended in the purchase of Negroes, & nothing is so much coveted as the pleasure of possessing many slaves.—These singularities are inherited from their Fore-Fathers—& many follow so closely in the path thru which their Ancestors trod as to deny themselves the Comforts & conveniences of life."[13]

There are local traditions that St. Helena planters, as well as those of Edisto and other Sea Islands, received fresh supplies of African slaves at their own private wharves after the closing of the slave trade, but no documentary evidence has been found to substantiate these traditions.

The plantation records which have been preserved for the sea-island districts show that planters tended to retain their slaves, sometimes even at great financial sacrifice, selling one only because of repeated insubordination or because of economic distress. In 1867 William Jervey, of Charleston, in attempting to settle the accounts of a plantation on Ladies Island, wrote to a member of the family that "the old gentleman several times had to sell negroes to pay . . . debts."[14]

When it was necessary to sell several Negroes, the planter usually attempted to dispose of them in family groups.[15] Negroes worked better and were more satisfied

---

[13] MS letter of Mrs. Gabriel Capers, March 25, 1791.
[14] MS in Sarah W. Ellis Papers, April 20, 1867.
[15] MS, A. F. Gregorie Account Book. A deed of sale dated Jan. 9, 1840, shows that A. F. Gregorie, of Greenwood Plantation, "Delivered to Mr J. E. Moore Mitchell the following Twenty five Negroes viz—

to make a change of masters when the whole or a part of their families went with them. When Sir Charles Lyell visited Beaufort in 1845, he observed the general unwillingness of planters to sell to Negro traders. If planters are "forced to part with slaves," he wrote, "they usually sell one to another, and are unwilling to dispose of them to a stranger. It is reckoned, indeed, quite a disgrace to a Negro to be discarded. When the former master bids for one of his 'own people,' at a sale of property forced on by debt, the public are unwilling to bid against him."[16] This tendency to retain a slave as long as it was possible to do so often led a planter into inefficiency and oversupply.

EXTENT OF SLAVEHOLDING

The average number of slaves per owner for Beaufort District in 1790 was twenty-four; in 1860, thirty. The average for the district in 1860 was twice as great as the average for the state as a whole. The following table shows the size of slaveholdings in the district in 1790 and in 1860:

```
Jan. 13th 1840
Sambo & Jenny his wife and their children
Ned
Tyrah
Rhynah
Pilot
Grace
Penny & her son Isaac & Jack
Island George & Bynah his wife
William & Nancy his Sister and her child Bess
Honor Elizabeths Maid
Charles and his Wife Hagar and their son Allen
Robert & his wife Caty & their children Peter
   Dunbee, and Caty's sister Dinah & her child
Bess brought back to stay with her Grand Mother Lucy."
```

[16] Sir Charles Lyell, *A Second Visit to the United States*, I, 233.

SIZE OF SLAVEHOLDINGS IN BEAUFORT DISTRICT[17]

Number of Slaves	Slaveowners Number		Per Cent	
	1790	1860	1790	1860
1 slave	73	78	12.5	7.3
2 and under 5	88	173	15.1	16.1
5 and under 10	95	204	16.2	19.0
10 and under 20	86	188	14.7	17.6
20 and under 50	150	216	25.6	20.2
50 and under 100	69	142	11.8	13.2
100 and under 200	20	51	3.4	4.8
200 and under 300	3	13	0.5	1.3
300 and under 500	0	4	0.0	0.4
500 and under 1,000	1	1	0.2	0.1
Total	585	1,070	100.0	100.0

Although the number of slaveholders in 1860 had increased 83.9 per cent over that of 1790, the distribution in the two periods, according to the size of holdings, did not vary appreciably. In 1790 some 58.5 per cent of the slaveowners had less than twenty slaves and in 1860 only 60 per cent had less than that number, a difference of less than two per cent. In 1790 those owning more than one hundred slaves were 4.1 per cent of the total, while in 1860 they were 6.6 per cent, a difference of 2.5 per cent. The only significant change in the distribution of the size of holdings occurred in the class possessing from twenty to fifty slaves. In 1790 this group was a fourth of the total, but in 1860 it had been reduced to a fifth.

While the general average for the district in 1860 would place every owner in the rank of a planter, it is significant that three-fifths of the slaveholders in the district owned less than twenty slaves. With less than this number a man engaged in the cultivation of sea-island

[17] *Agricultural Census, 1860*, p. 237; *Heads of Families at the First Census of the United States, 1790: State of South Carolina*, pp. 10-13.

cotton, the staple crop in 1860, could not hope to engage in large scale production. Only 19.8 per cent owned more than fifty slaves and only one planter owned more than five hundred. The conclusion must be, therefore, that the majority of those engaged in agriculture in this district, one of the most densely populated slave counties in the entire South, belonged to the small planter class.

It is difficult to estimate the exact number of slaves owned by St. Helena planters at any given time.[18] The first census of the United States shows that only four men in Beaufort District, none of whom lived on St. Helena Island, owned more than two hundred slaves in 1790. Frederick Witsell had 607; Thomas Heyward, 265; General Stephen Bull, 233; and John Rutledge (who lived in Charleston), 217. Of those living on St. Helena, the plantation of William Fripp with 153 slaves had the largest number; that of John Jenkins with 136 slaves, the next largest. The other holdings were considerably less. Thomas Chaplin had 65 slaves; William Chaplin, 50; John Chaplin, 30; Paul Fripp, 37; Thomas Fripp, 33; John Fripp, 38; Charles Capers, 45; William Capers, 15; John Cowen, 13; Peter Perry, 45; George Pope, 39.

Early in 1862 Edward L. Pierce, special agent for the United States Treasury Department, estimated that there was an average of forty slaves to a plantation on St.

---

[18] The courthouse at Gillisonville, the seat of Beaufort District, was destroyed by Sherman's Army in 1864. Later the county seat was changed to Beaufort, and in 1883 the courthouse there was destroyed by fire. Practically all of the antebellum county records have, therefore, been destroyed. The MS, "Return of Tax Collected by John M. Baker in the Parish of St. Helena for the Year Commencing Oct. 1, 1860" (in possession of William Elliott, Columbia, S. C.), does not contain a list of slaves. This MS is a duplicate of the original which Congressman William Elliott said in a written statement that he deposited in the Court of Claims. A search through some of the files of the Court has failed to reveal the original.

Helena. With the blockade of the coast and the capture of St. Helena Island on November 7, 1861, the planters on the Island left in great haste, in some cases not having time to take even a house servant along. After the hasty departure of their masters, the slaves on Ladies and St. Helena islands quite generally remained on their respective plantations so that Mr. Pierce's estimate included in his "Report to the Secretary of Treasury" of February 3, 1863,[19] closely approximates the number of slaves on the St. Helena plantations during the latter part of the plantation regime.

Mr. Pierce found 260 slaves at Coffin's Point, the plantation of Thomas Aston Coffin, who was generally conceded to have the best managed and the most prosperous plantation on St. Helena. On Dr. William J. Jenkins' plantation he found 130 slaves; on the Eustis plantation on Ladies Island, 120; on the others from 38 to 80 slaves.[20] On the "best peopled" plantations he found an average of eighty-one slaves but a general average, on all plantations, of about fifty-two. This estimate is much higher than the size of slaveholdings of the majority of planters in Beaufort District, for, as the foregoing table indicates, 60 per cent of the owners in the district possessed less than twenty slaves in 1860.

The price of slaves increased with the advancing years of the ante-bellum period until in 1859 the average price of prime field hands reached about $1,900.[21] In some instances prime men sold for almost three thousand dollars.

---

[19] *Rebellion Record*, I, 302-315.
[20] *Ibid.*, p. 303.
[21] Phillips, *American Negro Slavery*, p. 374. For the advance in prices and an explanation of the causes see *ibid.*, pp. 359-401.

The prices in Beaufort District, and, therefore, on St. Helena Island, followed closely the prices at Charleston, which were uniformly above the Virginia market but below that of New Orleans. The following table represents the investment in slaves of one planter in Beaufort District about 1860, James Gregorie, of Greenwood plantation. The prices may be taken as an average of prices for the district, and the proportion of prime hands, those valued at more than $1,000, to the entire holding as the average for the district.

VALUE OF SLAVES ON GREENWOOD PLANTATION IN 1860[22]

Value in dollars	Number	Per Cent
None	15	10.4
1-100	1	0.7
100-200	9	6.3
200-300	6	4.2
300-400	12	8.3
400-500	16	11.1
500-600	4	2.8
600-700	10	6.9
700-800	12	8.3
800-900	26	18.0
900-1,000	7	4.9
1,000-2,000	25	17.4
2,000	1	0.7
Total	144	100.0

Mr. Gregorie estimated the market value of his 144 slaves in 1860 to be $85,450. The average value of all his slaves was $593.40,[23] but the average price of the saleable slaves was $662.40. Fifty per cent of them would bring on the market something more than seven hundred dollars; while ten per cent had no market value whatever and

---

[22] MS in Gregorie Papers.

[23] Gregorie's estimate is probably too high. James Hamilton Couper, of Hopeton plantation, Glynn County, Ga., estimated the average price of the more than five hundred slaves on the plantation under his management to be $450.

were merely a liability to the owner. All slaves listed as worth more than a thousand dollars were men. Besides Solomon whose value was estimated at $2,000, there were Andrew at $1,500; Dublin, Israel, Sampson, Ben, Solomon, and Cato, at $1,200; John Cox, Phil, Toney, Quamina, and Buff, at $1,100; and John, Chester, Joseph, Jupiter, Paris, Frank, Pompey, Daniel, Hector, Richard, Jacob, Sam, and Abraham, at an even $1,000. Prime women who could go to the field and turn out as much work as a man were most often listed at $800, although a few, Beck, Sally, and Nanny, would bring $900. Thus, out of 144 slaves, the Greenwood plantation had about fifty-nine prime hands in 1860.

SIZE OF ST. HELENA PLANTATIONS

The exact number of plantations on St. Helena Island at the close of the plantation regime is difficult to determine, because the planters themselves were not always consistent in designating the same tracts as separate plantations. It sometimes happened, as in the cases of Captain John Fripp and Dr. William J. Jenkins, that a planter owned several tracts at various places on the Island which he operated as distinct plantations, but in paying his taxes he grouped all of his tracts as one large holding. The number of separate tracts was about fifty-four[24] as far as can be determined by statements made by the owners themselves, or their heirs, some thirty years after the close of the plantation regime; and the number of landholders,

---

[24] Petitions filed in the Court of Claims under the Compensation Act of 1891. Edward L. Pierce, special agent for the United States Government, listed the number of plantations at fifty. *Rebellion Record*, I, 303. This number includes Morgan, Coosaw, Datha, Wassaw, Pine, and Polowana islands, small islands separated from St. Helena Island by creeks.

forty. The size of individual landholdings is summarized in the following table:

SIZE OF LANDHOLDINGS ON ST. HELENA ISLAND IN 1860[25]

Size	Number	Per Cent
Less than 100 acres	4	10.0
100-300	14	35.0
300-500	7	17.5
500-800	8	20.0
800-1,000	1	2.5
More than 1,000	6	15.0
Total	40	100.0

In two instances, that of Captain John Fripp and the estate of Mrs. Mary Coffin, holdings amounted to more than two thousand acres,[26] while in one instance the holding was only twenty-seven acres. The average holding, however, was 573 acres. In some cases, persons owning plantations on St. Helena also had plantations elsewhere. Marion T. Chaplin, for example, owned not only the Marion Chaplin place of 303 acres on St. Helena Island but three other plantations on Ladies Island amounting to 861 additional acres.

A comparison of the size of the landholdings on St. Helena Island with the size elsewhere in the parish shows that the average holding for the Island was slightly less than the average holding for the parish. The following table indicates the size of landholdings in St. Helena's Parish:

---

[25] Petitions filed in the Court of Claims under the Compensation Act of 1891.
[26] William Fripp, Sr., died before 1860 and his estate, although not divided prior to the payment of taxes for that year, was soon distributed among his heirs. His land in the foregoing table is listed under the names of his children.

SIZE OF LANDHOLDINGS IN ST. HELENA'S PARISH IN 1860[27]

Size	Number	Per Cent
Less than 100 acres	10	7.3
100-300	39	28.5
300-500	33	24.1
500-800	24	17.5
800-1,000	8	5.8
More than 1,000	23	16.8
Total	137	100.0

Almost half, or 45 per cent, of the landowners on St. Helena Island had less than three hundred acres, while only 36 per cent in the parish as a whole owned a plantation that small. The average plantation on St. Helena, however, corresponded closely with the average for the parish, both containing almost six hundred acres.[28] A plantation of this size was larger than the average landholding for the state, the general average for the state being 488 acres.[29]

As has already been indicated, planters on St. Helena seldom operated their holdings as one large plantation, for in many instances the holdings were not contiguous. The actual size of the plantation unit was, therefore, in most cases smaller than the size of landholdings in 1860 would indicate. Although Captain John Fripp owned more than two thousand acres, the largest of his seven plantations contained only 460 acres. The following table, therefore, gives an indication of the working size of the plantation on St. Helena:

[27] MS, Return of Tax Collected by John M. Baker in the Parish of St. Helena for the Year Commencing Oct. 1, 1860.
[28] The average for St. Helena Island was 573 acres, and for the parish as a whole, 587 acres.
[29] *Eighth Census of the United States, 1860, Agriculture*, p. 222.

SIZE OF SEPARATE TRACTS ON ST. HELENA IN 1860[30]

Size	Number	Per Cent
Less than 100 acres	5	11.9
100-300	18	42.9
300-500	8	19.1
500-800	7	16.5
800-1,000	2	4.8
More than 1,000	2	4.8
Total	42	100.0

More than half of the plantations on St. Helena were operated in tracts of less than 300 acres, and only two, those belonging to the Coffins, were managed in tracts of more than a thousand acres each. Five plantations actually contained less than a hundred acres, and only eleven contained more than five hundred acres.

These lands were useful only for agricultural purposes and had no speculative value. Robert Mills in his *Statistics of South Carolina* estimated the price of land in 1826 in Beaufort District to vary from $60 an acre to twenty-five cents.[31] The best land brought from $50 to $60 an acre; the second quality, from $20 to $30; and the lowest grade, from 25 cents to $1. In 1860 Dr. Thomas Fuller's four plantations of 2,550 acres were valued at an aggregate of $63,750, or $25 an acre. The William Fripp estate of more than three thousand acres had the same valuation. William Elliott, congressman from South Carolina, estimated in a hearing before the Judiciary Committee in 1888 that the lands in St. Helena's Parish generally sold at $20 to $40 an acre in 1860.[32]

---

[30] This number does not include six of Captain John Fripp's plantations or five of Dr. William J. Jenkins' plantations, because the exact size of these plantations cannot be ascertained.

[31] Mills, *Statistics of South Carolina*, p. 372.

[32] MS, Before the Committee on the Judiciary of the House of Representatives, 1888. In possession of William Elliott, Columbia, S. C.

Here, as in the rest of the sea-island area, large landholdings and large slaveholdings were concentrated in the hands of a few planters, some of them as wealthy as any to be found in the coastal region of South Carolina and Georgia. Here was the quintessence of large scale plantation economy, the characteristic features of which were evolved out of the production of sea-island cotton.

CHAPTER IV

SEA-ISLAND COTTON CULTURE

THE PLANTING ROUTINE

THE CULTIVATION of sea-island cotton produced a characteristic system of agriculture. The average sea-island planter cultivated a little less than six acres to the hand. Had the plough been substituted for the hoe, the acreage per hand would have been twice as much. In addition to cotton, the planter raised corn and sweet potatoes as provision crops in the proportion of about seven-twelfths cotton, three-twelfths corn, and two-twelfths sweet potatoes. The average yield of cotton was about 135 pounds to the acre; of corn, fifteen to twenty-five bushels of the southern white-flint variety; and of potatoes, about 150 bushels to the acre.[1]

Since cotton was the main crop of the sea-island planter, he tended to consider that acres planted in provision crops were somewhat of a loss. It was seldom, therefore, that a planter raised enough corn and potatoes to furnish his plantation throughout the year, for the acreage in provision crops was determined not so much by the amount of provisions required as by the number of acres which the hands could attend while working the cotton crop. Factors' statements and the plantation books available indicate that sea-island cotton planters made frequent purchases of corn, rice, and bacon for provisions.

The planting season began about the middle of March, although the preparation of the soil started much earlier in

---

[1] Turner, *Cotton Planter's Manual*, p. 133. With reference to the crops of St. Helena see Pierce, "Report of the Government Agent," in *Rebellion Records*, sup., I, 306.

the year. Cotton was planted from about March 20 to April 10; corn about April 1; and sweet potatoes the latter part of March. The routine of labor on a sea-island cotton plantation from planting time until the crops were laid by is illustrated by that on John Fripp's Bluff plantation of 560 acres as recorded in his plantation book for 1856. The spring of this year was cold and wet so that Fripp was late in putting in his crops.

He did his first planting on March 20 and 21 when he banked and planted four acres of potatoes. The weather prevented his planting again until April 7 when he put in the rest of his potatoes, two more acres. On the tenth he commenced banking and planting cotton, and by the sixteenth he had put in thirty-eight acres which he recorded were doing "fine." Three days later he began putting in the corn crop and planted that day eighteen acres in the "Savannah swamp field." On the twenty-second he planted twenty-three acres of cotton in the "Marsh field." A week later he commenced the regular corn crop and by the first of May had planted in all sixty-three acres. The next day he planted twelve more acres of cotton in the swamp field and on May 3 put in three-fourths of an acre of rice in the small fresh water ponds by "Point field." On the twelfth and thirteenth he finished planting cotton, making a total of 121 acres.

The hands were busy hoeing cotton from that time until the twenty-second of May when they stopped to put in fifteen acres of "Shinney Peas." Two days later Fripp detailed a few hands to put in an acre of rice near the swamp field. All hands resumed cotton hoeing until July 5 when Fripp began to plant the first of his potato slips.

From then until August a few hands put in a half acre or less a day, planting in all sixteen acres of potatoes. Work on the cotton crop stopped about the middle of July. Fripp finished planting about the first of September when he had two acres of potato slips put in for seed and three-fourths of an acre of turnip seed sown.

By November 29 he had gathered and finished "breaking in" the corn crop, having made 650 bushels, less than 12 bushels to the acre. By December 9 he had finished digging potatoes, having made a poor crop, and four days later he had gathered all the cotton. On December 13 the hands began processing the cotton and did not finish ginning the crop of thirty-five bales until February 12, just in time to begin listing the soil in preparation for drilling in the cotton seed a few weeks later. During the slack periods, the hands had been engaged in digging and hauling marsh mud to manure the fields, cutting marsh grass for fodder and also for fertilizer, cutting and sawing wood, and ditching fields.[2]

St. Helena Island planters, as a rule, obtained the simplest of farm implements for their laborers. Most of the work in cultivating sea-island cotton was done with the hoe. In 1822 there was not a plough or scythe on Edisto, one of the best cultivated of the Sea Islands. The largest plantations had only two or three carts; the use of oxen was unknown.[3] By 1844 nearly every plantation on the island had a cart and mule or yoke of oxen to every six taskable hands. At the close of the ante-bellum period, however, John F. Townsend was the only planter who

[2] MS, John E. Fripp, Bluff Plantation Book.
[3] Seabrook, *Memoir on the Cultivation of Cotton*, p. 25.

used plows to any extent.[4] Only a few planters on St. Helena Island, such as Thomas A. Coffin and Dr. W. J. Jenkins, used plows, and when a plow was used it was more often drawn by an ox than a mule.[5]

In 1856 when John E. Fripp, of St. Helena Island, bought the Chechessee Bluff plantation of about 560 acres on Oakatee Creek, he equipped it as follows: a saddle, or sulkey, horse and a pair of carriage horses; four mules; eighty-eight stock cattle; six oxen; a large flat boat and two small ones; four good and three "indifferent" plows; three mule or horse carts, two ox carts, one good ox wagon, one ox wagon needing repairs, one mule, or ox, wagon needing a body, one carriage and one sulkey; four sets of cart harness; plow line chains; collars; one small corn mill, a small sugar mill and "fixings"; spades, axes, and hoes.[6]

Although various gins for extracting the seed from sea-island cotton were invented, the only kind used to any extent on St. Helena Island at the close of the ante-bellum period was the old foot-gin, the kind first invented for that purpose. Planters complained that the Negroes quickly broke the more complicated machines. The *Cotton Planter's Manual* described the foot-gins as follows:

These simple machines are 3½ feet high, 2 feet long, and 1 wide, with an iron fly-wheel like that of a "box corn-sheller," upon each side, working a pair of wooden rollers, made of hard oak, about ten inches long and nearly an inch in diameter, held together by screws. . . . These rollers wear out, and have to be replaced by new ones every day. . . . The rollers are moved by the foot, like

[4] Turner, *op. cit.*, p. 131.
[5] See MS, Port Royal Correspondence. In archives of U. S. Treasury Department.
[6] John E. Fripp, Bluff Plantation Book.

a small turning lathe, the operator standing at one end of the gin, feeding the cotton very slowly through the rollers, leaving the smooth black seeds behind. . . . Twenty or thirty of these little machines stand in one room; and, strange to say, none of those who have attempted to propel them by other power have succeeded. One very intelligent gentleman told me that he had spent $5,000 in trying experiments in machinery to gin this kind of cotton.[7]

BEGINNING OF EXPERIMENTAL AGRICULTURE

Although sea-island cotton in the early days of its introduction was one of the most profitable crops ever raised in the South, the increase of its production and the varying fineness of the fiber caused a wide fluctuation in the price. Thus while some planters realized considerable profits, others were hard put to make expenses. As early as 1826 the most progressive planters in nearly every parish which grew "sea-islands" began to inquire into the causes of this condition. They organized agricultural societies[8] in the attempt to improve the general methods of culture and to standardize the prices; they subscribed to agricultural magazines; they wrote articles; they sent out questionnaires.

In 1828 William Elliott, of St. Helena's Parish, writing in the *Southern Agriculturist*, expressed the general sentiment of sea-island planters on this important subject. He said:

I shall turn to the consideration of a question, which it is of a paramount importance that a Sea-Island Planter should examine and

---

[7] Turner, *Cotton Planter's Manual*, p. 135.

[8] The St. Helena Agricultural Society was organized prior to February, 1843. *The Southern Agriculturist* of that date contains a letter from Daniel Jenkins, the secretary, on the unsuccessful experiment of some St. Helena planters in packing sea-island cotton in square bales.

understand; viz. "What is the cause of the difference of price given for Cotton, grown even on adjoining plantations?" . . . latterly, the range of price has baffled all calculation, and has extended to such a pitch, that a favoured Planter has been known to obtain for his crop, *five times the price* obtained by his immediate neighbour. . . . Yet it must be confessed, that this unsettled state of things accompanied by its apparent system of favoritism, has a most discouraging effect on Planters. When they who enjoy equal advantages, as to salt exposure, practice equal assiduity in the application of salt manures, bestow equal care on the preparation of their staple, find that all these advantages and this care go for nothing—that the extra expense incurred by their superior preparation was equal to ten or twelve cents per pound—while one or two cents advance on the average price, was all their compensation; that the money thus profitably expended by the majority of growers, went to the exclusive profit of the foreign agent or manufacturer; while here and there some solitary, envied Planter, received a disproportionate reward for his labours. When these things are considered, it is not to be wondered at, that they are discouraged, and that they are ready to substitute any other culture which may offer to industry and skill, a competent and an equal remuneration. For, if the high rate of valuation, at which their lands and negroes have been acquired, whether inherited or purchased, be taken into the account, it will be confessed, that few investments of capital have yielded for the last ten years so trifling a return, as that of the Sea-Island Planters. The prices have never been high, and, whenever a full crop has crowned the wishes of the Planter, the price was sure to fall by anticipation.

. . . To the Vanderhorsts', the Seabrooks', Matthews', Coffins', and Popes', and others of that fortunate class, whose names give title to the highest prices in the agricultural lottery, I offer no advice. But, to the majority of Planters cultivating the Sea-Islands, or points of the mainland, inclosed by the arms of the sea, the debatable lands, as it were, of the culture, I would say, persevere yet a while in your efforts to approach the standard of these favoured names;—if that be, from physical causes impossible, hope yet longer, that, what happens in all other pursuits, will eventually happen in yours; viz. that a *gradation of prices may be established*, and that your cotton may meet the common justice, to be rated according to its fineness and cleanness, and not continue to be classed, as heretofore, with cotton the meanest, if it did not happen to equal the best.[9]

The Coffins and Popes, whose cotton Elliott mentioned as invariably receiving the top prices in market, were St. Helena Island planters.[10] Whitemarsh B. Seabrook, another successful planter, was one of the first to spread knowledge of the improved methods of cultivation. In 1826 he sent a questionnaire to several planters who were considered the most efficient growers of the staple. Thomas Aston Coffin, of Coffin's Point plantation, St. Helena Island, received one of these questionnaires.[11]

---

[9] Elliott, "On the Cultivation and High Prices of Sea-Island Cotton," *Southern Agriculturist*, I, 154-161.

[10] The Coffin trademark was a "pinch-toe" coffin.

[11] W. B. Seabrook, *A Report Accompanied with Sundry Letters*, pp. 25-27; Coffin's letter dated Dec. 26, 1826. His reply was as follows:

"1. Is all your cotton equally fine?

I think not, but I have never heard purchasers remark any difference . . .

"2. What manure do you esteem best?

I have generally used the marsh mud taken from the creeks; sometimes green marsh.

"3. Is your cotton so distinguished for one quality, remarkable for others, &c?

My cotton derives its character from its silkiness, strength and evenness of fibre.

"4. What has been your average crop for the last seven years? and what quantity do you plant to the hand?

Caterpillars and storms have destroyed some of my most promising crops; but I think 450 lbs. per hand are about the average. I generally plant nearly three and a half acres to the hand.

"5. Are you particular in the selection of your seed? . . .

I have generally preserved the seed from my earliest pickings; sometimes I have planted seed, exchanged with my friends, both North and South. I think the cotton produced from the seed, with a green tuft, the finest and most silky, though not the most productive.

"6. . . .

"7. Do you preserve your seed, &c?

I am not particular, so that it is kept dry.

The result of the wide differences in prices paid for sea-island cotton and the planters' subsequent attempt to remedy this situation led to improvements in the methods of agriculture, such as, the careful selection of seed, fertilization of the soil, soil analysis, and the rotation of crops. Instead of planting seed without regard to its origin, planters sought to obtain improved and tested strains. From 1826 to 1830 the Kinsey Burden seed was considered the most superior on the market; in 1854 "Owen's Selection," named for George C. Owens, was in highest favor.[12] At least three St. Helena Island planters gave their names to seed which was of high repute: Coffin, Pope, and Fripp. In 1868, when good sea-island cotton seed was extremely difficult to obtain, James Gregorie's factor in Charleston wrote to him, "I understand from

"8. Do you in gathering your crop pick those pods, which, from their immaturity, are imperfectly open, &c?
My orders are to pass over defective pods, to save the trouble of selecting them, when assorting; but, from the difficulty of seeing these executed, I presume they are much neglected, especially after frost.
"9. Do you dry your cotton in the sun or shade, and how long?
Generally one day on a scaffold, unless the cotton has been wet.
"10. What is your mode of preparation?
. . . I handle it as little as possible after it comes from the gin.
"11. Are you in the habit of using the whipper?
Before cotton goes to the gin, but not after.
"12. What is the character of your soil and situation?
High and low; mostly high; a yellow mixed sand on the hills, and black or grey in the narrow vallies which run N.E. and S.W. through the extent of the Island. I am on a neck of land, two sides are bounded by creeks, and one side by the ocean.
"I have *once* used a *machine gin* from St. Simons' Island, to the rollers of which, made of hickory, I gave as many as six hundred revolutions in a minute. I ginned about twenty bales of cotton with this gin, and heard no complaint about the staple being injured; but my negroes were continually putting it out of order, and my impelling power proving defective, I laid it aside. I introduced this remark, hoping the want of a gin, as well adapted to the Sea-Island Cotton as Whitney's saw gin is to the upland, may stimulate some of our planters, in this exertion, to produce one."

[12] Allston, *Essay on Sea Coast Crops*, p. 13.

Isaac his seed is the genuine old Fripp seed, if so take care & don't get it mixed with other seed so that you can furnish your friends with it next year."[13]

In the attempt to raise a staple with a fine, long fiber, sea-island cotton planters, while achieving this goal through a careful selection of seed, at the same time acquired a plant of small fruitage and consequently of slender yield, sacrificing quantity for the quality of the product. By force of circumstances, therefore, they were compelled to resort to every possible means of keeping the yield up to the maximum.

In the early days of the plantation regime when planters used any fertilizer at all it was for their potato fields, for they used only virgin land for their cotton. When the fields first selected for cotton became exhausted, as they invariably did in a few years, they again resorted to virgin land, clearing the land by girdling the trees, without taking the trouble to remove them, so that a cotton field was often a cemetery of dead oaks and palmettos which made the use of the plow impossible. In 1826 Robert Mills wrote, "The bulk of the planters, relying on the fertility of the soil, seldom plant any land but what is good, and change the same when it begins to fail for what is fresh, giving themselves little trouble to keep their fields in heart."[14] Even late in the ante-bellum period this expedient was still the most popular one.[15]

In some cases necessity forced the planter to drain the swamps and marshes and convert them into cotton fields.

---

[13] MS, John Colcock to James Gregorie, Charleston, April 9, 1868. In possession of Dr. M. G. Elliott, Beaufort, S. C.
[14] *Statistics of South Carolina*, pp. 155, 156.
[15] Seabrook, *Memoir on Cotton*, p. 24.

These reclaimed tracts often proved very fertile so that in the later ante-bellum period, a few sea-coast planters quite generally engaged in draining and embanking marshes and swamps. In 1844 Mr. Seabrook, of Edisto, thought that the immense tracts of unreclaimed swamps "which lie along the line where the salt and fresh water meet . . . are capable of yielding an amount of cotton wool equal to the yearly exports of the State."[16]

MARSH MUD AND SEA-ISLAND COTTON

A few planters fertilized their cotton fields soon after the introduction of the new staple; in fact, all the materials used as manure in the later ante-bellum period were employed as early as 1805 in a limited way by some sea-island planters, but it was not until 1825 that the methods of manuring became generally known.

Planters found that salt-marsh[17] mud which was within easy reach of most of the cotton fields, was the cheapest and one of the most profitable manures that they could obtain. It was usually applied to the soil at the rate of about forty-one cart loads to the acre. Planters employed various methods of adding it to their fields. On Edisto Island most of them preferred to use it as soon as dug. The Whaley plantation on Little Edisto was divided into halves, each half being planted in alternate years. Slaves went out in boats on the creeks and rivers to the nearby marshes, loaded their boats with the mud, and returned to empty it in ox-carts or hand-woven baskets

---

[16] *Ibid.*, p. 24.
[17] The term "saltmarsh" was used on the coast to apply to the mud and other matters of which the marsh is composed.

to be "toted" to the fields by other slaves.[18] The mud was then listed in. On the John F. Townsend plantation it was plowed in, but Mr. Townsend was the only man on the island who used plows to any extent.

Some planters dried the mud before spreading it upon the land. Tuomey's *Geological Survey of South Carolina* of 1848 recommends charring the mud to diminish its weight so that it might be transported profitably some distance up the rivers and so that it would fix the volatile products of decomposition on being added to a barn-yard manure heap.[19] Other planters made a compost[20] of the mud. R. F. W. Allston, writing in 1854 on the sea-coast crops, stated that the usual compost was prepared in summer "by mixing with farm-yard, cowpen and stable litter, salt marsh, marsh mud, and even salt."[21] It was applied to the land in winter at the rate of forty, fifty, and seventy cart loads. He considered that the best method of using this compost was, first, to prepare the land in the autumn by listing in the remaining growth as soon as the crop had been picked, even before the cotton had been prepared for market, and then in the spring to make a bed on the autumn listing by drawing up with a hoe the earth which had been well manured in the winter with the marsh-mud compost.

The proportion of marsh mud to barnyard manure used in this compost was based upon the character of the

---

[18] J. Swinton Whaley, "The History of Sea-Island Cotton." Unpublished manuscript.

[19] Tuomey, *Geology of South Carolina*, p. 232.

[20] For a discussion of composts see F. A. Procher, "Report on Manures," in *Southern Agriculturist*, new ser., V, no. I, 1-13; Turner, *Cotton Planter's Manual*, pp. 70-80, 85-93.

[21] Allston, *Essay on Sea Coast Crops*, p. 13.

land and the experience of the planter. Colonel Edward Barnwell, of St. Helena's Parish, considered his success in sea-island cotton planting to be due entirely to his method of preparing compost. He descanted so much on compost that one of his friends once remarked that Edward Barnwell would put compost into his will. He did. He left a certain Negro to a son who intended to be a planter "because he knows all about making compost, without which a plantation is of no value."

While some planters brought the marsh mud to the manure heaps, still others mixed the mud and the manure on the fields themselves by "running a cowpen." The plantation cattle, which numbered as many as could be pastured upon the "field at rest" and the woodland, usually twenty to every five hands,[22] were penned on succeeding nights in movable yards on the resting field, which was littered with fine straw and marsh grass. The tramping of the cattle excellently prepared the field for a top dressing of marsh mud. Sometimes marsh grass was laid between the old rows after running the cowpen but before the mud was applied. Then, the sod of one year's growth was hoed down into the alleys and the bed formed upon it.[23]

Some planters used as a fertilizer only the marsh grass, often called simply "saltmarsh." "St. Helena," writing in 1837 for the *Southern Agriculturist* on the cultivation of sea-island cotton, explained his method of applying marsh grass as follows:

It may . . . be gathered in the summer, and put up in heaps, for use in the following spring. Where the planter alternates his

[22] Turner, *Cotton Planter's Manual*, p. 87.
[23] *Ibid.*, p. 132.

fields, the marsh may be spread out in the alleys of the vacant field, and immediately listed in. This mode is decidedly preferable; because, putting in the marsh at so early a period, gives it abundant time to rot, by the ensuing spring. But where the same field is planted for any number of consecutive years, the marsh must be put up in heaps to rot during the summer; for the field is then occupied with the cotton. With a good scythe, it may be fairly estimated, that one fellow will do six times as much at cutting marsh, as in digging mud: and when it is considered that six cartloads of marsh, will manure a task better than 21 loads of mud, the balance is greatly in favor of marsh. Rushes do as well as marsh, where the land does not require salt. . . . Some planters object to marsh, and say that it produces "blue" in cotton; but no one need apprehend this, if the marsh has been put into the land so as to give it sufficient time to rot, before the cotton-plant reaches it.[24]

The value of the marsh mud as a manure for sea-island cotton land depended not only upon its effect in promoting retention of moisture but also upon the saline, organic, and calcareous matter which it contained. Most of the marsh mud, however, has a very low content of carbonate of lime and is not a sufficient fertilizer for soils deficient in calcareous matter. Some planters met this deficiency by the addition of crushed oyster shells which everywhere appear in great abundance along the banks of the rivers and creeks of the Sea Islands. John Couper, even before 1800, spread crushed oyster shells on his cotton lands on St. Simon's Island every other year and in the alternate years gave them a top dressing of marsh mud.[25] Yet the benefits of shells, or marl, to sea-island cotton land was so little known in the late ante-bellum period that Professor

[24] *Southern Agriculturist*, X, 175.
[25] MS in Couper-Wylly Papers.

Charles U. Shepard, in reporting on the nature of the soils of Edisto Island to St. John's, Colleton, Agricultural Society, suggested that "the peculiar fertility of new sea-island cotton land" may be "owing to the proportion of comminuted shells natural to such soils, and the deterioration of these lands under long cultivation, ascribable to the exhaustion of carbonate of lime."[26] He strongly urged, therefore, that planters add pulverized oyster shells to their cotton fields or be careful to use a marsh mud which abounded in a gravel of feldspar and hornblende.[27] The old indigo heaps, the refuse of the vats, offered the planter another source of lime for his cotton fields. The lime used in the preparation of the dye had become mixed with earthy matters and was especially beneficial to the cotton fields.

A few planters experimented with the commercial fertilizers, especially guano and its substitutes. The *American Agriculturist*, writing in the late ante-bellum period on the crops of Edisto Island, earnestly recommended planters to use guano, which contains "the same fertilizing properties of muck, in an hundredfold degree," and suggested that they apply about 200 pounds to the acre, plowed in deep, or buried in the bottom of the cotton beds, making sure, however, to use "none but the best Peruvian, and purchase it from a reliable merchant, so as to be sure it is genuine."[28] By the close of the ante-bellum period planters in the sea-island cotton belt quite generally used some kind of fertilizer.

[26] Tuomey, *Geology of South Carolina*, p. xlii.
[27] *Ibid.*, p. 234. Edmund Ruffin examined a specimen from a shell bank on Distant Island near Beaufort and found it contained 47 per cent of carbonate of lime.
[28] Printed in Turner, *Cotton Planter's Manual*, pp. 132-133.

ROTATION OF CROPS

Planters came much later to realize the importance of soil analysis as a means of determining what fertilizers were necessary to make their fields yield the maximum quantity of cotton. The first public organization to stress the importance of soil analysis was the Agricultural Society of St. John's, Colleton. In 1840 the Society asked Professor Shepard to analyze ten specimens of the soils of Edisto Island.[29] His report received considerable attention and helped to stimulate interest in improved methods of agriculture. Edmund Ruffin's geological survey and analysis of the mineral deposits of the state and Professor Tuomey's geological survey further contributed to the planters' increasing desire to know the exact nature of their soil so that they might succeed better in cultivating their plantations.

A few enterprising planters learned at an early date that a rotation of crops improved the quality of the land. For instance, John Couper, of Cannon's Point plantation, St. Simon's Island, a native of Scotland, practised rotation of crops before 1800, and his son, James Hamilton Couper, of Hopeton plantation, carried his father's work still further.

James Hamilton Couper, an honor graduate of Yale, later visited his uncle in Glasgow and from there went to

---

[29] Tuomey, *Geology of South Carolina*, pp. xxxviii-xliii. The soils analyzed were as follows: (1) virgin wet mud, (2) deposit wet mud, (3) close sandy soil from high land, (4) dark gray soil from land rather flat for cotton, (5) very light sandy soil (very high land), (6) dark gray soil from land rather low, (7) close yellow sandy soil (high land), (8) close yellow soil from the most productive part of Professor Shepard's tract, (9) mud that had been exposed to the sun for nearly two months, (10) mud taken from the cotton field in which it was buried the previous year.

Holland to study reclamation so that he might drain the fertile swamps and deltas of the Georgia coast. With slave labor he cleared the cypress brakes of the Altamaha delta, grubbing, diking, and ditching the land, sometimes at a cost of a thousand dollars an acre, until in 1826, when he bought a half interest in Hopeton plantation, he was cultivating at a profit 641 acres of improved swamp land. In 1832 J. D. Legare, editor of the *Southern Agriculturist*, of Charleston, said of Hopeton plantation:

> We hesitate not to say Hopeton is decidedly the best plantation we have ever visited, and we doubt whether it can be equalled in the Southern states. And when we consider the extent of the crops, the variety of the same, and the number of operatives who have to be directed and managed, it will not be presumptive to say that it may fairly challenge comparison with any establishment of the United States, for the systematic arrangement of the whole, the regularity and precision with which each and all of the operations are carried out, and the perfect and daily accountability established in every department.
>
> The proportions of the crop, at the time of my visit, were 500 acres in rice, 170 in cotton, and 333 in cane.[30]

Mr. Couper attracted attention as a scientific planter not only on the seaboard of Georgia and South Carolina, but in Europe as well. Sir Charles Lyell, Miss Frederika Bremer, and the Honorable Amelia M. Murray, distinguished European visitors who spent several days at Hopeton at different times during the late plantation regime,[31] also praised his plantation management and experimentation with crops.

---

[30] MS in Couper-Wylly Papers.

[31] Lyell, *Second Visit to the United States*, I, 261-273; Hon. Amelia M. Murray, *Letters from the United States, Cuba and Canada*, pp. 220-225; Frederika Bremer, *Homes of the New World*, pp. 485-491.

Mr. Couper seldom allowed any of his fields to rest, a method of improving the fertility of the land followed by most sea-island planters. Instead, he fertilized the land and rotated the crops in order to replace the minerals extracted by growing plants. The following table, made from Couper's Hopeton Plantation Book, indicates for ten years the crops planted on West Old Field of eighty-five and a half acres, one of the most fertile of the seventeen fields which he annually cultivated, and at the same time illustrates his experimentation with crops:

ROTATION OF CROPS ON HOPETON PLANTATION, 1820-1829[32]

Year	Cotton	Corn	Cotton and corn mixed	Potatoes	Sugar cane	Pumpkins
1820	79½	0	0	6	0	0
1821	55	23¼	0	7¼	0	0
1822	78½	7	0	0	0	0
1823	78½	5	0	2	0	0
1824	36¾	4	33	4¾	0	0
1825	81	0	0	3½	1	0
1826	66	16	0	0	3½	0
1827	26¼	33	14½	8½	0	1¼
1828	75¾	0	0	8½	0	1¾
1829	36¼	0	0	0	49	0

On other fields Couper rotated peas, cotton, corn, cotton and corn mixed, potatoes, and occasionally pumpkins.

Although Couper had mixed cotton with corn as early as 1824, in 1844 Seabrook spoke of this method of rotation as having been lately adopted by a few planters in Georgia.[33] They planted cotton on alternate ridges with corn, and the next year substituted the cotton rows for the corn.

---

[32] MS, Hopeton Plantation Book, 1818-1831. In possession of Mrs. W. S. Lovell, Birmingham, Ala. Hopeton Plantation, on the Altamaha River, in Glynn County, Ga., contained about eleven thousand acres and in 1826 was valued at $80,412. The map on page 63 was reproduced from a map in colors in Hopeton Plantation Book.

[33] Seabrook, *Memoir on Cotton*, p. 28.

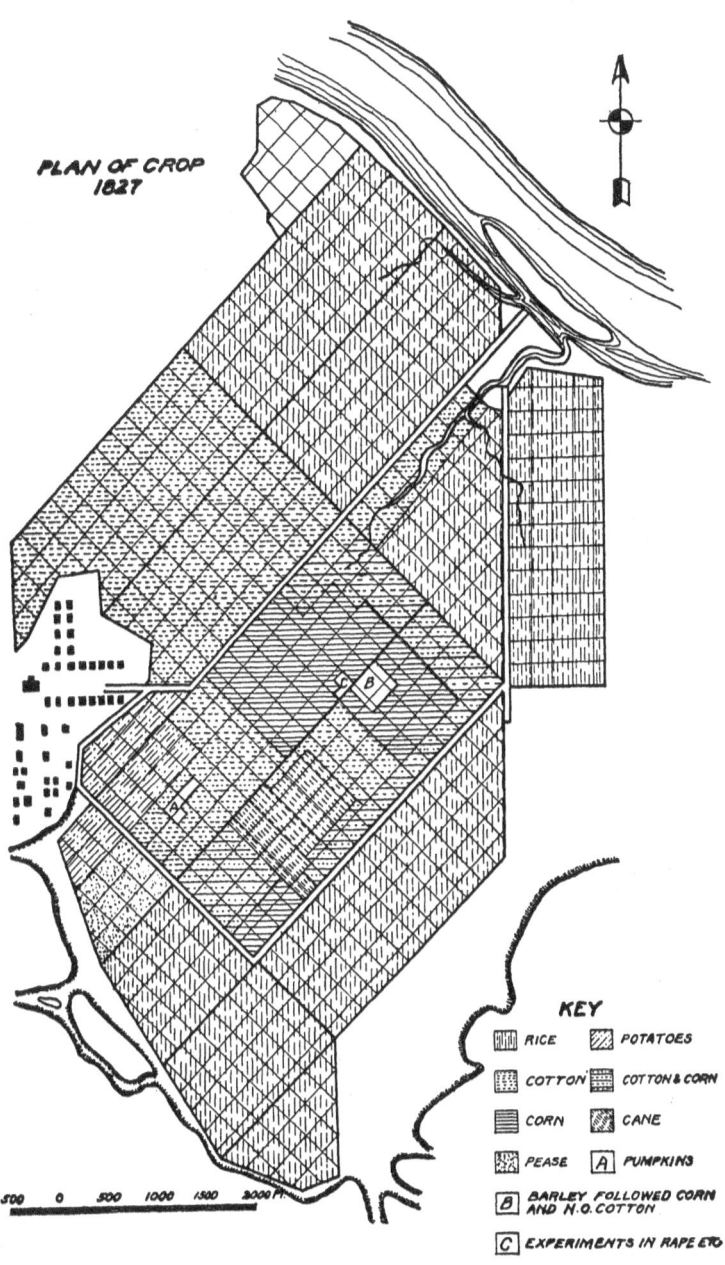

HOPETON PLANTATION ON THE ALTAMAHA

Seabrook, however, thought this rotation unfitted for the South Carolina Sea Islands "where the high lands, which are limited in quantity, and unfit for corn, are alone considered safe for cotton." Instead, he recommended as a good rotation to be followed " in a small way," potatoes, or spring peas, rest, and cotton.[34]

"Rest" was the common practice of "rotation" on the Sea Islands. When the land had become exhausted by repeated cropping, its fertility was restored not only by the application of manures, but by resting the field for a certain length of time. The time necessary for restoration was dependent, of course, upon the nature of the subsoil. Enterprising planters hastened the process by thoroughly breaking up the soil, thereby exposing fresh surfaces to the atmosphere and turning the grass and weeds under to enrich the soil.

THE AGRICULTURAL LOTTERY

Despite these efforts at scientific farming, which resulted in methods that are generally considered as belonging to present day agricultural development, sea-island cotton was an uncertain crop. In 1808 David Ramsay, writing the history of South Carolina, spoke of planting as an annual lottery, in which on an average of several years there were many blanks and many prizes. "A few of the latter," he wrote, "are very large, but the greatest number do not much exceed the price of the ticket."[35] In successful seasons, profits were large. One crop might purchase the land which raised it; two or three more, the Negroes who cultivated it. But in unsuccessful years,

---

[34] *Ibid.*, p. 29.
[35] David Ramsay, *The History of South-Carolina*, II, 396.

planters felt the pinch of hard times. A late, wet spring might defer planting until there could be no hope of maturing an average yield before frost. Had the spring been propitious, an unseasonable frost might blight the plant and decrease the crop. Excess of rain or drought might retard the crop or the plant might develop a disease. When the crop was made and ready to be gathered, a storm or hurricane might blast the labor of a year. When the crop was gathered and baled ready for market, economic conditions at home or abroad might reduce the price so low as to plunge the planter into debt.

The diseases to which sea-island cotton were subject, blight, rust, and "blue," were generally considered as arising from some defect in the soil.[36] They could be removed, or at least considerably remedied, by thoroughly draining the land and applying the proper fertilizer at the proper season. But the plant louse, cut worm, and the leaf worm, or caterpillar, as it was commonly known, could not be so easily combated. The plant louse was practically a yearly pest which planters fought by cultivation, attempting to raise a plant hardy enough to withstand the attacks of the insect. The cut worm often appeared in wet seasons and on low lands insufficiently drained. James Hamilton Couper recorded in his plantation book when commenting on the crop for 1818:

The cut-worm was so destructive, until the 18th. of May, as to have killed the cotton, as soon up, with the exception of the high parts of the old & new fields. They were universally found in the East River Field. It is believed that the Fresh, which covered the fields from the 5th. to the 21st. of March was the cause of their appearance in such numbers.[37]

[36] Allston, *Sea Coast Crops*, pp. 14, 15.
[37] Hopeton Plantation Book.

The leaf worm, although nearly always present, became destructive only when the conditions for its development were favorable, such as, a warm winter followed by a wet spring. Planters constantly attempted to fight the insect by seeking to raise a plant which would mature its pods sufficiently early to produce a paying crop before the worm reached its most destructive stage. Once the caterpillars appeared in great numbers, however, the average planter of the ante-bellum period knew little to do but curse the fate which sent them. By turning large flocks of turkeys into the fields, they could save many acres of cotton, but no plantation kept a drove large enough to protect all the fields in a bad year, for, when the caterpillars reached the final stage of development, they usually destroyed a crop within forty-eight hours. In 1846-1847, caterpillars reduced the estimated crop of the South from 2,400,000 bales to 1,779,000.[38] J. Swinton Whaley, of Little Edisto Island, recalls that caterpillars so greatly damaged three hundred acres of his father's cotton in 1867 that he saved only seven bags of cotton.[39] On this occasion, while driving along the main road to his summer home on the opposite side of the island, a distance of twelve miles, his father crushed caterpillars under his wheels the entire way. Having finished the fields, they were then in possession of the road. Doubtless some planters learned before 1860 that they could successfully combat the leaf worm by dusting their plants with Paris Green,[40] but this method was not common knowledge until much later.

[38] *DeBow's Review*, VI, 126.
[39] Whaley, "History of Sea-Island Cotton." Unpublished MS.
[40] Allston, in his *Essay on Sea Coast Crops*, p. 15, advises, "Destroy the enemy

The weather not only abetted the insects in their destruction of the cotton crops, but sometimes itself brought ruin. In 1819 James Hamilton Couper was found recording in his plantation book, "In the Spring, the Cotton was very generally destroyed by Frost," and "On the night of the 14th Octr. a sharp white frost destroyed about 70 acres of cotton at Hopeton."[41] In 1823 he wrote:

> The crop was set in good time; and was unusually promising until the excessive rains which commenced about the middle of July. These rains continued nearly two months, and occasioned the cotton to drop nearly the whole of the middle & under crop. The upper crop in quantity and maturity promised well, but from the diseased habit which the plant had acquired never opened.[42]

In 1826 he wrote, "This is the only cotton crop since 1818 which has not been cut off by spring freshes, early fall frosts, or gales of wind," and the following year he again recorded, "A very high fresh which occurred about the end of May nearly destroyed the Cotton in Carr's Is." There were heavy rains again in 1828 and 1829, and in 1830 "a very severe Hail Storm was so destructive to the cotton crop, that the failure . . . was nearly entire." With this year, Couper left off recording his observations on crops, but in a letter to his son in 1855 he wrote, "We have had a glut of rain during the week; and as was to be expected the cotton is shedding freely. Three fourths of the Cotton crops are destroyed by the August rains."[43]

---

in embryo, as the energetic planter . . . has already done." He doubtless refers to dusting the plants with a mixture of Paris Green, rosin, and damaged wheat flour.

[41] Hopeton Plantation Book. [42] *Ibid.*
[43] Couper-Wylly Letters, August 23, 1855, James Hamilton Couper to Hamilton Couper.

The southern sea coast is subject to autumnal storms which occasionally destroy the planters' entire crop. Sir Charles Lyell, in his second visit to the United States in 1841 and 1842, commented upon this fact, mentioning that in 1756 the entire coast from St. Simon's Island, Georgia, as far north as Charles Town (Charleston) was overflowed, the sea rising six feet above its ordinary level.[44] Parts of the Sea Islands were under water in 1804 and 1824. In the latter year the crops were unusually promising. John Couper had matured a crop of some six hundred bales worth $90,000, but he lost most of the crop in twelve hours by the hurricane of September 14.[45] The next year his crop was nearly destroyed by caterpillars. On September 8, 1854, the coast was again visited by a destructive hurricane,[46] and since the antebellum period by two, one in 1893 and one in 1911, which have caused great suffering and loss of life.

THE PLANTER AND HIS FACTOR

The very uncertainty of the crop, as well as the nature of it, tied the planter to the system of factorage so well known in England and other countries long before the settlement of the American colonies. Commission merchants in Charleston and Savannah readily credited sea-island cotton planters who might in one year make enough to pay off the debts of several years accumulation. It was customary, therefore, for the planter to spend his money before

---

[44] Lyell, *Second Visit to the United States*, I, 253.
[45] Couper-Wylly Letters. May 24, 1828, John Couper to his brother James Couper.
[46] U. B. Phillips, *Documentary History of American Industrial Society, Plantation and Frontier*, I, 141.

he had made it, and it was the factor who enabled him to do so.[47] He sold the planter's cotton on commission. He

[47] See factors' statements and letters in the McPherson and Gregorie Papers, and the John E. Fripp Papers. The following statement is John E. Fripp's account with his factor from September, 1856, to May, 1857:

Cr.———John E. Fripp, Esqr.———In Account———Current with———
Coffin & Pringle

1856
July 22   By Balance at your credit as pr. account rendered 86.77
November 20   By Nett Sales of 3 Bags sold in Liverpool
    say £50. 13.10
    £39.19.01 @ 9¼% 194
    £10.14.09 @ 8½ % 57.77   245.77

    £50.13.10
    Less advance recd. 17th June last   194
    " 127 days Interest on advance
        from 5th
    September last to maturity
        of Sales
    10th January 1857 @ 6%   4.01
    " our commission @ 2½%
    on balance say on $51.77..   1.29   199.30   46.47

1857
January 5   By received for T. M. Hanckel's order upon
    Legare & Colcock........................... 135.75
February 20   By received for 3 Hides 11.10
April 13   By Nett Proceeds of 11 Bags Cotton as pr.
    Sales rendered 1,718.85

                                                   $1,998.94

"Dr.———John E. Fripp, Esqr.———In Account———Current with———
Coffin & Pringle

1856
September 30   To Sundry Postages paid to date........... .28
November 26   " remitted him 50.00
    " 94 yds California Kersey @ 40c........ 37.60
    " 124½ yds Brown Plains @ 34c........ 42.33
    " 44½ yds Union Plains @ 25c........ 11.12
    " 56 Blankets 129.20
    " 20 yds Satinet @ 62½c............... 12.50
    " 1 ps Red Flannel 35 yds @ 25c........ 8.75
    " 1 ps Long Cloth 40½ yds @ 15c....... 6.07

sold him on credit the provisions on which his plantation operated: his Negro cloth, his farm implements, frequently his cotton seed, and much of his corn and bacon. He paid the planter's taxes and cashed his drafts.

Frequently the planter and his factor were related by blood ties so that the agent had an additional incentive to treat him as a preferred creditor. While the relation between individual planter and factor was often friendly, there was in general a feeling of resentment between the two. When the planter's crop failed, his factor might consider that the failure was due, in part at least, to mismanagement; while the planter constantly regarded his factor's commissions as too high. An Edisto planter who once raised large crops of sea-island cotton still speaks with bitterness of the more than hundred years of bondage in which Charleston factors held sea-island planters.

		"	1 ps Bleached Homespun 47 yds @ 12½c	5.88
		"	48 pair Shoes @ $1.10................	52.80
		"	Freight $2.72 Drayage 19c	2.91
1857				
January	1	"	paid his order to B. S. Screven........	50.00
March	3	"	paid him	500.00
	4	"	paid 8 Months & 13 days Interest on his Bond for $3415 to John Webb to date	154.60
			& on account of the Principal of said Bond	1,345.00
			& one year & 1 Month Interest on his Bond for $4000 to same to date....	303.33
	10	"	paid his order to Wm. C. Danner & Co.....	104.26
May	5	"	paid his order to O. P. Law, Tax Collector..	95.56
				$2,902.40
			To Balance brought down at your debit this day......	$ 903.55
			E. E.	

Charleston 10th June 1857
Coffin & Pringle
for John P. Matheson

Without his factor, however, the planter would have been hard put to it to operate his plantation. The factor often held the planter's cotton in storage waiting higher prices, paying storage and insurance, which, of course, were deducted from the sale of the cotton. Sea-island cotton was usually later in reaching the market than the short-staple cotton because of the longer time required in ginning it. It did not begin to move freely into market until the first of the year, but some planters had their factors hold their cotton as late as July and August.

It usually cost the planter about 4 per cent of the value of the bale to market his cotton after it had been ginned. For instance, in June, 1835, Miss Mary B. Elliott, daughter of William Elliott, the first successful planter of sea-island cotton in South Carolina, sold ten bales of prime cotton from her plantation "The Battery"[48] for $1,258.65, the freight, storage and factor's commission of which were $48.64, or 4 per cent of the receipts.[49] In July it cost her 4.6 per cent of the receipts to market five bales of stained cotton and two bales "a shade better." In June, 1840, she was paying 4.1 per cent for freight, storage, and commission. In 1859 John E. Fripp, of St. Helena Island and Bluff plantation on the Oakatee, was paying 4.1 per cent.[50] Freight ordinarily cost $1 a bale; landing, weighing, and storage about 26 cents a bale; insurance, about 37 cents a bale, and the factor's commission 2½ per cent of the sale price.[51] Planters on St. Helena Island ordinarily

[48] The town of Port Royal was built on this plantation during the Civil War.
[49] Miss Mary B. Elliott Account Book, 1835-1849.
[50] John E. Fripp Papers.
[51] Based upon statements which Coffin & Pringle, factors, made to John E. Fripp, in Fripp Papers.

sent their cotton to Beaufort by their own sail boats which were loaded at the plantation docks. At Beaufort they put the cotton, which they billed to their factor, on a boat for Charleston, paying the usual $1 a bale for freight.

The price paid for sea-island cotton varied with the yield and demand for the staple throughout the antebellum period, as did that of upland cotton. Between 1806 and 1816 the price varied from 25 cents to 47 cents a pound.[52] At this time, sea-island cotton was not graded, as William Elliott pointed out in 1828,[53] but sold generally as either fine or inferior. The account book of Miss Mary B. Elliott, his sister, in which she recorded her sales between 1830 and 1849 indicates that she sold during this time four grades of cotton: extra fine, prime, inferior white, and stained or yellow.[54] The price which she received for prime cotton varied from 21 cents in 1843 to 62½ cents in 1836. The inferior white brought 4 or 5 cents a pound less than the prime cotton and the extra fine about that much more. The stained cotton sold usually from 7 to 9 cents a pound.

A sea-island cotton planter of Liberty County, Georgia, analyzed his cotton crops from 1830 to 1847 and found that the average price he received a pound in the eighteen years varied from 13½ cents in 1842 to 41 cents in 1838.[55] At the same time his yield per acre varied from 68 pounds in 1846, when he received net proceeds of $41 a hand, to 223 pounds an acre in 1842, when he

---

[52] *DeBow's Review*, IV, 412.
[53] *Supra*, p. 51.
[54] The classes of long staple cotton on the market were: Floridas, Santees, Maines, and Sea Islands. Each of these was usually classified as common, medium and fine.
[55] Turner, *Cotton Planter's Manual*, pp. 128-129.

realized $80 a hand. The net proceeds per hand were highest in 1835 at $137 a hand and lowest in 1846 at $41, with an average of $83 for the eighteen years.

Miss Mary B. Elliott received over a period of eleven years an average of $87.54 a bale for her sea-island cotton, receiving as high as an average of $183.57 a bale in 1836 and as low as $54.61 in 1848.[56] If it cost an average of $27 a bale to gin the cotton, as Seabrook of Edisto Island estimated,[57] and 4 per cent of the receipts to market it, then the planter had $57.04 a bale out of which to care for his slaves, pay the general overhead on his plantation, and realize interest on the investment of his capital.

[56] Elliott Account Book, 1835-1849.
[57] *Supra*, p. 30.

CHAPTER V

PLANTATION MANAGEMENT

WHILE MOST sea-island planters were ready to agree upon the unsuccessfulness of growing long staple cotton, at least one of them was unwilling to attribute their failure to caterpillars, storms, and the Charleston factors. Whitemarsh B. Seabrook, writing on this subject in 1834 for the *Southern Agriculturist*, was of the opinion that it was due rather to the planter's mismanagement: to his absence from the plantation in the summer months, to his want of strict personal supervision when he was at home, to over-planting, and to ignorance.[1]

THE OVERSEER

St. Helena planters quite generally employed overseers to supervise the detailed operations of their plantations, at the same time reserving the right to lay down the general rules of management.[2] When the planter had several large holdings, as for instance, Captain John Fripp and Dr. W. J. Jenkins, it was impossible for him to attend personally to all the affairs of his crops and his laborers. Had the planter been disposed to undertake so arduous a task, he likely would have done so at the risk of his health, for the whites were subject to the diseases of the summer months, especially malaria, or the "intermittent fevers." No planter, therefore, who could borrow the price of an overseer's wages would spent the "sickly season" on his

---

[1] Whitemarsh B. Seabrook, "On the Causes of the General Unsuccessfulness of Sea-Island Planters," *Southern Agriculturist*, VII, 177-183.

[2] For a list of regulations made by a planter for his overseer, see Phillips, *Plantation and Frontier*, I, 115-122.

plantation. Some St. Helena planters, however, who were unwilling to leave their plantations for long, built a health resort on a bluff on the seaward side of the Island so that they might direct the general management of their plantations during the summer months, the period so important in the growth of sea-island cotton.

While practically every cultivated tract of land on St. Helena Island had its overseer, not every tract had a resident overseer. The owner might employ only one overseer, who had general supervision over his various tracts, and delegate the details of management to a trusted Negro, known as the driver. Consequently, on some plantations there was not even a house for an overseer, the plantation being superintended by the driver and visited by the overseer living on another plantation.

The overseer's position was a difficult one, for his employer expected him not only to manage the plantation economically and raise a good crop, but also to keep the Negroes satisfied and happy. It was customary to furnish the overseer with a house, provisions, and one or two house servants in addition to his money wage.[3] The salary varied with the overseer's ability and the planter's prosperity. James Hamilton Couper, who for several years was the head overseer, or "general manager" of Hopeton plantation, in Glynn County, Georgia, received $2,000 a year and "the general run of the plantation."[4] When he bought half of the plantation in 1826, he retained the general management under the following conditions: "$1000 to be allowed [me] for management, I am

---

[3] For a planter's contract with his overseer see Phillips, *Plantation and Frontier*, I, 122-126.

[4] Couper-Wylly Papers, John Couper to James Couper, May 24, 1828.

also to make the same use of plantation money for maintainance as heretofore. I am also to be allowed a cook, washerwoman and boy as houseservants, a woman for poultry and a stable boy,—or an equivalent. . . . One-half the wages of an overseer and one-half his finding to be allowed by you, and the other by me. The salary not to exceed $600."[5]

At the time James Hamilton Couper was receiving $2,000 a year, Charleston papers were printing advertisements of overseers who offered their services for as low as $50.[6] Miss Mary B. Elliott, of "The Battery" on Port Royal Island, had seven different overseers between 1834 and 1849 whom she paid from $200 to $350 a year.[7] From 1842 to 1861, H. M. Stuart had six different overseers for his Oak Point plantation in St. Helena's Parish whom he paid at a rate of $165 to $320 a year.[8] Both Miss Elliott and Mr. Stuart were forced on one occasion to change overseers in the middle of the year, and the longest that either of them retained the same overseer was six years.

Planters were often willing to make many concessions to their overseers, for a frequent change demoralized the Negroes and led to the general deterioration of the plantation. In 1828 the *Southern Agriculturist* attributed the good condition of the Butler plantation on Butler's Island, Georgia, to the fact that the management of the estate had been kept in the same family for twenty-six years, R. King

---

[5] Couper-Wylly Papers, James Hamilton Couper to James Hamilton, May 22, 1826.

[6] *Charleston Courier*, Feb. 20, 1828. "A Married Man, whose Wife has been brought up in the Country, will take care of a Plantation as Overseer, for fifty dollars a year."

[7] Elliott Account Book.

[8] H. M. Stuart Receipt Book.

having assumed management in 1802, finding the gang good, but "very disorderly which is invariably the case when there is a frequent change of managers."[9] Later his son succeeded him.

Louis Manigault, after having made only half a crop due to his new overseer's inexperience, wrote, "He says 'he will do better another year, that now he sees into it,' and as is well known, 'Never change an Overseer if You can help it.' We try him once (but only once) more."[10] But he proved no better the second year than the first. "Elated by a strong and very false religious feeling he began to injure the plantation a vast deal, placing himself on a par with the Negroes, by even joining in with them at their prayer meetings, breaking down long established discipline, which in every Case is so difficult to preserve, favouring and siding in any difficulty with the people, against the Drivers, besides causing numerous grievances."[11] And so Manigault was forced to look for a new overseer.

ORGANIZATION OF SLAVE LABOR

Planters learned early in the use of slave labor that it was necessary to give certain trusted Negroes limited authority over the others so that with a change of overseers the plantation routine might be disturbed as little as possible. On the large plantations the seasoned Negroes trained the new ones and were responsible for their behaviour. In the early days of the plantation regime, when a gang of fresh Africans was purchased, they were assigned

---

[9] R. King, Jr., "On the Management of the Butler Estate," *Southern Agriculturist*, Dec., 1828.
[10] Phillips, *Plantation and Frontier*, I, 143.
[11] *Ibid.*, p. 145.

in groups to certain reliable slaves who initiated them into the ways of the plantation. These drivers, as they were called, had the right of issuing or withholding rations to the raw recruits and of inflicting minor punishments. They taught the new slaves to speak the broken English which they knew and to do plantation work which required little skill, gathering oyster shells to be burned for making lime, mixing concrete from sand, lime, and shells, cutting wood, and ditching fields. At the end of a year, the master or overseer for the first time directed the work of the new Negro who now had become "tamed," assigning him to a special task of plantation work along with the other seasoned hands who had long since learned to obey orders, to arise when the conch blew at "day clean," to handle a hoe in listing and banking, to stand still when a white man spoke.

The planter usually divided his hands into four classes: drivers, tradesmen, house servants, and field hands. The number of drivers on a plantation depended upon its size. Only the largest of the St. Helena plantations had as many as two. It was the driver's business to superintend generally the field hands, and he carried a small club or whip as his "wand of office." He issued rations; he saw that each laborer's task was properly performed; and he inflicted corporal punishment whenever he saw fit, always, however, subject to the overseer's or master's order. In the absence of the overseer or owner, the driver usually succeeded to much of their authority, and in many cases knew more about the details of plantation affairs than the owner himself. For instance, when St. Helena Island was captured by Federal troops in 1861, the drivers quite generally remained at home issuing rations and directing the work of the plantation.

R. King, Jr., overseer of the Butler estate, thought that the selection of drivers was one of the "grand points" in plantation management. A cruel driver could demoralize the whole plantation, while an honest one could keep the slaves busy and happy. "An order from a driver," he said in explaining his method of plantation discipline, "is to be as implicity obeyed as if it came from myself, nor do I counteract the execution, (unless directly injurious,) . . . It would be endless for me to superintend the drivers and field hands too, and would of course make them useless."[12] Miss Harriet Ware, a missionary to St. Helena Island in 1862, described Limus, a driver on one of the St. Helena plantations, as being "very smart" and easy to learn. "He has the energy and *cuteness* and big eye for his own advantage of a born New Englander. He is not very moral or scrupulous, and the church-members will tell you 'not yet,' with a smile, if you ask whether he belongs to them. But he leads them all in enterprise, and his ambition and consequent prosperity make his example a very useful one on the plantation."[13]

Next to the driver in importance and authority were the tradesmen and the house servants. While the num-

[12] *Southern Agriculturist*, Dec. 1828. "But the grand point [in managing the Butler estate] was to suppress the brutality and licentiousness practiced by the principal men on it; (say the drivers and tradesmen). More punishment is inflicted on every plantation by the men in power from private pique, than from a neglect of duty. . . . The driver to screen favourites, or apply their time to his own purposes, imposes a heavy tax on some. Should they murmur, an opportunity is taken, months after, to punish those unfortunate fellows for not doing their own and other tasks. . . . As an evidence of the various opportunities that a brutal driver has to gratify his revenge, . . . let any planter go into his field, and in any Negro's task he can find apparently just grounds for punishment."

[13] *Letters from Port Royal*, pp. 37-38.

ber of tradesmen on a plantation depended upon the size of the slaveholding and the plantation economy of the owner, every planter on St. Helena Island who owned as many as thirty slaves had at least one tradesman, usually a carpenter. Sometimes the planter had a head carpenter and several subordinates. The Trescot house on Barnwell Island near St. Helena, which had just been completed at the outbreak of the Civil War, was built entirely by Trescot's own carpenters, such work as window sashes and panellings being done in Charleston.[14]

The carpenter did the building and repair work of the plantation, and when work was slack at home he was usually hired out to neighboring plantations or to some reliable person in Beaufort or Charleston. For instance, in August, 1841, Miss Mary B. Elliott, of Beaufort, paid $69.50 "to Mrs. Oswald's York for carpenter work."[15] In 1851 H. M. Stuart, of Beaufort, paid Joe $19 for plastering a room and $1.50 for mending a chimney.[16] Thus, some of the plantation tradesmen exercised as many liberties as free Negroes, and they commanded a position of respect among their fellow slaves. Miss Laura M. Towne, a missionary to St. Helena during the Civil War, found Will, a cabinet-maker on one of the Capers plantations, "very discontented because he was ordered to the field, there being no work at his own trade to do." He was able to read and was "very intelligent and self-respecting."[17] Sir Charles Lyell, who visited James Ham-

---

[14] William Howard Russell, *My Diary North and South*, p. 145. Congressman William Elliott took this house down in 1876, floated it to the town of Beaufort, and erected it just as it had been on Barnwell Island. The house is now owned and occupied by Dr. M. G. Elliott.

[15] Elliott Account Book.   [16] Stuart Receipt Book.

[17] *Letters and Diary of Laura M. Towne*, p. 27.

ilton Couper's Hopeton plantation in 1841, was agreeably surprised to see the rank held there by the black mechanics. "When these mechanics come to consult Mr. Couper on business," he wrote, "their manner of speaking to him is quite as independent as that of English artisans to their employers."[18]

Besides the tradesmen, Edward L. Pierce, in 1862 found on the St. Helena Island plantations among the group of laborers "more intelligent than the average," plowmen, watchmen, and religious leaders. Each plantation also had its stock minder who attended to the breeding and care of the stock; and on the better managed plantations, its poultry minder as well. The stock minder frequently served also as coachman for the overseer's family, while the coachman for the planter's family was usually one of the house servants.

Negroes unable to do a full day's work, "quarter hands," "half hands," and "three-quarter hands," usually performed the house work. For instance, the usual house servants on Henry A. Middleton's Weehaw plantation near Georgetown were "a cook that is not a full task[,] a girl of twelve, a boy of fourteen."[19] An old woman did the gardening for the overseer's family, and an old man attended to the overseer's and the owner's horses and served as coachman for the overseer. The house servants attached to the planter's family went back and forth with the family from the plantation to the summer house.

[18] Lyell, *A Second Visit to the United States*, I, 267.
[19] Henry A. Middleton, Jr., Weehaw Plantation Book. In possession of Langdon Cheves, Charleston, S. C.

THE TASK SYSTEM

Less than half of a planter's total number of laborers could usually be counted upon for a full day's work.

When Captain Basil Hall visited the United States in 1827 and 1828 he found on a sea-island plantation on St. Simon's Island, Georgia, 122 slaves. Of these, seventy were men and women between the ages of fourteen and fifty; forty-eight were children under the age of fourteen; and four were superannuated. The seventy workers were classified as follows: thirty-nine full hands, sixteen three-quarter hands, eleven half hands, and four quarter hands. Out of seventy persons, therefore, the planter had fifty-seven and a half "taskable hands," but those working in the fields were only forty-four taskables, while the other thirteen and a half were employed as cart drivers, nurses, cooks for the Negroes, carpenters, house servants, and stock minders.[20]

The number of taskable hands on a plantation varied from year to year. Children were not sent to the field until they were fourteen, but were put to work at minor jobs, pulling weeds, "minding child," picking up trash, washing dishes. Superannuated slaves were also given tasks calling for little physical exertion; such as, gardening, tending horses, nursing, sewing. *Enceinte* women did half tasks until confinement, and women with suckling babies also did half task until the child was eight months old. A slave who had been sick did a portion of a task until he had sufficiently recovered to resume his accustomed amount of work.

[20] Captain Basil Hall, *Travels in North America in the Years 1827 and 1828*, II, 229.

The basis of work on a sea-island cotton plantation was the task. In time the term came to signify a quarter of an acre laid out 105 by 105 feet. The acre was laid out square, 210 by 210 feet. A day's work for a full hand depended upon the time of year and the kind of work he was doing. When listing, the full hand's task was a quarter of an acre. Listing was the first process of preparing the land for cotton after the field had been manured, and consisted of hoeing the grass off the old bed into the alleys. Next the old beds were hauled on top at the rate of a quarter of an acre a day to the full hand. When a plow was used, as it seldom was, the hands followed with hoes, finishing off the beds at the rate of three tasks a day, or three-fourths of an acre. A plowman's allotment was usually four tasks, or an acre a day.

When the bed had been made, two hands made holes the width of the hoe cross-wise on the top of it at intervals of about eighteen inches. Another hand followed, scattering ten or fifteen seeds in each hole, while two other hands covered them to a depth of about an inch and a half, patting the soil down. Since this was light work the day's assignment in this process was usually three tasks.

A day's work at hoeing after the cotton came up was ordinarily two tasks. Picking, which was done generally by the women and children, was accomplished at the rate of about ninety to a hundred pounds a day for a full hand. The task at assorting was from thirty to fifty pounds of seed cotton a day, at ginning from twenty to thirty pounds a day, at moting from thirty to fifty pounds a day.

The tasks involved in plantation work as laid down

for Weehaw plantation near Georgetown, which were also observed on St. Helena plantations, were as follows:[21]

Corn: Sowing done in gang. Covering done in gang.
   Hoeing ¼ acre Hauling up ½ acre.
   Plowing corn 2½ to 3 acres; a man & mule will tend 30 acres. Stripping fodder ¾ acre on first day—after that strip 1 acre & carry home that of the previous day.

Potatoes & Slips:
   Planting—3 [hands] in a ¼ acre, who also bed it up.
   Hoeing—2 in a ¼ acre. Hauling up 20 Compass.[22]
   Digging slips—men, 5 rows—Women, 4 rows & carry home.
   Digging roots for allowance—5 to 7 rows, as they bear.
   Weeding is usually done by the shufflers.[23]

Peas: 3 hands to 3 acres when planted between corn.
   Harvesting—2 large blankets.

Ditching . . . 6 to 8 tasks. Spreading straw[24]—if wet ½ acre. if dry ¾ acre. Listing in straw—½ acre.

Getting task stakes, 500 to a hand[25]

Splitting Rails—100 Rails 12 ft long & heavy

Cutting Wood—1 cord. . . .

Splitting garden railings—500 to 3 men. . . .

Cutting down & piling up corn stalks, 1 to 1¼ to 1½ acres.

Digging ditches . . . —600 cubic feet.

The tasks at cutting marsh grass and digging marsh mud for fertilizing the fields were estimated by the cart load and varied with the weather and the distance of the marsh from the field.

---

[21] Henry A. Middleton, Jr., Weehaw Plantation Book.
[22] A compass was five feet as measured by a wooden triangle called a compass.
[23] Children or superannuated men and women.
[24] On St. Helena plantations marsh grass was used instead of the rice straw spread on the Weehaw fields.
[25] Each hand's task was staked off.

BRINGING IN MARSH GRASS

SLAVE RATIONS

The amount and type of rations which were issued to the hands varied with the plantation. For instance, four different plantations on Edisto Island observed the following practices.[26] One plantation master issued to each hand one bushel of potatoes a week from about October 1 to February 1, and then one peck of corn, ground or unground as preferred, or one peck of broken rice. The owner gave out meat occasionally. On another plantation the rations were: one bushel of potatoes, or ten quarts of corn meal, or eight quarts of rice and four quarts of peas. In addition to this, the slaves, numbering 170, were allowed during the year twenty barrels of salt fish, two barrels of molasses, and fresh meat occasionally. On a third plantation the diet was varied by a weekly ration of a half bushel of potatoes, six quarts of meal, and twenty-one pounds of fresh meat, or ten quarts of meal or rice. A fourth plantation gave out, in addition to the usual half bushel of potatoes, a quart of vegetable soup once a day during hard labor and twice a week at all other times.

In 1862 Edward L. Pierce reported that the customary rations issued by St. Helena planters were a peck of corn a week to each hand and meat at Christmas and in June when work was hardest.[27] While a few plantations allowed meat only at Christmas, a few others dealt it out as often as once a month or once a fortnight. Some plantations also gave molasses and sugar occasionally. Children were allowed from two to six quarts of corn a week, the amount varying with the age of the child. Edward S. Philbrick, one of the Government's superintendents of

---
[26] Turner, *Cotton Planter's Manual*, p. 134.
[27] Pierce, "Report," in *Rebellion Record*, sup., I, 310.

plantations in 1862, reported that Thomas A. Coffin gave his 250 slaves twelve beeves in summer and four at Christmas, four barrels of molasses in summer, and from April to June, when work was heavy, two pecks of corn and two and a half pounds of bacon per slave.[28] He also regularly gave every hand a quart of salt a month and every man two "hands" of tobacco a month and four "hands" at Christmas.

In addition to the rations issued by the master, the slave might gather from the plantation creeks and rivers all the oysters and crabs which he desired. The practice in regard to the fish varied with the plantations, as will be indicated later.[29] Each family was also given a small patch of ground, about one task, back of the cabin to cultivate as desired. Most families planted three or four rows of corn and put the rest in potatoes. They ate part of the corn, but fed most of it to the pig and chickens which each hand was permitted to keep. Some planters on St. Helena even permitted their Negroes to have cattle. Nor did the hands usually eat their stock and poultry, but sold it to the master or to the island storekeeper or to merchants in Beaufort.

When Captain Basil Hall visited a plantation on St. Simon's Island in 1828, he found that the master's family was supplied entirely with poultry and eggs by his Negroes at these prices: eggs, 12½ cents a dozen; chickens, 12½ cents each; fowls, 20 to 25 cents each; ducks, 50 cents each.[30] They were given the liberty to carry their produce to a better market if they could find one. With

[28] MS in Port Royal Correspondence. In Archives of U. S. Treasury Department.
[29] *Infra,* p. 142.
[30] Hall, *Travels in North America,* II, 232.

the money thus obtained they bought extra clothing, coffee, sugar, and what was with them the chief necessity of life, tobacco.[31]

R. W. Roper estimated in 1844, in an address delivered in Columbia, S. C., before the State Agricultural Society, that it cost a planter $11.52 annually to feed a slave.[32] His estimate was based upon the following rations: twelve bushels of corn at 50 cents a bushel, twelve quarts of salt at 1 cent a quart, two pounds of bacon a week at 4½ cents a pound, and twelve pounds of tobacco a year at 6 cents a pound. While the prices quoted in 1844 were, of course, not the same for each year of the ante-bellum period, they approximated fairly closely the general average.

Clothing cost the planter considerably less. St. Helena planters ordinarily allowed each slave two suits a year, one for summer and another for winter. Thomas A. Coffin, of Coffin's Point plantation, gave out in April for every 200 hands 500 yards of men's blue cotton cloth, like the material used in workmen's clothes in the North, 600 yards of coarse unbleached cotton shirting for the men, 600 yards of the same material for women's underclothes, 600 yards of calico in gay colors for frocks, 100 handkerchief pieces, and 100 straw hats for men. In November he issued 550 yards of stout woolen cloth for men's clothes and 600 yards of thinner woolen for women, 1,200 yards of unbleached cloth for shirts and underclothes, 100 turban handkerchiefs for the women, 100 warm caps for the men; 200 pairs of shoes, and 67 blankets of assorted sizes. The house servants got hose and flannels in addition to

[31] Pierce, "Report," *Rebellion Record,* sup., I, 310.
[32] R. W. Roper, "Address," *Southern Agriculturist,* new ser., V, no. 3, p. 89.

these supplies,[33] and the drivers four suits a year, instead of the usual two suits received by field hands.

Roper estimated that the average yearly cost of clothing was $6.12 a slave as follows: six yards of woolens at 55 cents a yard, six yards of summer homespun at 10 cents a yard, a pair of shoes at 90 cents, a hat, cap, or handkerchief at 25 cents, a blanket every three years at $4 a blanket, and needles, thread, buttons, and trimmings at 24 cents a year.[34] This estimate brought the average cost of food and clothing to $17.64 a slave.[35]

Upon adding to this estimate the expense of providing a house, medical care, and incidentals, one finds that the cost to the master amounted to a little less than $50. When it is remembered that two or more slaves were fed and clothed for every taskable hand, it will be seen that the cost per hand ran between $75 and $100 a year, equivalent to wages of about $7 or $8 a month. In 1860 a day laborer was receiving in South Carolina 82 cents a day without board and a farm hand $11.37 a month with board, only a few dollars more than it cost a planter to maintain each taskable hand.[36] When it is considered that slaves, unskilled and often poorly supervised, cultivated only six acres to the hand, it will be seen that the plantation operated not only at a low wage level, but also at a low level of efficiency.

The type of houses provided for the slaves varied with the plantation management, as did every other phase of the plantation routine. When Timothy Ford, of Morris

---

[33] MS in Port Royal Correspondence.
[34] Roper, *op. cit.*, p. 89.
[35] Phillips, *Plantation and Frontier*, I, 135. Louis Manigault, of Argyle Island, estimated that food and clothing for 1838 cost him about $21 a slave.
[36] *U. S. Census of Mortality and Miscellaneous Statistics*, 1860, p. 512.

Town, New Jersey, visited Beaufort and the neighboring Sea Islands in 1785 he recorded in his diary, "The planters all fix at a distance from the road with avenues cut through the woods leading up to their houses. The Negro houses are laid out like a camp & sometimes resemble one."[37] The Negro quarters, or "nigger-house yard," or "nigger street," as they were variously called, did, indeed, resemble a camp spread out a quarter of a mile back of the master's or overseer's house. Edward L. Pierce in 1862 described the houses of the field hands on St. Helena Island as being "ranged in a row, sometimes in two rows fronting each other. They are 16 feet by 12, each appropriated to a family, and in some cases divided with a partition. They numbered on the plantations visited 10 to 12, and on the Coffin plantation they are doubled, numbering 23 double houses intended for 46 families."[38] Later he reported that on some of the plantations the cabins were "ill-conditioned being without chimneys,"[39] so that when there was a fire inside, the occupants were engulfed by a great cloud of smoke. In 1862 Miss Laura M. Towne described the quarters on the Eddings Point plantation, the Edgar Fripp plantation, and on one of the Jenkins plantations as "wretched hovels" with wooden chimneys and general squalor.[40] Later in the same year Charles P. Ware, another missionary to St. Helena Island, found the houses on the McTureous plantation "terribly out of repair, with wooden chimneys and mud floors."[41]

[37] Joseph W. Barnwell (ed.), "Diary of Timothy Ford, 1785-1786," *South Carolina Historical and Genealogical Magazine*, XIII, 145.
[38] Pierce, "Report," in *Rebellion Records*, sup., I, 304.
[39] MS in Port Royal Correspondence, E. L. Pierce to S. P. Chase, April 1, 1862.
[40] *Letters and Diary of Laura M. Towne*, p. 57.
[41] *Port Royal Letters*, p. 77.

William Howard Russell, who visited Barnwell Island in April, 1861, several months before the capture of the region by the Federal Army, has left a vivid picture of the Negro quarters on the Trescot plantation:

> The huts stand in a row, like a street, each detached with a poultry-house of rude planks behind it. . . . No attempt at any drainage or any convenience existed near them, and the same remark applies to very good houses of white people in the south. Heaps of oyster shells, broken crockery, old shoes, rags, and feathers were found near each hut. The huts were all alike windowless, and the apertures, intended to be glazed some fine day, were generally filled up with a deal of board. The roofs were shingled, and the whitewash which had once given the settlement an air of cleanliness, was now only to be traced by patches which had escaped the action of the rain.[42]

Captain Basil Hall, another English visitor to the United States, found the quarters on Edisto Island at a much earlier date, "uncommonly neat and comfortable." He thought the "cottages" might "have shamed those of many countries" he had visited. Each was "divided into small rooms or compartments, fitted with regular bed places"; all had chimneys and doors, and some, though only a few, possessed the luxury of windows. There was one cabin to every five persons.[43] In 1846 Sir Charles Lyell described the Negro houses on Butler's Island as "neat, and whitewashed, all floored with wood, each with an apartment called the hall, two sleeping rooms, and a loft for the children." On Hopeton plantation he found the Negro houses "as neat as the greater part of the cot-

---

[42] Russell, *My Diary North and South*, pp. 146-147.
[43] Hall, *Travels in North America in 1827 and 1828*, II, 210, 211.

tages in Scotland." In each was a chest, a table, two or three chairs, and a few shelves for crockery.⁴⁴

Although it was customary for sea-island planters to provide their Negro quarters with floors, occasionally temporary quarters were built without floors as a means of combating some contagious disease. For instance, after the slaves on his plantation had suffered from a disastrous attack of Asiatic cholera, E. M. Whaley, of Little Edisto Island, burned the old quarters and built temporary ones without floors at a considerable distance from the former location. It was to the planter's interest to keep his "people" well and as comfortable as he deemed consistent with his plantation economy, for a slave was the most valuable piece of property he possessed. Cattle were valued at $7 a head, a yoke of oxen and wagon at $45, a mule at $100, but a prime slave might bring as high as $2,000.

MEDICAL CARE OF THE SLAVE

Sea-island planters, aside from humanitarian reasons, carefully guarded their people's health because it was good business to do so. In the lists of rules which the planter included in his contract with his overseer, there invariably occurred specific instructions concerning the medical care which the Negroes should receive. P. C. J. Weston's instructions to his overseer on his rice plantation in South Carolina began with the statement, "The Proprietor, in the first place, wishes the Overseer most distinctly to understand that his first object is to be, under all circumstances, the care and well being of the Negroes." The instructions further read: "Strong medicines should be left to the

⁴⁴ Lyell, *Second Visit to the United States*, I, 249, 264.

Doctor; and since the Proprietor never grudges a Doctor's bill, however large, he has a right to expect that the Overseer shall always send for the Doctor when a serious case occurs."[45] But the Overseer was cautioned against permitting persons to lie up when "there was nothing or little the matter with them."

Many plantations had hospitals, or "sick houses," as the Negroes called them. The hospital on Prospect Hill plantation on Edisto Island was a brick building. Sir Charles Lyell found the hospital on Hopeton plantation in 1845 to consist of "three wards, all perfectly clean and well-ventilated." One was for men, another for women, and a third for lying-in women.[46] The hospital was in charge of the mistress of the plantation, or the overseer's wife, assisted by a Negro woman whose special task it was to look after the sick. Sir Charles observed that the Negroes refused to take medicine from any hands other than those of their master or mistress. When a Negro child was sick it was usually the mistress who sat up all night giving medicines rather than the mother. After Mrs. Trescot, of Barnwell Island, had been up all night nursing a Negro woman, she said to her English guest next morning, "When people talk of my having so many slaves, I always tell them that it is the slaves who own me. Morning, noon, and night, I'm obliged to look after them, to doctor them, and to attend them in every way."[47]

Since the owner and his wife or his overseer attended to all the simple illnesses of his people, he sometimes attempted to school himself in medical knowledge. The

[45] *DeBow's Review*, XXI, 38; Phillips, *Plantation and Frontier*, I, 116, 120.
[46] Lyell, *op. cit.*, p. 264.
[47] Russell, *My Diary North and South*, p. 141.

Southern Agriculturist, in an article on "The Plantation Doctor," issued the warning that "the planter of all others, should be acquainted with medical remedies, to cure those diseases and injuries to which his Negroes, from their occupations, are so frequently liable."[48] The planter might obtain for his own instruction in the treatment of minor diseases numerous books of "family medicine." One such book, *The Planter's Guide and Family Book of Medicine,*[49] published in Charleston in 1848, lists all the diseases common to the Negro together with the treatment therefor.

Despite the planter's own ministrations, his plantation medical bill was often high. Miss Mary B. Elliott's Account Book gives the medical bill for her plantation for seven of the years between 1837 and 1849. It was lowest in 1849 at $25 and highest in 1845 at $124.94 with an average for the seven years of $68.89. E. M. Whaley's bill of 1862 for his Little Edisto Negroes whom he had moved to Georgia amounted to $329.50. The bill, which is itemized for the year, indicates that the doctor was frequently called at night to treat a sick Negro. For six days in April the doctor visited Jim every day and gave him medicine, charging $2.50 or more a visit. From November 4 to December 2 he visited Louisa's child, sometimes every day, at other times only once a week.[50] Some planters made a contract with their doctors to attend to their Negroes at a given price per head for the year. For example, a planter near Savannah paid his doctor a flat rate of $1.50 a slave, while a certain Dr. Pritchard

---
[48] *Southern Agriculturist,* X, 561.
[49] J. Hume Simons, *The Planter's Guide and Family Book of Medicine.*
[50] MS in Whaley Papers dated December 6, 1862.

offered his services to another planter in that vicinity at $1.25 a head.[51] On St. Helena Island at least four of the planters were doctors.

Negroes seem to have been especially susceptible to cholera, "peripneumonia," and dysentery, or bloody flux, as it was most commonly called. When once cholera appeared among the Negroes, it usually could not be controlled until several had died. In 1852 and again in 1854 cholera swept off many of the best slaves on Louis Manigault's plantation on Argyle Island, Georgia. After these losses, Manigault bought 771 acres of "high land" on the Georgia main which he used partly for cholera camps and for the summer residence of the Negro children.[52] In 1855 when about fifty cases of cholera appeared among James Hamilton Couper's Hopeton plantation Negroes, he wrote to his son in alarm, "The causes I cannot discover, they [the Negroes] live at various settlements, are employed in every kind of work, and have the same food."[53]

Couper considered "peripneumonia" almost as alarming as cholera.[54] "Peripneumonia" was the ante-bellum term for pleuropneumonia, a combination of pleurisy and pneumonia. Although it did not occur in epidemics, it was nearly always fatal to the slaves. Although dysentery did not always appear among the plantation Negroes in a severe form, in 1857 Henry A. Middleton, Jr., lost forty of his people on Weehaw plantation, near Georgetown, from an epidemic of this disease.[55] After the epidemic,

[51] Phillips, *Plantation and Frontier*, I, 166.
[52] *Ibid.*, pp. 141, 143.
[53] Couper-Wylly Papers, March 9, 1855.
[54] *Ibid.*, April 13, 1857.
[55] Weehaw Plantation Book.

the village was moved about three-fourths of a mile away to the pine woods and the houses built farther apart.

Smallpox and yellow fever also caused the planters considerable alarm, although there were more widespread efforts to prevent these infectious diseases than others to which the Negroes were subject. The state quarantine laws greatly reduced the number of cases of yellow fever and the planter's general use of vaccine lessened the epidemics of smallpox. Henry A. Middleton, Jr.'s, Weehaw Plantation Book indicates that he regularly had the black children vaccinated.

Although sea-island planters usually considered that the winter months were the hardest for the Negroes and the summer months for the whites, the Negroes also suffered from malaria, although not to the same extent as the whites. In 1857 James Hamilton Couper wrote to his son James that the illness of another son was "induced by the same state of the atmosphere which has caused a very general malaria of typhoid fever among the Negroes." For four weeks during this attack there was an average of forty ill in the plantation hospital.[56]

The death of a trusted slave often brought a deal of sorrow into the planter's family. In recounting the deaths on the plantation in a letter to his son, Couper wrote in 1857:

To myself personally the most painful loss has been that of poor old Sandy and his wife Joan. . . . I requested Mr. Brown to read the funeral service at his grave; and your mother, myself and the family attended. He was an honest, faithful and good man; and I part with him as with a devoted and tried friend. He was

[56] Couper-Wylly Papers, April 13, 1857.

among my earliest playmates, and during my whole life his attachment never varied. I shall gratify myself by placing a stone on his grave.[57]

INFANT WELFARE

The children's diseases were sometimes more disastrous than cholera or dysentery, despite the general precautions observed in caring for the plantation children. Planters usually insisted that the young be given special attention, and they also urged mothers to take proper care of themselves during pregnancy. Henry A. Middleton, Jr., would not permit any woman to work on his island lands in midwinter, and he immediately put *enceinte* women on half task until confinement. Every planter who had a hospital for his people insisted that the mothers come there for confinement, for there they could be better cared for and kept more quiet, but the women invariably preferred their own houses where they could gossip with their friends without restraint, and they usually managed, as Couper told Sir Charles Lyell, to be taken by surprise at home. Mothers were allowed a month of rest after confinement, an advantage rarely enjoyed by hard-working English peasants, and were not put at full tasks until the child was eight months old.

Doctors were seldom called at the confinement of a Negro woman,[58] for the woman's mistress herself seldom received such attention. In every group of plantation slaves there were one or more midwives listed on the plantation record as the "granny," or nurse, but known

[57] *Ibid.*
[58] MS in Hawks Letters, Library of Congress. Dr. J. M. Hawks to Esther Hawks, May 17, 1862, from Edisto Island: "In midwifery here, Drs. are not called, several births have occurred since I have been here all attended by the Negro women on the place."

to the people themselves by the respectful title of Maum. The mistress herself or the overseer's wife was also usually present to assist the midwife at the confinement of a Negro woman. At Christmas the planter rewarded the granny by giving her 75 cents for each delivery during the year. He also might seek to encourage the mother to care for her child properly by giving her, perhaps, as much as a $1 for every living child she had at Christmas. Henry A. Middleton, Jr.'s, practice was to give every woman with an infant one month old $1 and the same amount to every woman with a year-old child. At Christmas in 1859, he rewarded twenty-six mothers with month-old infants, and fourteen mothers with year-old infants.[59]

St. Helena planters allowed new-born infants "two of each garment and six diapers."[60] The garments were flannel dresses, dresses of cotton checks, and jackets of homespun.[61]

As soon as a mother resumed work after confinement, she was often required to take her infant to a nurse or granny, whose task it was to take care of both the "lap babies" and the "knee babies" during working hours. Sometimes the same granny looked after the plantation babies year after year, while on other plantations this task was assigned to a group of women who took turns every month "minding child." Henry A. Middleton, Jr., rewarded the "monthly nurses" on his plantation "75c. for infants that live." As long as a mother suckled her infant, she left her work in the field at stated intervals to do so, or an older child brought the baby to the field to be fed.

[59] Weehaw Plantation Book.
[60] *Port Royal Letters*, p. 44.
[61] Weehaw Plantation Book.

After eight months the child was put on a diet of vegetables, milk, and starches prepared, on the best managed plantation, by a special cook assigned to that task. On Weehaw plantation the children's allowance was given out every morning and cooked for them three times a day. They had vegetable soup every day and rice for dinner three times a week. While the potatoes lasted, they had potatoes every day for breakfast. During the winter they had molasses three times a week and milk on alternate days. After May first, however, they had molasses every day until milk was again used in winter.[62]

Despite this special attention, the proportion of children in the total number of deaths on Weehaw was high. In 1856 six out of eleven deaths were of infants under one year; in 1857 thirty-three out of forty deaths were of children under three years; in 1858 twelve out of fourteen were of children under two; in 1859 fourteen out of eighteen were of children under one; in 1860 thirteen out of twenty were of children. The causes of death as listed by the planter were as follows: diarrhea, pneumonia, debility, fever, spasms, lockjaw, dysentery, convulsions, accident, cholic, worms, and teething, with the largest number dying of lockjaw.

It must not be overlooked that the infant death rate among the whites was also high. Planters on St. Helena Island seem to have had as much difficulty in rearing their own children as those of their Negroes. The tombstones still standing in the cemeteries there show that parents sometimes lost four or five infants in succession. James A. Pope lost five children under six years of age

[62] *Ibid.*

between 1833 and 1850. Within a period of five years William Jenkins lost three infants in succession.

Data for the comparison of the death rate of whites and Negroes in the ante-bellum period are meager. The death rates for Charleston from 1830 to 1845 are as follows:

COMPARISON OF WHITE AND BLACK DEATH RATES IN CHARLESTON[63]

Year	Deaths Per Thousand	
	Whites	Blacks
1830	25.4	25.0
1831	21.4	26.3
1832	19.2	18.1
1833	18.2	17.9
1834	23.8	22.7
1835	23.2	21.5
1836	24.6	51.0
1837	21.1	21.4
1838	54.6	30.3
1839	33.4	25.6
1840	19.7	21.5
1841	15.2	22.3
1842	19.9	20.9
1843	16.4	30.4
1844	14.4	23.1
1845	18.9	20.6

The death rate of the whites was highest in 1838 when 54.6 persons per 1,000 died due to an epidemic of yellow fever, and lowest in 1841 when only 15.2 per 1,000 died, with an average for the sixteen years of 23.1 per 1,000. For the blacks the death rate was highest in 1836 when 51 per 1,000 died from an epidemic of cholera, and lowest in 1833 when only 17.9 per 1,000 died, with a general average of 24.8. The general average for the whites was lower by only 1.7 persons per 1,000 than the general average for the blacks. At the same time the average

[63] J. D. B. DeBow, *Industrial Resources of the United States*, II, 294.

death rate for the whites in Philadelphia from 1831 to 1840 was 23.2 per 1,000 and for the blacks 32.3 per 1,000.[64]

The data available showing the ratio of births to deaths in the slave population of the sea-island region are likewise meager. Henry A. Middleton, Jr.'s, Weehaw Plantation Book records the births and deaths on his plantation from 1845 to 1860, as follows:

BIRTHS AND DEATHS ON WEEHAW PLANTATION, 1845-1860[65]

Year	Births	Deaths	Increase	Decrease
1845	21	24	..	3
1846	17	20	..	3
1847	28	16	12	..
1848	21	25	..	4
1849	22	20	2	..
1850	26	9	17	..
1851	18	19	..	1
1852	25	20	5	..
1853	29	22	7	..
1854	24	20	4	4
1855	25	59	..	34
1856	27	11	15	..
1857	22	40	..	18
1858	28	14	14	..
1859	20	18	2	..
1860	31	20	11	..
Total	384	357		

Beginning in 1845 with approximately 252, the slave population of Weehaw plantation showed after sixteen years an increase of births over deaths of 27, giving an increase of 10.7 per cent in the slave population. The number of deaths was highest in 1855 when an epidemic of whooping cough and measles among the children brought the number up to 59 and lowest in 1850 when

[64] *Ibid.*
[65] The high death rate is probably accounted for by the fact that planters usually included stillbirths in the numbers of deaths.

only nine died. The number of births was greatest in 1860 with thirty-one and lowest in 1846 with only seventeen.

Some idea of the child-bearing period of the slave women on St. Helena Island may be obtained from records in the John E. Fripp papers. One record gives a list of births from 1802 to 1860. Of the twenty women whose child-bearing records seem to have been complete, two women had ten children each; one, nine children; two, eight children; three, seven children; one, five children; four, four children; four, three children; and three, two children. It is possible to ascertain from the records at what age ten of these women first bore a child. Die, who was the youngest mother in the group, was fifteen when her first child was born; Jenny was seventeen; Daphney, eighteen; Jane, Judy, Matilda, Olive, and Martha, nineteen; Doll, twenty; and Hetty, twenty-two. Four of Hetty's ten children died in infancy as did four of Olive's eight children. The others lost from one to two children each.

PLANTATION PROFITS AND LOSSES

James Hamilton Couper, who administered the James Hamilton estate for forty years, often said that the estate realized a higher percentage of profit on an investment in Schuykill River bonds issued by the city of Philadelphia than it did upon an investment in 600 slaves and 1,500 acres of Georgia seacoast farming land.[66] Data for a tract of 800 acres of this estate raising sea-island cotton have been preserved as follows:

AVERAGE RECEIPTS AND DISBURSEMENTS ON HAMILTON
PLANTATION FOR FORTY YEARS[67]

Investment	Valuation
120 slaves @ $450	$54,000
800 acres land @ $20	16,000
Stock: horses, mules, oxen, cattle	2,000
Farm implements	2,000
Total	$74,000
Receipts	
Sale of cotton	$ 5,277
Increase of slave stock, av. of 4 @ $450	1,800
Total	$ 7,077
Disbursements	
Support[68] of 120 slaves	$ 2,200
Taxes	162
Depreciation @ 2% of investment	1,480
Total	$ 3,842
Profits	$ 3,235

The profit realized on one well-managed sea-island cotton plantation over a period of forty years was, therefore, only 4.37 per cent. With so small a profit as this, it is no wonder that planters complained of the general unsuccessfulness of planting sea-island cotton. Yet on rare occasions, those marvelous years when both the price and the weather conspired to give fabulous yields, the profits might rise as high as 100 per cent on the investment. Planters considered their lands and their labor fit for no crop other than sea-island cotton, and the occasional high returns made them willing to gamble on the results.

[66] Wylly, *Seed That Was Sown in the Colony of Georgia*, p. 59.
[67] *Ibid.*, pp. 60, 61. Table made from data given.
[68] This item includes clothing, food other than provisions raised on the plantation, physician's bill, overseer's and manager's salaries.

CHAPTER VI

THE PLANTERS

THE HOME-SEEKERS

IN THE EARLY days of the settlement of South Carolina, St. Helena Island attracted both the home-seeker and the speculator. Landgrave Joseph Morton, for instance, in 1703 had a grant for 1,270 acres of land in the vicinity of St. Helena, although he already had a prosperous plantation on Edisto Island where he had established his home.[1] Earlier than this, John Bailey had a grant for 4,800 acres which included a section of St. Helena Island, but before many years he was selling parts of it in small tracts.[2] Of the home-seekers, the Caperses, Fripps, Eddingses, and Chaplins were planting on St. Helena by 1725. Such pioneer families as these remained generation after generation adding to their holdings by grant, purchase, or marriage, gradually dispossessing the improvident planters and the speculators.

By 1760 the Jenkinses, Scotts, and Perrys had plantations on St. Helena, and later came the Popes, the Coffins, the McTureouses, the Pritchards, the Whites, the Wallaces, the Bakers, the Fullers, and the Crofts.[3] At the close of the plantation regime in 1860 the Capers family

---

[1] Grants for Land in South Carolina, XXXVIII, 430.
[2] Memorial Book, III, 313-314.
[3] The Reynolds family was also among the earliest settlers on St. Helena Island and owned land there until after 1825, but by 1860 they no longer had holdings on the Island. Those who had lived on St. Helena prior to 1860 include a long list of names, among whom are the following: Cowan, Norton, McKee, Waight, Fendin, Oswald, Sams, Ellis, Bland, Clark, Greaves, Ladson, Evans, Morgan, Greene, Hall, Goodman, Adams, Betterson.

had a record of 151 years of planting on St. Helena and the Fripp family had a record of 136 years.

The case of the Fripp family is especially interesting because members of that family finally came to possess a large portion of the Island. As early as 1707 John Fripp had bought land on Edisto Island,[4] but it was not until 1724 that he made a purchase of 480 acres of the tract on St. Helena Island[5] which had been granted to John Cowan[6] in 1706/7. After that, he and his sons and their children gradually added to their holdings until by 1860 they owned more than twelve thousand acres of land on St. Helena and neighboring small islands which were distributed among some twenty plantations. Indeed, William Fripp, Sr., owned 3,472 acres, the greatest acreage of any planter in the parish, and Captain John Fripp had 2,210 acres divided among seven plantations besides a controlling interest in Hunting Island, 2,000 acres of uncultivated land which was set aside as a game preserve for the planters who owned it.

The social life of St. Helena seems to have been less pretentious than that of some of the other Sea Islands of South Carolina and Georgia; but, due to the destruction of most of the family records during the occupation of the Island by the Federal Army during the Civil War,[7] the data on this subject for the whites of St. Helena are so meager that one cannot be dogmatic in this respect.

[4] Memorial Book, III, 313-314.   [5] *Ibid.*
[6] Cowan Creek which separates Ladies Island from St. Helena was named for him.
[7] *Rebellion Record*, III, 309. A reporter for the *New York World* wrote shortly after the capture of Port Royal, "In the forts and in plantation residences around, were found a mass of documents, letters of all descriptions, and official papers."

Mrs. Abigail Capers, evidently a woman of northern birth, writing from Laurel Hill plantation to a friend in the North in 1791, has left an admirable picture of life among the planters on St. Helena Island in the early days of the plantation regime. She says:[8]

Most of those whom I have had an opportunity of knowing are far from discovering any trace of extravagance; in proportion to their Fortunes, they are the plainest people I ever met with wholly attentive to the Cultivation of Indigo, the profits of which article is mostly expended in the purchase of Negroes, & nothing is so much coveted as the pleasure of possessing many slaves.— These singularities are inherited from their Fore-Fathers—& many follow so closely in the path thru which their Ancestors trod as to deny themselves the Comforts & conveniences of life—

As there is no general Rule without an exception you will naturally conclude that there are some families amongst us, who are more liberal in their sentiments, & who do not believe that happiness is confined within the narrow limits of a plantation, where a great majority are slaves—As yet I have not given Carolina the praise it merits.—The country is beautiful & were it not for the intense heat of the summer months, the Climate would be charming—if a spirit of Industry & emulation prevailed, a great alteration would soon be visible, but the want of Education in both Sexes prevents their striving for the general good, & a patriotic spirit is as strange amongst our neighbours as the term. However, these defects will be amended whenever it becomes the practice for parents to procure the means of knowledge for their Children, were they half as careful to lead them good examples as they are to bestow a large Inheritance, I will venture to say the Country would be considered vastly more important. Many eyes are already opened, & it is now thought necessary for a young man to know something besides reading[,] writing & arithmetic,— . . .

[8] Copy of original in possession of Penn Normal, Industrial, and Agricultural School, St. Helena Island, S. C.

As I have already exposed the faults of the natives, I will proceed to acquaint you with their virtues, which are for the most numerous.—Hospitality to strangers & Charity toward the poor, every where prevails [.] Strong attachments reign in families, and Quarrels among Neighbours are rarely known— . . . St. Helena . . . contains Seventy families, forty of whom are eminent planters, . . . we are seated in a Genteel neighborhood, & few sundays pass but we see good deal of Company, as that is high visiting day—

SOCIAL CLASSES

Sixty-nine years later there were still only forty landowners on the Island.[9] If there were still seventy families on the Island, the white population numbered about three hundred and fifty,[10] while the slave population was more than two thousand.[11] The slave population, therefore, greatly outnumbered the white population. Indeed, in 1860 the slave population of Beaufort District was 81.2 per cent of the total, a proportion of blacks to whites exceeded only by one county in South Carolina, that of Georgetown, and by few others in the entire South. The following table gives a comparison of the black and white population for the last three decades of the ante-bellum period:

WHITES AND BLACKS IN BEAUFORT DISTRICT[12]

Year	Whites	Slaves	Free Negroes
1840	5,650	29,682	462
1850	5,947	32,279	579
1860	6,714	32,530	809

---

[9] *Supra*, pp. 41-42.
[10] Estimating five members to the family.
[11] In 1862 Edward L. Pierce, special agent for the United States Government, reported the Negro population of St. Helena to be 2,721. Some slaves had left with their masters in 1861; others had fled, others were working at Hilton Head and Beaufort; while still others were in the army. See Pierce's "Report" in *Rebellion Record*, sup., I, 316.
[12] *United States Census, 1840*, pp. 226-227; *United States Census, 1850*, p. 338; *Eighth Census of the United States, 1860, Population*, pp. 448-449.

The proportion of whites to blacks remained practically the same during these three decades, the whites being 15.8 per cent of the total population in 1840 and 16.8 per cent in 1860.

Even with such a small percentage of whites in the population, there were, as Mrs. Capers suggests in 1791, social classes among the whites. There were three general classes with various shadings of social differentiation between them: the "genteel," the middle class, and the poor. Some of the "eminent planters," of whom Mrs. Capers spoke, belonged to the gentry. They were the ones whose sea-island cotton sold at the top prices. They educated their sons in England in the days before the Revolution and afterward in South Carolina or in the North. They spent the hot summer months at a health resort; they had their hunting clubs and their literary societies. They entertained on their plantations and at Beaufort and Charleston.

The middle class was composed chiefly of the overseers and trades people, although no strict line was drawn between classes. It sometimes happened that an overseer was himself a planter and a member of the gentry. Even on St. Helena Island there were storekeepers who sold small supplies to the planters and traded with the slaves. The agent for the Federal Government found a German storekeeper on the Island in 1861 who had taken considerable quantities of cotton in payment of debts which he claimed some of the planters had allowed to accumulate.[13]

It has often been claimed that St. Helena's Parish con-

---

[13] MS in Port Royal Correspondence.

tained no poor whites, but the *Minutes of the Vestry of St. Helena's Parish,* as well as other records, refute this tradition. In 1737[14] the parish assessed itself £100 currency for the support of the poor, and in 1820[15] the poor tax amounted to 25 per cent of the general tax, or $725. The poor whites kept small shops, worked on the rivers as boatmen or fishermen, or did a little planting.

THE "BIG HOUSE"

It was customary for the planters of St. Helena Island to spend the winter months at their plantation houses and the sickly months, from June until October, at a health resort. At the eastern end of St. Helena Island stood the plantation of Thomas Aston Coffin at whose house began a public road, called the Sea-side road, that extended thirteen miles to a Jenkins plantation at Land's End on Port Royal Sound. Two miles from the Coffin plantation a road diverged to the right, leading to Ladies Island and Beaufort on Port Royal Island, a distance of some eleven miles. Along these roads were most of the plantation houses on the Island.

When Edward L. Pierce investigated conditions on St. Helena Island for the United States Government early in 1862 he found that the master, if a man of wealth, was likely to have his main residence at Beaufort, sometimes having none on the plantation, but having a small house for the overseer or for the driver. "He may, however, have one," continued Mr. Pierce in his report, "and an expensive one too, as in the case of Dr. Jenkins, at St.

---

[14] A. S. Salley, Jr. (ed.), *Minutes of the Vestry of St. Helena's Parish, South Carolina, 1726-1812,* p. 25.

[15] Mills, *Statistics of South Carolina,* p. 372.

THE "BIG HOUSE" ON COFFIN'S POINT PLANTATION, ST. HELENA ISLAND

Helena, and yet pass most of his time at Beaufort, or at the North. . . . The houses for overseers are of an undesirable character. Orchards of orange or fig trees are usually planted near them."[16]

Ordinarily the plantation home, or "big house," as the slaves called it, was built in a clump of fine live oaks, approached by a stately avenue of magnificent oak trees gracefully draped with gray moss. Back of the house were usually to be found orchards of peach, orange, and fig trees. Scattered among these trees were the corn houses, the stables, cotton houses, the well which supplied the house with water, and the cabins of the house servants.[17] A few hundred yards back of these stood the fence and gate, invariably left open, which shut off the slave quarters and the fields.

The houses of the owners and of the overseers were usually built high off the ground. At The Oaks, one of the Pope plantations, the residence, which was just completed at the outbreak of the Civil War, is high enough above ground for the present occupant to use the space underneath as a garage. In some cases this ground floor was enclosed and made a part of the house. In such instances, the kitchen, dining room, and sometimes the sewing room were located there.[18]

Miss Harriet Ware, who came from Massachusetts in 1862 as a missionary to the Negroes on St. Helena Is-

---

[16] Pierce, "Report" in *Rebellion Record*, sup., I, 304.

[17] For a description of William Fripp's Pine Grove plantation see *Letters from Port Royal*, pp. 23-24.

[18] Prospect Hill on Edisto Island is a beautiful example of this type of house. It was built about 1790 and was designed by James Hoban, who was also the architect for the White House. In 1860 the house was owned by William Grimbal Baynard.

land, described the plantation houses as "being all built of hard pine, which is handsome on the floors, but the rest of the woodwork is painted in this house[19] an ugly green, which is not pretty or cheerful. The walls are always left white. Clapboards are unknown, but hard-pine boards, a foot or more broad, are put on in the same way, and everything outside is whitewashed. The place is very attractive-looking, grapevines and honeysuckles and pine woods near."[20] Miss Laura M. Towne, a volunteer from Philadelphia for missionary work among the Negroes, thought The Oaks "not a pretty place, but the house is new and clean, about as nice as country-houses in Philadelphia, without carpets though, and few of the civilized conveniences."[21] Some of the other houses the missionaries found to be "two-story affairs, old, dirty, rickety, poorly put together and shabbily kept."[22]

Not all of the planters left the Island for Beaufort or for the North during the summer months. Some of them went to the Island's own health resort, St. Helenaville.[23] Here was a long, sandy beach where one might bathe in the salt water at high tide and where one might have fresh cool breezes from the ocean through most of the hot summer days. A missionary from the North found St. Helenaville to be in the spring of 1862 "a Deserted Village of a dozen or more mansions[24] with their house-servants' cabins behind them, and two churches in a large pine wood,

---

[19] Pine Grove plantation.
[20] *Letters from Port Royal*, p. 21.
[21] *Letters and Diary of Laura M. Towne*, p. 13.
[22] *Letters from Port Royal*, p. 77.
[23] There is now scarcely a trace left of St. Helenaville. It was practically destroyed in May, 1866, by a tornado. *Nation*, II, 658.
[24] Most of these houses were small.

free from underbrush, . . . The village is directly on the creek on a bluff like that on which Beaufort is situated, about eight feet high, and is the place the white people used to spend the summers for health and society—those who did not go North to travel, or to Beaufort."[25] Some planters, such as William Fripp, had a house both in the village and in Beaufort as well as the family house on the plantation.

The houses in Beaufort were more pretentious than the ones on St. Helena Island. Here planters vied with one another in building imposing mansions. Sir Charles Lyell who visited Beaufort in 1845 described it as "a picturesque town composed of an assemblage of villas, the summer residences of numerous planters, who retire here during the hot season, . . . Each villa is shaded by a verandah, surrounded by beautiful live oaks and orange trees laden with fruit."[26] Although Miss Harriet Ware thought in 1862 that the Coffin home at Coffin's Point plantation must have been handsomely furnished, judging from the pieces which were left—"rosewood tables, side-boards and washstands with marble tops . . . sofas that must have been of the best"[27]—the St. Helena homes were plainly furnished in comparison with the display to be found in the houses in Beaufort. On the walls of some of the Beaufort houses there were portraits of the owners drawn by the famous American painter, Thomas Sully, and some done even by French and Italian artists; on their floors were expensive Turkish and Persian carpets; on their

---

[25] *Letters fom Port Royal*, pp. 30-31.
[26] Lyell, *A Second Visit to the United States*, I, 231. For a description of the houses in Georgetown, S. C., see Russell, *My Diary North and South*, pp. 129-130.
[27] *Letters from Port Royal*, p. 60.

shelves, volume after volume of masterpieces in English and French handsomely bound. Edward S. Philbrick, of Massachusetts, writing to his wife in 1862 after the Federal Army had occupied Beaufort, said, "There is something very sad about these fine deserted houses. Ours has Egyptian marble mantles, gilt cornice and centrepiece in parlor, and [a] bath-room, with several washbowls set in different rooms."[28]

Beaufort was significant only as a summer resort, for it had little, if any, commercial importance.[29] During the hot weather when the planters were in their summer residences, the population was about 2,000, but at other periods of the year it was less than half that number.[30]

Besides St. Helenaville and Beaufort, there were several other summer resorts in that region. They were generally located in the sandy ridges in the attempt to get away from the swamps and marshes where the disease-bearing mosquitoes bred most freely. Most of these settlements bore the names of their founders, as McPhersonville, Gillisonville, Grahamville, Heywardsville. Today they still exist as small villages.

EARLY INTEREST IN EDUCATION

St. Helena's Parish seems to have been interested early in the education of its youth. In 1747 the Reverend Lewis Jones bequeathed a legacy of £100 sterling to the church wardens and vestry of the parish "towards the Education of poor Child.ⁿ of this Parrish,"[31] and the vestry contracted with the parish schoolmaster to teach a selected group of

---

[28] *Ibid.,* p. 8.
[29] *Official Records,* ser. I, vol. LIII, sup., serial no. 111, p. 71.
[30] *Ibid.* The Census of 1850 lists the population of Beaufort at 879.
[31] Salley, *Minute of the Vestry of St. Helena's Parish,* pp. 39, 43. .

poor children for a specified number of months each year. Those who could afford it or did not care to patronize the parish teacher employed private tutors, several families sometimes joining to pay a teacher's expenses. This practice, begun in the colonial days, was continued during the ante-bellum period, but wealthy planters who had been in the habit of sending their sons to England to be educated prior to the Revolution,[32] sent them in the ante-bellum period to the College of Charleston, the South Carolina College,[33] and to Harvard, Princeton, and Yale.

The General Assembly of 1786-1788 incorporated the Beaufort Society and the St. Helena Society, organizations which had been formed both for religious and educational purposes, and in 1795 a group of citizens of Beaufort obtained a charter for the establishment of Beaufort College which was to be supported from the sale of vacant lots in the town and from the sale of escheated and confiscated property in the parish. In 1811 the General Assembly passed an act providing free schools.[34] The act granted neighborhoods with schoolhouses $300 a year for free elementary instruction, preference being given to poor orphans and children of impoverished parents. Beaufort qualified for state aid, and in 1826 had a grammar school, three schools for boys, one for girls, and three for young children.[35] These schools had a combined enrollment of about two hundred pupils. In 1850 there were twenty-eight schools in Beaufort District supported in part by

---

[32] See Edward McCrady, "Education in South Carolina prior to and during the Revolution," *South Carolina Historical Society Collections*, IV, no. 5.
[33] Later the University of South Carolina.
[34] H. G. Cutler, *History of South Carolina*, I, 532.
[35] Mills, *Statistics of South Carolina*, p. 373.

public funds which amounted to $1,800. The enrollment was 598 pupils.[36]

In ante-bellum days Beaufort was distinguished throughout South Carolina for the learning and culture of its citizens, and St. Helena Island lived in the reflected glory of its health-resort town. As early as 1802 a library society was organized in Beaufort; in 1826 the volumes numbered between six and eight hundred,[37] while by 1860 they had climbed to the thousands.[38] There were also many private libraries both in Beaufort and on the plantations.[39] On St. Helena, the libraries of Dr. William J. Jenkins, Thomas Aston Coffin, and J. J. Pope were sufficiently large to attract the attention and admiration of the conquering army officers in 1861. A reporter of the *New York World*, in describing the capture of Port Royal, mentioned "a rich old plantation mansion, not far from the fort, on an estate belonging to a family by the name of Pope. Here was a splendid library, a mass of papers and documents, and a file of the *Charleston Mercury*, for the last thirty or forty years. One was seen dated as far back as 1812."[40]

George P. Elliott, writing in the *Charleston Mercury* in 1857, called attention to the high order of society in St. Helena's Parish. Among the natives of Beaufort, he

---

[36] Cutler, *op. cit.*, II, 605-606, 639.
[37] Mills, *op. cit.*, p. 375.
[38] When Beaufort was captured by the Federal Army in 1861 the library was considered confiscated property and sent to Washington where it was placed in the Smithsonian Institute and subsequently burned when the building housing it was destroyed by fire.
[39] The Receipt Book of Henry M. Stuart and Account Book of Miss Mary B. Elliott show frequent purchases of books.
[40] *Rebellion Record*, III, 309 (*New York World* narrative of capture of Port Royal).

mentioned such men as Thomas Heyward, Jr., signer of the Declaration of Independence and a circuit judge of South Carolina; Robert Barnwell, a distinguished speaker of the House of Representatives of South Carolina; Stephen Elliott, botanist and editor of the *Southern Review;* John A. Stuart, editor of the *Charleston Mercury.* "There are distributed from the Beaufort postoffice annually," he wrote, "thirty-three thousand one hundred and twenty-four newspapers, three thousand four hundred and sixty magazines and other periodicals, and we have not been able to find a single man or woman, native of the Parish, that cannot read and write.[41] The public schools have been always of the first character and the evidence of this is, that our young men, at various times, have carried off the first honors, at Yale, at Princeton, at Columbia, and at Charleston College; and this is a Parish that has not above 1,200 white inhabitants."[42]

RELIGION

Prior to the Revolution the Church of England was the established church of South Carolina. In 1712 when the parish of St. Helena was established, a group of inhabitants elected the Reverend Mr. Guy, assistant to the rector of Charles Town, resident minister, "after having first obtained the consent of the Reverend Mr. Johnson, the Bishop of London's Commissary, then at Charles-

---

[41] There were 206 illiterate white adults in Beaufort District in 1850, *Census of 1850,* p. 343. Beaufort District was composed of Prince William's, St. Helena's, St. Luke's, and St. Peter's parishes and included what are now Beaufort, Hampton, and Jasper counties.

[42] "Beaufort and Its People," *Charleston Mercury,* Sept. 25, 1857; also in Benjamin R. Stuart, *Magnolia Cemetery, an Interpretation of Some of its Monuments and Inscriptions.*

Town."[43] The Society for the Propagation of the Gospel in Foreign Parts allowed Mr. Guy a salary, and continued for many years to give the parish aid, "in compassion to their great wants." When Mr. Guy arrived, "the people had no teacher of any persuasion, and lived all without using any kind of publick divine worship."[44] He performed the service in the parishioners' houses in different parts of the parish.

In 1724 the parish obtained a grant from the provincial government to which some of the wealthy citizens added contributions, and erected a small, neat brick church in Beaufort. The Society sent the Reverend Mr. Lewis Jones to be rector of the parish church, and he served there with much good to the community until his death in 1747.[45]

As early as 1734 the Reverend Mr. Jones was ordered to go to "St. Helena Island to perform Divine Service once in 6 weeks for Six Months."[46] Later a small church of tabby and brick, sixty by forty feet, was built in the center of the Island on the road leading to Jenkins' plantation at Land's End, serving as a Chapel of Ease to the parish church in Beaufort. After the Revolution, the church was enlarged, and the Island became a separate cure about 1794. Several of the planters donated land for the glebe and the Reverend John S. I. Gardiner, later rector of Trinity Church, Boston, was minister there for some time, having " a respectable congregation."[47]

---

[43] David Humphreys, "An Account of the Missionaries Sent to South Carolina," in Carroll, *Historical Collections*, II, 546.

[44] *Ibid.*, p. 547.

[45] Salley, *Minutes of the Vestry of St. Helena's Parish*, p. 38.

[46] *Ibid.*, p. 22.

[47] Frederick Dalcho, *Historical Account of the Protestant Episcopal Church in South Carolina*, p. 395.

Although the official religion of the province of South Carolina was the Protestant Episcopal, this denomination was not the first to have teachers in the vicinity of St. Helena Island. Before 1712 Anabaptist and Presbyterian preachers had been there, although none were living in the region in that year.[48] St. Helena's Parish Register refers occasionally to persons who were not of the Episcopal persuasion, labeling them "Dissenters" and "Anabaptists." The Euhaws,[49] in Beaufort District, was the center of the Anabaptist denomination prior to the Revolution,[50] and from that group missionaries went out winning converts. Hugh Bryan, one of the most active Presbyterian leaders in South Carolina before the Revolution, was a resident of St. Helena's Parish.[51] By 1820 the Baptists had become the most numerous sect in the District,[52] and also in 1860 the Baptists outnumbered the other denominations in Beaufort District, there being in 1860 twenty-seven Baptist churches, twenty-three Methodist, eleven Episcopal, and two Presbyterian.

It is not known when the first Baptist church was built on St. Helena Island, but the large brick church situated near the center of the Island, still known as "Brick Church" and still used by one of the Baptists groups on the Island, was erected in 1855. The Baptists and Episcopalians seem to have been the only denominations hav-

---

[48] *Ibid.*, pp. 376-377; Humphreys, "Missionaries Sent to South Carolina," in Carroll, *Historical Collections*, II, 547.

[49] That is, the land formerly occupied by the Euhaws.

[50] See John O. B. Dargan (?), *Christian Fellowship: Or the Solemn Covenant of the Baptist Church of Christ in Beaufort, S. C.*; Morgan Edwards, *Materials Toward a History of the Baptists in South Carolina*.

[51] See Hugh Bryan and Mary Hutson, *Living Christianity Delineated in the Diaries and Letters of*.

[52] Mills, *Statistics of South Carolina*, p. 373.

ing churches on St. Helena in 1860. After the Civil War there were still enough whites on the Island to maintain the Episcopal, or "White Church," as it was sometimes called, but the Negroes took possession of "Brick Church." Today there is only one Methodist church on the Island; the Episcopal church was destroyed by a forest fire and has not been rebuilt; the remaining eight churches are of the Baptist denomination.

RECREATION

"Hunting is the principal amusement of the planters, and its consequent associations at the club house," wrote Robert Mills in 1826 in his sketch of Beaufort District.[53] In 1860 hunting was still one of the chief amusements of the planters.[54] Hunting Island, an island of 2,000 acres separated from St. Helena Island by Harbor River, which had long borne that name, was set aside as a hunting preserve for its owners, Captain John Fripp, John G. Barnwell, General Stephen Elliott, Edward M. Capers, Dr. W. J. Jenkins, and others. In 1860 it was well stocked with deer.

It was customary on the Sea Islands from Charleston to Savannah for the planters to maintain a hunting preserve and a club house where monthly dinners were given, each member furnishing in rotation dinner, service, and liquors. Captain Charles S. Wylly has left a description of the club dinners which were held at St. Clair house, St. Simon's Island. "Let us picture," he said, "the dinner of December 7th, 1851:

The hour is five p. m. . . . The room is warmed and cheered

---
[53] Mills, *Statistics of South Carolina*, p. 376.
[54] See William Elliott, *Carolina Sports*.

by the glowing coals in a great fire-place; the table with cover laid for fourteen, is clothed in the snowiest of damask and lit by a score of candles made from the wax of the myrtle berry which cover the salt marshes; the brass candlesticks shine like virgin gold; the dishes are of the palest blue, East Indian China. The waiters, James Dennison from The Village, Sandy and Johnny from Cannon's Point, assisted by old Dic and Sam Froid, have since nine in the morning been busy in the kitchen. The guests arriving, . . . are mounted on wiry steeds, whose only living had been drawn from moss, marsh and shucks . . . but who shew in gait and mettle their descent from Spanish and Arab stock. They are met each by one, or oftener two black boys, . . .

The dinner was not served in courses, save that the two soups, one a clam broth, the other chicken mulligatawny, were brought on first, the fish, shrimp pies, crab (in shell) roasts, and vegetables were all placed in one service; the dessert was simple, tartlets of orange marmalade, dried fruits and nuts. The dishes disposed of, amid general gossip and talk, and the cloth drawn, the great punch bowl with its mixture of rum, brandy, sugar, lemon juice and peel, was brought in. The wine glasses were pushed aside and stubby bottle-shaped glass mugs were handed round; and the chairman of the meeting, rising, announced that the health of the President of the United States would be drank, standing and with cheers.[55]

After this opening of the evening, there followed, according to Captain Wylly's account, "scenes of extraordinary conviviality verging, I fear, into hard drinking and the recountal of the most surprising adventures and experiences."

Planters also entertained frequently at their homes with house parties, dinners, and teas. A former slave of Thomas A. Coffin, of St. Helena, has left an account that his master entertained very little at his plantation house on the Island, choosing rather to entertain in more elaborate

[55] Wylly, *The Seed That Was Sown in the Colony of Georgia*, pp. 55, 56.

style in Charleston.[56] The planters of St. Helena seem to have made frequent trips to Charleston, going a part or all of the way in their own small boats, leaving from their private wharfs on their plantations.

Sir Charles Lyell who visited the Sea Islands in 1845 wrote from James Hamilton Couper's Hopeton plantation with much warmth concerning "the perfect ease and politeness" with which the planters entertained in their homes. "There is a warm and generous openness of character in the southerners," he wrote, "which mere wealth and a retinue of servants cannot give; and they have often a dignity of manner, without stiffness, which is most agreeable. The landed proprietors here visit each other in the style of English country gentlemen, sometimes dining out with their families and returning at night, or, if the distance be great, remaining to sleep and coming home the next morning."[57]

These visits always entailed extra burdens on the mistress of the plantation, who was already over-burdened with many household duties. Captain Wylly, a relative of James Hamilton Couper, recalls the busy lives of the plantation mistresses in his own family:

> The mistress of one of these plantation houses, and hostess of this never-ending house-party, led an arduous life. Servants she had in numbers; but, excepting perhaps a butler or a head housemaid, they were often idle, incompetent, and needed her constant oversight and care. Almost every half hour during the day would she be called to administer to some want or to grant or refuse some request from her many dependents. At nine the plantation nurse arrived with a list or "tally" of the sick.

---

[56] MS in possession of Penn Industrial, Agricultural, and Normal School, St. Helena Island.

[57] Lyell, *Second Visit to the United States*, I, 246.

The serious cases had to be visited first, and, if necessary, a physician summoned; for the others, medicine to be prescribed, weighed and measured. At eleven the wagon from the quarters came, with probably the whole carcass of a beef or sheep, and she was required to direct the cutting of the joints reserved for the table and kitchen and order the disposal of the remainder. The cook must have a personal interview and minute directions. The same was demanded by the fisherman, who wishes to show his catch and receive orders regarding the opening of oysters, clams, or the boiling of crabs or prawn. At twelve the three seamstresses, whose perpetual work was the fashioning of plantation garments, arrived with their baskets of completed coats, pants or shirts. These must be "checked up" against the cloth, buttons and thread that had been issued them and other woolens and home-spuns measured and delivered. And by now the butler wishes to know what he had best serve to the gentlemen returning from their hunt.

At two a tired and weary woman sank into a chair, hoping for a brief rest. Vain hope—a frightened mother calls for "Missis" to "just run up to de quarters to see little Nancy, who is fall into a fit." A half mile of unshaded road intervenes. But go she must. The fit is found to be but indigestion; . . . old Simon stops to say he would like some pain killer, also tobacco. Bella says she *must* tell her Missis she and Tom, her husband, have agreed to part; a lesson on marital duties is to be read, and after that some kind words are to be spoken.[58]

When at last the Mistress reaches the "big house" it is after three, and dinner is to be served in half an hour to a number unknown until her husband returns. But it is certain that he will bring with him someone whom he has met by chance upon the road. The Mistress must busy herself with the final preparations for dinner, and if she is the mother of a growing family not even the few minutes left before dinner can she claim as her own.

[58] Wylly, *The Seed That Was Sown in the Colony of Georgia*, pp. 24, 25.

The people of Beaufort had various societies in which the planters of St. Helena and their wives took some part. The women had their Dorcas Society which corresponds to the present-day church societies, and their missionary societies to encourage home and foreign missions. In 1835 there were in Beaufort also a Tract Society, a Bible Society, and a Benevolent Society, which seem to have had a fairly continuous existence through the ante-bellum period.[59] The men also had a literary society besides the library society already mentioned.

In 1850 a group of citizens organized the Southern Rights Association of St. Helena's Parish. Two councils of safety were appointed, one for Beaufort and one for St. Helena Island. Those serving for St. Helena were Joseph J. Pope, Sr., Joseph D. Eddings, Daniel Jenkins, Edgar Fripp, F. O. P. Fripp, and Dr. J. A. P. Scott.[60] Later in 1851 when the association began to talk of secession, a group of members, including John M. Fripp, William Fripp, Sr., and J. J. T. Pope of St. Helena objected, stating that they had understood that the purpose of the organization was not secession but the following words of the constitution:[61]

To organize more effectually the people of St. Helena Parish, in support of Southern interests; to insure concert of action among the citizens of this and other Southern States for the vindication of their rights; to maintain the Federal compact in its original purity and simplicity, as the only means of preserving the Union, and to support the State authorities in any measure South-Carolina may adopt for her defence or that of her sister States against the injustice and oppression of those of the North.

[59] MSS, Elliott Account Book and Stuart Receipt Book.
[60] Moore, *Rebellion Record*, sup. I, 197-202.
[61] *Ibid.*, pp. 200-201.

Twenty-nine of the 135 members, including three from St. Helena, withdrew from the association, but the organization continued to function, sending delegates to the various Southern Rights meetings held in the state.

The planters of St. Helena were, thus, not all of one mind nor all of one class. They varied in political belief and in social customs from the cultured Coffins, leaders of society in the aristocratic coastal country of South Carolina, to the storekeeper who was the first to confiscate the planters' cotton when they fled from the conquering Federal troops in 1861.

CHAPTER VII

THE SLAVE COMMUNITY

THE SLAVE AND THE LASH

THE EVERY-DAY life of the slave people on a St. Helena plantation was by no means crowded with constant toil. In the late spring when the cotton had to be hoed at the critical stages and again in the autumn when the cotton was in "good blow" they might work from "day clean" to "fust dark," but these were unusual periods, and, as a reward for the extra labor, their masters dealt out choice rations of molasses and meat and passed around presents of tobacco and gay headcloths. The ordinary task of a full hand kept him in the field only four or five hours a day so that the "smart" ones were habitually through by two o'clock. Only the "t'ick headed" remained as late as five. The rest of the day was theirs to spend as they chose.

A southern youth, Hamilton Couper, who had spent all his life on his father's sea-island cotton and rice plantation on the Georgia coast was surprised to find the white servants working so hard in New Haven where he was attending Yale. The Irish maid-of-all-work in his rooming house, so he wrote to his mother, "does more than any servant I have ever seen."[1] The Honorable Amelia Murray of England who visited Couper's parents at their Hopeton plantation was also impressed with the difference in work required of the southern slave and the northern "saucy help." "I never saw servants in any old English family," she observed, "more comfortable, or more de-

[1] Couper-Wylly Papers. Hamilton Couper to Mrs. J. H. Couper, 1846.

voted; it is quite a relief to see anything so patriarchal, after the apparently uncomfortable relations of masters and servants in the Northern States."[2] Sir Charles Lyell, another distinguished English guest in this coastal family, thought the condition of the slaves was "more like that formerly existing between lords and their retainers in the old feudal times of Europe, than to any thing now to be found in America."[3]

Even the slaves themselves admitted that they were generally well-treated. All on St. Helena Island agreed that, while most of them had "good Massa," certain planters were "Massa Debil heself."[4] The Coffin Negroes reproached the northern missionaries who came to the Island after the capture of Port Royal in 1861 with the fact that there was no "confusion" when they belonged to "Ole Massa."[5] Yet other Negroes were careful to show the missionaries their scars from the lash, and one woman solemnly reported that four babies had been "killed within her by whipping."[6] Miss Laura M. Towne found in one dining room "a whipping-post and pulley for stretching and whipping,"[7] which was probably a fly brush with which some facetious person had tried Miss Towne's credulity.

There was far less cruelty practised on the sea-island slaves than northern sympathizers were inclined to be-

[2] Murray, *Letters From the United States, Cuba and Canada*, p. 220.
[3] Lyell, *Second Visit to the United States*, I, 261.
[4] MS in Arthur Sumner Papers, Port Royal, May 18, 1862.
[5] *Letters from Port Royal*, p. 165.
[6] *Letters and Diary of Laura M. Towne*, p. 58. For other instances of cruelty practised by St. Helena planters see Sarah M. Grimké, *American Slavery As It Is*. It must be remembered that this book was published to prove a case against slavery and that many of the accusations are obviously absurd.
[7] *Ibid.*, p. 13.

lieve. Whipping made a rebellious and sullen slave who shirked his work and stirred up trouble. This was the reason that a driver was permitted to inflict stripes only in the presence of the overseer and that some planters forbade whipping altogether. No driver on the Butler plantation on St. Simon's Island was permitted when R. King was overseer to inflict punishment until after a regular trial. "When I pass sentence myself," said King, "various modes of punishment are adopted; the lash least of all,— Digging stumps, or clearing away trash about the settlements, in their own time; but the most severe is, confinement at home six months to twelve months, or longer."[8] All planters admitted that punishment was necessary in order to carry on the plantation routine; it was inherent in the system of slave labor; but the lash was the least effective mode.

CULTURAL DEVELOPMENT

Before 1860 it had frequently been pointed out by travelers in the South and by masters themselves that the coastal Negroes, especially the sea-island Negroes, were less advanced culturally than the "Up-Country," or Piedmont Negroes, because they had less association with civilizing forces. It was evident to even a casual observer that on the sea-island cotton plantations, where the slaves had contact with few whites except the overseer and his family and but little intercourse with the slaves of other islands or even of other plantations on the same island, they must remain more stationary than where they equaled in number the whites or even formed a minority, as was true in a large part of Piedmont South Carolina.

[8] *Southern Agriculturist*, Dec., 1828, p. 524.

Sir Charles Lyell even found a difference in the cultural development of the various sea-island Negroes. Those on the smaller plantations on St. Simon's Island were, for instance, more civilized than those on the larger estates.[9]

When Edward L. Pierce visited St. Helena Island in 1862 to observe the plantation conditions as an agent for the Federal Government, he arrived at the conclusion that slavery had bred out of the Negro all manly qualities. They had become "an abject race, more docile and submissive than those of any other locality." They did not want to fight; they did not want to be uplifted; they wanted to be left alone. "Nowhere has the deterioration of the Negroes from their native manhood," he wrote in an article for the *Atlantic Monthly*, "been carried so far as on these Sea Islands,—a deterioration due to their isolation from the excitements of more populous districts, the constant serveillance of the overseers, and their intermarriage with one another, involving a physical degeneracy with which inexorable Nature punishes disobedience to her laws."[10]

On St. Helena Island, where there were some two thousand slaves to a little more than two hundred whites, the Negroes learned very slowly the ways of the whites. Their mastery of English was far less advanced than that of the Piedmont slaves. They spoke a garbled English, imperfect words and expressions which they and their parents and grandparents had learned from the few whites with whom they came in contact. Their speech mystified the northern missionaries who came to the Island

---

[9] Lyell, *Second Visit to the United States*, I, 268.
[10] *Atlantic Monthly*, Sept., 1863; also in E. L. Pierce, *Addresses and Papers*, p. 106.

after the Federal occupation in 1861. Arthur Sumner, from Cambridge, Massachusetts, tried to describe to his cousin their way of speaking. "These negroes speak with an inarticulate jabber. The sounds roll around in their great chops, and come pouring out through their huge mouths, so that I find it easier to understand a foreign language than confused utterance. Their idioms, too, are funny. I told Byron, a boy who waits upon me, that I was going to distribute clothing on his place. 'Talk *we* house?' said he:—meaning, 'Are you speaking of our house?' . . . Byron came to me with a message from his mother—'Ma says if you give her some trade'—Imagine such a sentence uttered as if it were a word of many syllables. Can you make it out? . . . 'Ma wants to know if you will give her some thread?' "[11]

These missionaries from the North, who, of course, knew nothing first-hand of slavery, thought that the St. Helena Negroes were the most degraded and backward of all the coastal slaves in the South.[12] After the northern whites had become acquainted with other sea-island Negroes from such places as St. Simon's Island, Georgia, and Edisto Island, South Carolina, who were quartered temporarily on St. Helena Island by the Federal Army, they were still of the opinion that the St. Helena slaves were the most retarded in the South except those on the sugar plantations in Louisiana. Arthur Sumner wrote late in 1862, "The Georgia and Florida negroes are vastly superior in appearance, character, and intelligence, to the natives of these Islands. It is the testimony

---

[11] Arthur Sumner Papers. Port Royal, May 18, 1862. The last word was pronounced as if spelled tred, not trade.

[12] *Letters from Port Royal,* p. 181.

of all those who knew the South, that the colored people of the Sea Islands, are the lowest grade of Negroes in America. I'm sure I hope I shall never see a worse set than those who live on our part of St. Helena Island."[13] Miss Harriet Ware, who had been conducting a school on St. Helena, concluded in 1863 that "as a general thing the Edisto people are a better class of blacks, more intelligent and cultivated, so to speak."[14]

It is not surprising that the St. Helena slaves should have been less advanced than those even of neighboring islands, for as it has already been pointed out, St. Helena Island was one of the most isolated of the Sea Islands. It is a buffer from the Atlantic for two other large islands, and the Island itself is cut up into various small islands by the broad tidal creeks which interlace it. It is likely that at least half of the more than two thousand slaves who inhabited St. Helena in 1860 had never been off the Island, for Beaufort was difficult to reach and only the most privileged were allowed to go there. Shut off from contact with the outside world, they were thus unfamiliar with many of the cultural traits of the whites which had sprung up since their own forebears had become "tamed."

It is remarkable, then, that the slaves should have achieved as much of the culture of the whites as they did. They were quick to learn from the few whites with whom they were thrown and from the house servants who went back and forth with the master's family from the Island

---

[13] Arthur Sumner Papers. Dec., 26, 1862.
[14] *Letters from Port Royal*, p. 150. See also the opinion of Charles P. Ware, *ibid.*, p. 97; of W. C. Gannett, *ibid.*, p. 178; and see James S. Pike, *The Prostrate State: South Carolina Under Negro Government*, ch. XXXII; Whitelaw Reid, *After the War: A Southern Tour*, p. 94; Hazard Stevens, *The Life of Isaac Ingalls Stevens*, II, 354.

to Beaufort, Charleston, and the North. Some of the St. Helena people were as alert and ambitious as the whites themselves. Charles Ware, of Massachusetts, in 1862 described Charles, the carpenter on Hope plantation, as "a man after my own heart." "He attracted me first by his dignified and respectful demeanor, and by his superior culture. He has a little touch of self-consideration. He, more than any other negro I know, seems to me like a white person."[15]

SOCIAL CLASSES

The Negroes themselves perhaps unconsciously set a premium on a knowledge of "buckra" ways, for they placed in the upper classes of their social scale those who had superior advantages of learning the customs of the dominant race. The "swonga" people were the drivers who took their orders directly from the overseer, the house servants who were intimately associated with the master's and the overseer's families, the mechanics who were permitted to hire their own time from their masters and work in Beaufort or Charleston. To this group also belonged any among them who from superior rank or intelligence acted as their official or self-appointed leaders. The religious leaders and the plantation watchmen were usually "swonga" Negroes, as were also the witch doctors and those who could boast of physical prowess. It is obviously difficult to point out definitely the various gradations in the social classes among the slaves, but in general the drivers and mechanics stood at the head, followed by the house servants, and at the bottom of the scale stood the field hands.

[15] *Letters from Port Royal*, p. 82.

Edward S. Philbrick was surprised in 1862 to find the St. Helena Negroes so sensitive to social distinctions and "caste feeling." "There is no race in the world," he wrote from Coffin's Point plantation, "with whom a little *state* gives so much power as the African. They have always been accustomed to see men of any power treated as such, and receiving the attention corresponding thereto. They have always seen a white man on a horse, and have got to think it so far a badge of power & caste, that they will hardly lift their hats to a white man on foot. In fact the Negroes themselves, while moving about from one plantation to another always find some old mule to straddle & look down with contempt upon a 'walking nigger.'"[16] Miss Laura M. Towne, a missionary like Philbrick, also observed the Negroes' sensitiveness to class feeling. Upon visiting two Negro women, she was made to understand that they were "both of the colored aristocracy, had lived in the best families, never did any work to speak of, longed for the young ladies and young 'mas'rs' back again, because April was the month they used to come to Beaufort and have such gay times."[17]

SLAVE MARRIAGES

The amount of interference in the domestic life of the slave varied with the opinions and attitudes of the master. A Charleston planter told his English guest, Captain Basil Hall, in 1827, that he made no attempt to regulate the habits and morals of his people except in matters of police. "We don't care what they do when their tasks are over—we lose sight of them till the next day," he said. "The

---

[16] Port Royal Correspondence, E. S. Philbrick to E. L. Pierce, March 27, 1862.
[17] *Letters and Diary of Laura M. Towne*, p. 14.

men may have, for instance, as many wives as they please, so long as they do not quarrel about such matters."[18] Nevertheless, most planters insisted that their slaves give up their African customs of polygamy and accept the Christian standard of monogamy as the rule of their family life.

St. Helena planters quite generally required their slaves to choose a mate for life, and they attempted to impress the solemnity of the marriage upon the contracting parties by the observance of a ceremony. The engagement of a slave couple was formally recognized on the plantation when the black man asked the master's permission to marry, designating specifically the chosen girl. Many owners encouraged their men to choose from among the girls of their own plantations, but they did not always insist upon it.[19] A man might select his wife from another plantation on the Island, but if he did so he must suffer the inconveniences of not having a woman to look after his clothes, grind his corn into grits, and cook his meals. On the other hand, a wife on a neighboring plantation gave the husband an excuse for leaving his own plantation frequently.

Upon gaining permission to marry, the couple might request that the ceremony be performed at once, whereupon the planter, if without too many religious scruples, might informally "pronounce" them man and wife. The master was more likely to insist, however, upon a marriage by a white preacher or by one of the religious leaders

---

[18] Hall, *Travels in North America*, II, 216.
[19] Mr. J. Swinton Whaley, of Little Edisto Island, possesses today a bill of sale for a Negro girl his father paid $1,200 for in order that one of his slaves might have the wife he loved.

from among his own slaves. A wedding was often made the occasion of a general celebration on the plantation. The master gave special provisions, such as beef and rice for making a stew, and molasses for sweetened water to wash it down, and the young ladies made the cake.[20] The mistress and her daughters also influenced the bride to come to the ceremony properly gowned in white with a flowing veil improvised from a discarded window curtain from the master's house. The mistress might provide this extra finery or the bride herself might purchase it with her hoarded savings. If it were the marriage of a house servant, the ceremony might be performed in the kitchen or dining room of the "big house" or in a nearby grove of trees. Marriages of field hands were frequently performed in the open or in the praise house, as the plantation church was called.

After the feasting and the merrymaking were over, the couple went home to the cabin which the master or overseer had set aside for them. But they did not always go home destined to remain faithful to the vows which they had just taken. The looseness of the slave's code of morality was one of the evils most often cited against him.[21] Despite the preachers' instructions upon the nature, sacredness, and perpetuity of marriage many slaves did not hold themselves to such a doctrine. This circumstance is not surprising when one considers the polygamous customs of their African ancestors and the failure of law either to recognize or protect Negro marriages. The issue of an extra-marital relation placed but little additional

[20] Murray, *Letters from the United States,* p. 224.
[21] Lyell, *Second Visit to the United States,* I, 272, 273.

burden upon the parents, for the master provided for all children alike. A violation of marriage vows was accompanied by no disgrace or punishment other than that inflicted by the master or by the church if the culprit were a member. There seems to have been very little intimacy between the white men and the Negro women on St. Helena Island. The northern missionaries found not more than five or six mulattoes on the whole Island in 1861.

There were forces sufficiently strong to keep many slaves faithful to their marriage vows. Chancellor Harper, of Charleston, called attention in 1854 to the fact that slave marriages were often faithfully adhered to during life.[22] In 1857 a sea-island planter, in recounting the deaths among his people, mentioned with sadness that of "poor old Sandy and his wife Joan." "The latter died apparently of mere debility; and her husband, after watching until her death, went to bed at midnight, complaining merely of a sore throat, and expired the next evening without any one suspecting that he was seriously ill." The planter concluded that the faithful old man had died of "mental depression, operating on a feeble constitution."[23] On Edisto Island there still lives "Old Jeff," born in slavery, who, although as devoted to his wife as Sandy, lived on after her death. Every day he went to her grave to mourn and there he slept at night. After several months his friends became alarmed at his behavior. Upon being questioned he explained that he intended to dig up

---

[22] "Memoir on Slavery," DeBow, *Industrial Resources of the United States*, II, 219.

[23] Couper-Wylly Papers, James Hamilton Couper to James Couper, April 13, 1857.

his wife's bones and take them to his house so that he could have 'he wit' me always."[24]

FAMILY LIFE

In their attempt to impress the sacredness of marriage upon their slaves, the whites were often discouraged by the low value which the slave women placed upon chastity. Wives were as prone as husbands to break the marriage vows. In fact, the female tended to be the dominant sex in slave life. It was decidedly to the advantage of a black man to have the good will of one of the women of the plantation, for life thereby was made much easier. On the plantations where clothes were issued by the yard, it was customary for the women to do the sewing for the family so that a husband was almost as dependent upon his wife for a new suit of clothes as he was upon his master; but, on the plantations where superannuated women were delegated to do all the plantation sewing and mending, the slave men were somewhat more independent of their women.

The weekly issuance of rations, a predominant portion of which was corn, was also dealt out in the bulk and must not only be shelled but pounded into grits before being cooked. It was customary for the women and children to assemble at the cornhouse on Monday, an hour or so before "fust dark," to receive the weekly allowance from the driver. Kneeling or sitting upon the ground with her children about her, each woman shelled the corn, using a cob to increase her speed. On some of the plantations there were improvised mortars for shelling corn, made of

[24] Information obtained from J. Swinton Whaley, Little Edisto, S. C., and from a personal interview with the Negro.

huge logs hollowed at one end. At these, two stood with their rude pestles striking alternately up and down. After the corn was shelled, the driver poured all upon a large hide or blanket and measured each person's portion into a basket, made by hand from pine straw and palmetto. After receiving the corn, the women ground it into grits, each waiting her turn at one of the hand-mills near the cornhouse.

With the aid of her children, the mother prepared supper from the rations just issued, supplementing the corn and salt pork with "turnip salad" or cow-peas from the "patch" back of the cabin, sweet potatoes roasted in the ashes, oysters or crabs from the creek, or with luxuries which she had bought at one of the island stores. Into the black pot placed on a bed of coals on the hearth went the grits to be boiled until thick and tender, or, perhaps, vegetables and fat pork might be cooking there. If so, the corn meal, which had come out of the mill together with the grits, would be made into a pone, cooked either on the open hearth or, if the family were thrifty, in a frying pan over the coals. The elders first helped themselves from the pot, and then turned it over to the children who ate to their satisfaction, and finally relinquished it to the dogs, invariably a part of the slave family, who licked it clean for the next meal.[25]

The mother also prepared the hasty breakfast eaten just after the conch blew at "day clean," if, indeed, the workers took time for breakfast, and filled her own and

[25] See Laura M. Towne, "Pioneer Work on the Sea Islands," *Southern Workman*, July, 1901.

her husband's pails which they took to the field with them for dinner.²⁶

If the wife were frugal, she might have a portion of the weekly rations left when Monday came around again, and these she might either feed to her pigs and chickens or sell to the overseer or to an island storekeeper. The money was hers to use for the good of the family, but it was hers, nevertheless. It was the woman of the family who, with the aid of her children, worked most of the family patch, and it was usually the woman who marketed the produce and pocketed the money received in exchange.

The planters helped to make of woman the dominant sex in the family life of the slave by the position which they gave her in the plantation regime. The cabin was hers. The children, too, were listed on the plantation records as belonging to the mother. Seldom was the father's name indicated. Thus a person might go through life known as Binah's Toby or Moll's July. Likewise the mother had the privilege of naming the new baby unless she graciously yielded the right to its father or to a friend or relative. In this right she often exercised a singular taste, for one child might be called Jupiter, another Quash, a third January, and a fourth Hard Times.

Miss Towne was amused at the jealousy of their "natural rights" which the men on St. Helena Island began to show after that region had come under the jurisdiction of the Federal Army during the Civil War. "Political freedom they are rather shy of, and ignorant of," she

---

²⁶ Some planters, as it has already been pointed out, delegated plantation cooks to prepare the noon meal for the field hands so that they might have something hot to eat at this time. Some planters also allowed an hour's rest at nine o'clock for breakfast.

wrote, "but domestic freedom—the right just found, to have their own way in their families and rule their wives—that is an inestimable privilege! In slavery the woman was far more important, and was in every way held higher than the man. Several speakers have been here who have advised the people to set the women in their proper place —never to tell them anything of their concerns, etc., etc.; and the notion of being bigger than women generally, is just now inflating the conceit of the males to an amazing degree. When women get the vote, too, no people will be more indignant than these, I suppose."[27]

The care of the children was divided between the mother and the plantation nurse, with the other children also doing their share of "minding child." When Captain Basil Hall visited a plantation near Charleston on his tour of the South in 1828 he found the mothers in the field at their work and "a sober old matron in charge of the three dozen shining urchins, collected together in a house near the center of the village. Over the fire hung a large pot of hominy, a preparation of Indian corn, making ready for the little folks' supper, and a very merry, happy-looking party they seemed."[28] At all other times, the children were in the mother's care. It was not an uncommon sight to see a woman going about her home work with an infant tied securely to her back.

Parents were severe in the discipline of their children, for they did not want their offspring to grow up to be "no-manners." They taught them to curtesy when approached by a white person and to hold out their hands to

---

[27] *Letters and Diary of Laura M. Towne*, p. 184.
[28] Hall, *Travels in North America*, II, 210; *supra*, pp. 97-98.

shake; to keep silent in the presence of elders and otherwise to show respect for age. Some of the missionaries who arrived on St. Helena Island shortly after the opening of the Civil War were indignant at the harsh treatment the children received at the hands of their parents. "I don't suppose these children ever received a caress or a word of tenderness since they were infants," wrote Arthur Sumner. "The children are invariably spoken to in harsh and peremptory tones by all grown niggers, and are whipped unmercifully on the least offence. Yet they are very obedient to their parents, and certainly stand much more in awe of adult darkies than they do of us mild-eyed missionaries."[29] Miss Towne concluded that parents were not really harsh to their children, but that their rough way of ordering them about, threatening to "skin um 'live" and to "bro'k um back," merely sounded savage. All visitors to the Sea Islands, either as guests of the master before the War or as missionaries, agreed that the children, despite the rough treatment from their parents and despite the fact that they seemed to have no games,[30] were a happy, carefree lot. Sir Charles Lyell thought the Hopeton plantation children had "such bright, happy faces when three or four years old, and from that age to ten or twelve . . . such frank and confiding manners, as to be very engaging."[31] Yet all were horrified by the fact that their mothers permitted them to run about in summer completely nude, a practice which people of today, with their recent adoption of the sunbath theory, would be inclined to approve.

[29] Arthur Sumner Papers, St. Helena Island, July 9, 1863.
[30] *Letters from Port Royal*, p. 192n.
[31] Lyell, *Second Visit to the United States*, I, 263.

Obviously, there was not the opportunity for home life in the slave family that there was in the free family, nor was meal time the institution that it was in the white family, for there was rarely to be found in the slave cabin a "family table."[32] Some observers of slave life thought also that there was little family affection among them. Edward S. Philbrick wrote to a friend that there was far less family affection and attachment among members of slave families than existed among the Irish peasants, adding, however, that he did not know "how much allowance to make for their being so much less demonstrative in their emotions, and more inured to suffering."[33]

LEISURE TIME

When task was done, the slave was his own master within the limits of plantation regulation. He might go home to work on his piece of ground, tend his pigs and chickens, play with his children, or fish in the creek. The slave had several ways of making money for his own use, in which he was encouraged by his master. As has already been pointed out, the black people ordinarily supplied their masters with chickens and eggs for which they usually received the market price.[34] They often sold their hogs and the truck from their garden patches; they wove baskets, and made boats and canoes. An overseer on the Butler plantation on St. Simon's Island said that he regularly allowed a certain number to go to town on Sundays

---

[32] Pierce, "Report," *Rebellion Records*, sup., I, 304. "Except on Sundays, these people do not take their meals at a family table, but each one takes his hominy, bread, or potatoes sitting on the floor or on a bench, and at his own time. They say their masters never allowed them any regular time for meals." In this connection see *supra*, p. 137n.

[33] *Letters from Port Royal*, p. 15.

[34] *Supra*, p. 86.

to dispose of eggs, coopers' wares and canoes, but required that they be home by twelve o'clock unless by special permission.[35] When it became illegal for a slave to hold personal property, the master, overseer, storekeeper, and slave all found ample means of evading the law as the cases arising on this statute indicate. Masters often paid their people for extra work done on the plantation, such as, gathering corn blades for fodder or collecting rice straw. Miss Mary B. Elliott, of Beaufort, gave her slaves 5 cents a pound for blades.[36] The master also gave them presents of money, especially at Christmas or New Year.

By thus being permitted to possess personal property of his own, the slave felt his condition to be less abject. Some planters tried to help their people to accumulate more than they could ordinarily obtain through the sale of "nigger truck" so that they might have some degree of independence. James Hamilton Couper set apart a field for the benefit of twenty-five picked men and allowed them half of their Saturday's labor in which to work it. He required all to work faithfully in the common field during the first year, and at the end of that time divided the $1,500 arising from the sale of the crop equally among them. But when they were left to work the field as they chose, they did very little and at the end of two years abandoned it entirely.[37]

While some slaves wisely spent their money for comforts which the master did not provide, others laid out their pittances in indulgences: liquor, tobacco, and fancy

[35] "On the Management of the Butler Estate," *Southern Agriculturist*, Dec., 1828.
[36] Elliott Account Book.
[37] Lyell, *Second Visit to the United States*, I, 268.

clothes. An English visitor at Hopeton noticed that whenever the mistress paid a visit to Savannah she was overwhelmed with commissions from her slaves who wished to obtain the latest fads in articles of dress, "of which they are passionately fond." "The stuff must be of the finest quality, and many instructions are given as to the precise color or fashionable shade. White muslin, with figured patterns, is the rage just now."[38]

The Negro spent a part of his spare time in simple recreation. Indeed, many masters thought that he spent most of it that way. If a tidal creek bordered the plantation, as was true of most plantations on St. Helena Island, the master permitted his people to fish freely for crabs, shrimp, bass, whiting, and catfish, sometimes, however, reserving for his own use the choicest sea foods, such as shrimp and whiting. It was seldom that a master permitted his people to go at will in boats upon the creeks, and only by special permission could they go upon the Sound for one of the most exciting of all water sports, drum fishing. In the fishing season, it was customary for the master to commission a certain number, usually three or four picked men, to do the drum fishing for the week, the fish, of course, being intended for the master's table. But when the men came in with a big catch, probably as many as five or six twenty-five pound fish, the fishermen not only had their reward from the catch, but the steaks were distributed among all the people as well. The slaves invariably considered the head the choice part of the fish. Even today it is not difficult to start an argument over who shall claim the head when a fish is about to be divided.

[38] Lyell, *Second Visit to the United States*, p. 265.

By plantation rule and by law of the state only one slave to a plantation was permitted to carry a gun for hunting, and he did so only to provide ducks for the master's table or to kill the crows and blackbirds which ate the seeds and the young plants in the fields.

The Negroes were also fond of singing and dancing, and most planters indulged them in this propensity. One South Carolina planter who had been having trouble in disciplining his slaves supplied his people with fiddles and drums and "promoted dancing." To his gratification the ill temper of the slaves disappeared and peace was once more established on the plantation.[39] Their dancing was a sort of shuffle which animated the whole body, and was performed individually rather than by couples. The dance was usually held at night in the open or in one of the cabins and the entire group participated in the merrymaking. Miss Towne frequently complained after she reached St. Helena Island in 1862 that the Negroes on her plantation had been up singing and dancing all night.

Most visitors to the Sea Islands wondered at the slaves' "passionate fondness" for singing. Fredrika Bremer, a Scandinavian visitor to coastal South Carolina, was of the opinion that "one must see these people singing if one is rightly to understand their life." After attending a Negro church service, she declared that "they sang so that it was a pleasure to hear, with all their souls and with all their bodies in unison; for their bodies wagged, their heads nodded, their feet stamped, their knees shook, their elbows and their hands beat time to the tune and words

[39] N. Herbemont, "On the Moral Discipline and Treatment of Slaves," *Southern Agriculturist*, IX, 70-75.

which they sang with evident delight."[40] Captain Basil Hall, who was rowed down the Altamaha in a cypress dugout by "five smart negroes," was impressed by the "wild sort of song" with which they accompanied their labor. He thought the song "not very unlike that of the Canadian voyageurs, but still more nearly resembling that of the well-known Bunder-boatmen at Bombay."[41] Whitelaw Reid, who heard the Negroes singing at "Brick Church" on St. Helena in 1865, described their song, "Roll Jordan Roll," as having "a curiously monotonous melody."[42] Miss Towne thought that the St. Helena folk "in their lowest state . . . could always do one thing well—sing." "At first," she said, "they sang melody alone, but after having once been given the idea of harmony, they instantly adopted it."[43]

A holiday was always the occasion for much singing, dancing, and general merrymaking. It was the custom on St. Helena Island to give the Negroes Saturday afternoon and all of Sunday, three days at Christmas, and an occasional day at the end of a hard season of work. These were holidays which the master set aside for his people and instructed his overseer to observe. P. C. J. Weston clearly indicated in his "rules to the overseer" the holidays which he wished the Negroes on his South Carolina rice plantation to have:

No work of any sort or kind is to be permitted to be done by negroes on Good Friday, or Christmas day, or on any Sunday, except going for a Doctor, or nursing sick persons; any work of this kind done on any of these days is to be reported to the Proprietor, who

---

[40] Bremer, *Homes of the New World*, p. 393.
[41] Hall, *Travels in North America*, II, 228.
[42] Reid, *After the War: A Southern Tour*, p. 103.
[43] Towne, "Pioneer Work on the Sea Islands," *Southern Workman*, July, 1901.

will pay for it. The two days following Christmas day; the first Saturdays after finishing threshing, planting, hoeing, and harvest, are also to be holidays, on which the people may work for themselves. Only half task is to be done on every Saturday, except during planting and harvest, and [except by] those who have misbehaved or been lying up during the week.[44]

Most of their holidays the slaves spent "pleasuring themselves." Christmas was the great event of the year, for it was at this time that the master distributed rewards to his people as well as extra provisions of beef and molasses and "hands of tobacco." The master of at least one sea-island plantation also provided his slaves with "plenty of whiskey." At the end of the three-day orgy the Negroes were often "completely done up with eating, drinking, and dancing."[45]

A holiday was also the occasion for many requests to visit the island stores and neighboring plantations, but most planters discouraged inter-plantation visits and required the overseer and the drivers to check up frequently on the activities in the "street." An overseer was supposed to see that all was well in the quarters before he went to bed, and the drivers were also responsible for keeping the street quiet. It was by this means rather than by the patrol system that sea-island planters kept peace on their plantations at night, although occasionally the planters or their overseers joined in "riding a patrol." No slave was permitted either by law or by plantation regulation to be absent from home without a ticket. While some planters permitted every well behaved slave to have one whenever he requested it, others issued tickets more

[44] Phillips, *Plantation and Frontier*, I, 117.
[45] Hall, *Travels in North America*, II, 232.

reluctantly. To check upon the comings and goings of the people it was customary to have "list" twice a day on Sunday when the names of all the men were called, from which none was excused except those who were sick or who had tickets. At the evening list "every negro must be clean and well washed."[46]

RELIGION AND EDUCATION

While it is undoubtedly true that some planters in the early days of the introduction of slave labor into South Carolina were hesitant about allowing their Negroes to become christianized for fear that it might elevate them above their chattel state,[47] by the opening of the antebellum period masters quite generally came to look upon the conversion of the Negroes as one of the justifications of slavery. They not only encouraged the various religious denominations to send missionaries to their slaves, but they often built plantation churches for the special use of the Negroes and permitted their sons and daughters to instruct the slaves from the Bible. Missionaries, appointed by the church but chiefly paid by the planters, preached to the Negroes and catechized them. Ministers prepared special sermons and catechisms for them. Bishop Meade of the Episcopal denomination published his *Sermons, Dialogues and Narratives for servants, to be read to them in families* in Richmond in 1836, and the second edition of Rev. Charles C. Jones' *The Catechism for*

---

[46] Phillips, *op. cit.*, p. 116.
[47] *The South-Carolina Gazette*, March 27, 1742.

"WE [the Grand Jury at Charles Town] present, . . . that, by influence of . . . HUGH BRYAN, Great Bodies of Negroes have Assembled together on Pretence of religious Worship, Contrary to Law, and destructive to the Peace and Safety of the Inhabitants of this Province."

Colored Persons was published in Savannah in 1837. These are only two of many such works published in the South.

The Missionary Society of the South Carolina Conference of the Methodist denomination collected for their missions to the Negroes between twelve and fifteen hundred dollars in 1837 and in 1840 reported nineteen missionaries, thirteen missions, 232 plantations administered unto, 5,482 members, and 3,811 children.[48] Very little data can be obtained concerning the activities of the Baptist denomination among the sea-island Negroes, although it is known that more of them adhered to the Baptist faith than to any other. In the summer of 1838 a revival of religion commenced among the Negroes of Liberty County, Georgia, and spread throughout the entire coastal region of South Carolina and Georgia, continuing for two years. During that time the Congregational Church in Liberty County and the Baptist churches throughout the region greatly added to their colored membership.[49]

In addition to the space reserved for slaves in the rear and in the gallery of "Brick Church" on St. Helena Island, practically every plantation had its own "praise house" where the people held their weekly services. In case the planter provided no separate building, services were held in the cabin of the religious leader. Miss Towne wrote to a friend shortly after she reached St. Helena Island in 1862 that the praise house was "always the cabin of the oldest person in the village of negro houses."[50] She was

[48] Charles C. Jones, *The Religious Instruction of the Negroes in the United States*, pp. 82, 83.
[49] *Ibid.*, p. 83.
[50] *Letters and Diary of Laura M. Towne*, p. 20.

doubtless speaking from a knowledge only of the plantation where she was then residing, for her co-workers have left descriptions of various praise houses on the Island. W. C. Gannett wrote in April, 1862, that the praise house on Pine Grove plantation was "quite a nice little house,— the best on this part of the island."[51] The praise house of Eustis plantation on Ladies Island which their mistress, then living in Massachusetts, had built them was a church indeed.[52]

Once, twice, or even three times a week, those who were religiously inclined met at the praise house to sing, pray, and exhort. Edward L. Pierce estimated that about half of the adult Negroes on St. Helena were members of a church.[53] The praise meeting usually opened with a "sperichil" followed by a hymn which the leader "deaconed out" two lines at a time, reading from a well-worn psalm book, if perchance he had learned to read, pretending to read, nevertheless, holding the book nearer the flickering light as if to make out the words, all the while calling out the lines from memory. Cuffy, the leader of the praise house on Pine Grove plantation, always made his own hymns, improvised from hymns of the whites, "praying to de Lord Jedus teach um as he in de woods [to] jine one word 'ginst t'oder."[54] After another hymn and perhaps a spiritual, the leader would ask for a prayer, then

[51] *Letters from Port Royal*, p. 20 n.
[52] See also Wm. Henry Trescot, "Address on Gen. Stephen Elliott, delivered in the House of Representatives of South Carolina, Sept. 8, 1866," p. 5. For many years preceding the War, Rev. Stephen Elliott, father of General Elliott, of Beaufort, "had declined the rectorship of a regular congregation, and, having built a church upon his own plantation, preached regularly and most efficiently to the slaves of the neighborhood."
[53] Pierce, "Report," *Rebellion Record*, sup., I., 305.
[54] *Letters from Port Royal*, p. 27.

A ST. HELENA ISLAND PRAISE HOUSE

read a long passage from the Bible and after another prayer call upon a member to speak.

Edward L. Pierce attended several praise meetings on St. Helena in 1862 and reported that "their exhortations to personal piety were fervent, and though their language was many times confused, at least to my ear, occasionally an important instruction or a felicitous expression could be recognized. In one case, a preacher of their own, commenting on the text, 'Blessed are the meek,' exhorted his brethren not to be 'stout-minded.' "[55]

After another prayer and song the "shout" began.[56] Although the prayer meeting invariably preceded the shout, the members considered the shout a part of their worship, explaining that "it exercise de frame."[57] Pushing the benches back to the wall and perhaps putting another piece of lightwood on the fire in the hearth and on the one which burned red before the door, the worshipers began the recreation which for the church members took the place of the informal dance.

"Old and young, men and women, sprucely-dressed young men, grotesquely half-clad field hands—the women generally with gay handkerchiefs twisted about their heads and with short skirts—boys with tattered shirts and men's trousers, young girls barefooted," wrote Miss Harriet Ware who attended many a shout on St. Helena in the

[55] Pierce, *op. cit.*, p. 305.
[56] Mr. William Elliott, of Columbia, S. C., a relative of the William Elliott frequently quoted in these pages, states that "the 'shout' is the object of the meeting to which the rest is the introduction." Mr. Elliott speaks from an intimate knowledge of sea-island customs. The shouts, however, which the writer attended on St. Helena Island in 1928 were invariably commenced after the praise meeting had been dismissed.
[57] *Letters from Port Royal*, p. 27.

early days of the Civil War, "all stand up in the middle of the floor, and when the 'sperichil' is struck up, begin first walking and by-and-by shuffling around, one after the other, in a ring. The foot is hardly taken from the floor, and the progression is mainly due to a jerking, hitching motion, which agitates the entire shouter, and soon brings out streams of perspiration. Sometimes they dance silently, sometimes as they shuffle they sing the chorus of the spiritual, and sometimes the song itself is also sung by the dancers. But more frequently a band, composed of some of the best singers and tired shouters, stand [sic] at the side of the room to 'base' the others, singing the body of the song and clapping their hands together or on their knees. Song and dance are alike extremely energetic, and often, when the shout lasts into the middle of the night, the monotonous thud, thud of the feet prevents sleep within half a mile of the praise-house."[58]

Miss Towne thought the shout to be "certainly the remains of some old idol worship." "I never saw anything so savage," she said. "They call it a religious ceremony, but it seems more like a regular frolic to me."[59] The shout was, indeed, a modification of the Negro's regular dance. After a Negro was converted he no longer attended dances in the cabins where "de sinners cross um feet," for the Methodist and Baptist preachers and missionaries taught the slaves that dancing was evil. He went instead to the praise house where the same dance, recently in vogue today as the "Charleston," was performed, with-

[58] *Ibid.*, p. 27n; also in *Nation*, May 30, 1867. For other descriptions of shouts on St. Helena Island see *Letters and Diary of Laura M. Towne*, pp. 20, 21, 22, 23.
[59] *Letters and Diary*, p. 20.

out crossing the feet, to the tune of a spiritual. Nor did the Negroes take their violins into the praise houses, for the missionaries also taught them that fiddle music was sinful since the fiddle furnished the tunes for the old dances. The last violin on St. Helena Island before the Civil War is said to have been owned by a Negro on Coffin's Point, but he got rid of it before "big gun shoot," as the Negroes called the battle of Port Royal.

Sir Charles Lyell observed the same kind of religious worship on the Georgia Sea Islands and mainland. "On the Hopeton plantation above twenty violins have been silenced by the Methodist missionaries," he wrote in 1845. "At the Methodist prayer-meetings, they are permitted to move rapidly in a ring, joining hands in token of brotherly love, presenting first the right hand and then the left, in which manœuvre, I am told, they sometimes contrive to take enough exercise to serve as a substitute for the dance, it being, in fact, a kind of spiritual *boulanger* [?], while the singing of psalms, in and out of chapel, compensates in no small degree for the songs they have been required to renounce."[60]

The religious life of the slaves was organized by the whites upon the same plan as their own. On plantations of any size, slaves who had joined the church were formed into a class, at the head of which was one of their own number, acting as deacon or leader, who was also sometimes a licensed preacher.[61] The leader who was the head of the praise house often decided in council with his subordinates, the watchmen, whether a candidate for member-

---

[60] Lyell, *Second Visit to the United States*, I, 269, 270.
[61] "Negro Slavery at the South," DeBow, *Industrial Resources of the United States*, II, 251.

ship was worthy of admittance. The Reverend Charles C. Jones, after many years spent in preaching to sea-island and mainland slaves concluded that they were inclined to place true religion in profession, in forms and ordinances, and in excited states of feeling, and true conversion in dreams, visions, trances, and voices, "all bearing a perfect or striking resemblance to some form or type which has been handed down for generations, or which has been originated in the wild fancy of some religious teacher among them."[62] They offered these dreams and visions to the church sessions as evidences of conversion just as the whites were inclined to do in camp meetings.

They were also quick to follow the custom of the whites in "churching" offending members. "The discipline of colored members," wrote the Reverend Mr. Jones, who, no doubt, had taken part on many such occasions, "is involved, tedious, vexatious and disgusting." Excommunications and suspensions were of "perpetual occurrence, for crimes shocking in character, and of themselves sufficient to show the general state of morals; such for example as adultery, fornication, theft, lying, drunkenness, quarreling, and fighting." The Reverend Mr. Jones thought that the Negroes perverted the gospel and colored their religious practices with their African superstitions. Thus their "doctors, prophets, and conjurers" modified the teachings of the white preachers.[63]

The church was not only responsible for giving Christianity to the Negroes, but also to a large extent for teaching a few of them to read and write. The early statutes

---

[62] Jones, *Religious Instruction of the Negroes*, pp. 125, 126.
[63] *Ibid.*, pp. 131, 127, 128.

against teaching slaves to read had long been in abeyance when Sunday schools began to be organized among them early in the ante-bellum period. Masters usually encouraged their people to attend these Sabbath schools and often delegated their own children to do the teaching. The reaction against the Abolition agitation led many planters to fear the consequence of their people's learning to read. Accordingly, the Sunday school movement was largely abandoned after 1835; nevertheless, on every plantation there were always some slaves who either were taught to read with the permission of the master or who picked up the knowledge clandestinely. Miss Towne found on St. Helena Island in 1862 a cabinet maker, Will Capers, who could read and write and who hoped the Government would pay him for teaching his fellows. He told her that he conducted a secret night school for men during plantation days.[64] Nevertheless, it was unusual for a slave to know his letters, and most of them could not count beyond, "one, two, five, eight, ten."[65]

For the most part, sea-island planters found their laborers mild and forgiving, quick to start a quarrel, but as quick to forget it. Sir Charles Lyell thought that there were more broken heads among the Irish in a few years when they came to dig the Brunswick Canal than had been known among the coastal Negroes for half a century.[66] They were a good natured, happy people, making the most of their lot, forgetting the work of the day in their hours of "pleasuring."

[64] *Letters and Diary of Laura M. Towne*, p. 27.
[65] Towne, "Pioneer Work on the Sea Islands," *Southern Workman*, July, 1901. Miss Towne, however, could not have come in contact with the house servants, but only with the field hands.
[66] Lyell, *Second Visit to the United States*, I, 266.

CHAPTER VIII

"CONTRABAND OF WAR"

THE CAPTURE OF PORT ROYAL

FOR THREE DAYS the Federal fleet had been collecting in Confederate waters, until by the afternoon of November 6, 1861, Confederate scouts were able to count forty-five steamers and gunboats outside Port Royal Sound. Only the most timorous were fearful of an attack on the two forts guarding the entrance to the Sound, Fort Beauregard at Bay Point on Eddings' Island and Fort Walker upon Hilton Head, and the consequent capture of Beaufort. The planters themselves could not conceive of any military strategy which would make the possession of Beaufort important to the enemy. It was Charleston's scalp which the fleet had come to take and the display outside Port Royal was a subterfuge. So they remained on their plantations with their families quietly waiting for the enemy to sail on.

The Confederate officers were not to be taken by surprise, although they were fervently hoping that Beaufort with its inadequate defense was to be spared. They asked for reinforcements at once and began preparations for an attack. At dawn on the morning of November 7 the "armada," led by the sixty-gun flagship of Captain DuPont, advanced in battle array upon the two forts with their feeble batteries, twenty guns at Fort Walker and nineteen at her sister fort across the Sound. At 9:25 o'clock a nine-inch gun from one of the forts opened fire. Soon firing was general upon land and water, but the advancing fleet came on safely beyond the range of the Confederate barrage. Passing both batteries, they turned and delivered, in their changing rounds, a terrific shower of shot and shell in flank and front. By 3 o'clock in the afternoon, the Confederate forces commenced retreating to Ferry Point, leaving the Sea Islands about Port Royal Sound in the possession of the Federal Army during the remainder of the war.[1]

When word came that Beaufort was actually to be attacked, the confusion on the plantations was overwhelming. Hastily gathering together what clothes they could, wives prepared themselves and their children for the flight to the main, while husbands got ready the flats and boats for the trip. They took with them only the house servants most urgently needed in the care of the family, the nurses and cooks, instructing the field hands to remain at work under the direction of the drivers until their return. In their flight they had little time or space for family heirlooms or valuables. They left their houses and their fields just as they were. By afternoon when the Federal troops took possession of the district, not a white person of Confederate sympathies could be found in Beaufort or on the plantations.[2]

[1] See "The Capture of Port Royal, S. C.," *Rebellion Record,* sup. I, pp. 192-197; *Official Records,* ser. I, vol. VI, serial no. 6, pp. 186-193.

[2] A few weeks later a general outcry arose in Charleston over this unpremeditated flight. Women and politicians alike declared that the planters should at least have taken time to destroy the crops which were evidently going to be of such benefit to the enemy. To this attack, a St. Helena planter replied in the *Charleston Daily Courier,* Dec. 2, 1861:

"Our sacrifices already have exemplified our patriotic devotion, and our failure to have entailed greater, by the destruction of our several crops, resulted in our having been steadily employed in providing ways and means for the retreat of the forces at Bay Point . . . it is . . . true that the successful conduct of that retreat was entirely due to the exertions of the little band of men composing the St. Helena Mounted Riflemen, Captain Fripp [in command]. . . .

General W. T. Sherman, in command of the "Expeditionary Corps" arriving at Port Royal, as this region was now to be called, on the fleet in command of Captain DuPont, described in two official reports conditions as he found them after the battle:

The effect of this victory is startling. Every white inhabitant has left the island. The wealthy islands of Saint Helena, Ladies, and most of Port Royal are abandoned by the whites, and the beautiful estates of the planters, with all their immense property, left to the pillage of hordes of apparently disaffected blacks.

. . .

The surrounding country evacuated by the whites, as described in my last, has upon it an abundance of valuable property, including ungathered crops and cotton mostly gathered. I have directed all the means of transportation, such as boats, scows, wagons, &c., to be collected for the use of the Army; but in regard to other private property, such as can be made of no injury to us in the operations of the enemy, I have directed not to be interfered with. This, however, is a difficult matter, and there exists too great a propensity to rob and pillage the houses and plantations left in charge only of the blacks.[3]

Later Hazard Stevens who also witnessed as an officer of the Federal Army the capture of Port Royal attributed much of the looting to the Negroes whom he de-

"The facts are briefly these. So soon as it was understood by the St. Helena Company that a retreat of our forces from Bay Point might become necessary, every hand was employed and every individual busied in gathering together the flats and boats from every quarter of the Island. This duty was rendered doubly arduous by the unwillingness displayed by some of the negroes, who shrunk from executing the order from fear, and in many instances secreted themselves at the appointed time. So excited and disorganized had they become from fear inspired by the terrible cannonading only three miles distant from their point of rendezvous, that it was found necessary to have the flats, as they were manned, each superintended by a member of our little company, who were instructed to make an example of the first rebellious negro who hesitated to row."

[3] *Official Records*, ser. I, vol. VI, serial no. 6, pp. 6, 188.

scribed as being in "the densest ignorance, some of them the blackest human beings ever seen, and others the most bestial in appearance." "These ignorant and benighted creatures flocked into Beaufort on the hegira of the whites," wrote Stevens, "and held high carnival in the deserted mansions, smashing doors, mirrors, and furniture, and appropriating all that took their fancy. After this loot, a common sight was a black wench dressed in silks, or white lace curtains, or a stalwart black field hand resplendent in a complete suit of gaudy carpeting just torn from the floor. After this sack, they remained at home upon the plantations, and reveled in unwonted idleness and luxury, feasting upon the corn, cattle, and turkeys of their fugitive masters."[4]

The Negroes were inclined to hold aloof from the invading army. They had been told by their masters that the enemy was likely to seize them and carry them off to Cuba. They, who were accustomed to look upon persons even from neighboring islands as "foreigners," were startled by the presence of so many white persons. The officers had expected to put the Negroes to work at once in getting ready the new camps, after the example of General Butler, who had earlier captured Hampton Roads and solved his labor problem and the status of the Negro simultaneously by declaring the slaves contraband of war. But, after the army had been at Port Royal more than a month, the Negroes still were suspicious. A great many would come in to watch the operations of the white soldiers, bringing with them wives and children, but when work was suggested most of them would again take to the

[4] Stevens, *Life of Isaac Ingalls Stevens*, pp. 354, 355.

woods and the swamps, often leaving their families to be fed by the army.[5] By February, 1862, however, 600 Negroes had collected at the Federal camp at Hilton Head.

The Negroes on the islands more remote from Beaufort and Hilton Head quite generally remained on their respective plantations under the direction of the drivers who still held the keys to the corn-houses. With the same sense of responsibility that they felt before their masters fled, they dealt out rations and directed the work of the field hands. In one instance a Federal agent was called upon to settle a dispute between a driver and a field hand, as being the only white man to whom an appeal might be made. The driver was refusing the hand his peck of corn because he had been absent visiting his wife on a neighboring plantation when the corn was gathered, the work having been done after "gun shoot," as the Negroes termed the battle of Port Royal. The hand protested that he had helped to plant and hoe the corn and had been absent when it was gathered only because of sickness. Upon this evidence the agent advised the driver to deal out the peck, and the driver promptly did so.

The St. Helena Negroes seem to have had little part in the looting of their masters' houses. They were accustomed to the absence of their owners and to seeing the "big house" closed many months during the year. They could not believe, as the soldiers told them, that their masters were gone for good. After a while they did begin to take a few simple articles such as sugar and soap,[6] and

[5] *Official Records,* ser. I, vol. VI, serial no. 6, p. 202.
[6] Their attitude is in striking contrast to that of the Combahee River Negroes who usually to a man went off with the Federal Army when a raid was made up the River. On one such occasion, seventy-three Negroes on the plantation where

later, when they saw the soldiers entering the houses, they also took pieces of furniture, but by far the greater portion of valuables was taken by the soldiers and Government agents.

THE PROBLEM OF THE CONQUERING ARMY

When the Federal Army captured Port Royal, it found that it had also taken possession of some ten thousand Negroes who might be "contraband of war," but whose status was doubtful, nevertheless. They could not be treated as northern laborers, put to work at the camps, and then ignored. It was even possible that the Army might in the last extremity have to feed and clothe them. But in the meantime there were valuable provisions for the Army on the plantations and valuable crops in the fields which could not be left to the uncertain course of the Negroes.

One of the first orders to the troops was to collect boats and mules for transportation service and corn and cattle for the commissary. Edward L. Pierce later reported that the Army had taken nearly all the corn from Ladies Island, hoping that the surplus on St. Helena would be sufficient to feed the Negroes of both islands, and from all the plantations it had taken the workable mules and horses and many of the oxen, which they slaughtered for beef, sometimes killing as many as "fifty or more head on a plantation."[7]

two Federal boats anchored aided in the destruction of their own and three neighboring plantations. They set fire to the "big house," containing a library of 3,500 volumes, to the steam threshing mill, rice barn, corn house, kitchen, storeroom, mule stable, and three Negro houses. They put on board 6,000 bushels of rice from the plantation barn and then, with their clothing tied in bundles and with their chickens and pigs squealing a protest, climbed on the vessels to the last woman and child. See *Charleston Mercury*, June 19, 1863.

[7] Pierce, "Second Report," *Rebellion Records*, sup., I, p. 319.

To the Treasury Department, the War Department turned over the task of collecting and selling the cotton. For this purpose, Secretary Chase hastily appointed certain men whom he called cotton agents to direct the work of the Negroes. William H. Reynolds, lieutenant colonel of the First Regiment of Rhode Island Artillery, was appointed resident agent and placed in charge of the cotton agents. His motives appear to have been superior to those of many who worked under him. In making a report on the progress of work to Secretary Chase the first of the year he wrote:

> I find on most of the Plantations corn, and Sweet Potatoes, in sufficient quantities to support the Negroes.
> I have made arrangements to furnish them with salt, molasses & other small stores in moderate quantities deducting the cost of these articles from the amt due them for labor.
> . . . I find it is impossible to hire the Negroes by the day, on many of the Plantations, & have authorized my clerks to allow them a dollar for every four hundred pounds of stone cotton which they deliver at the steamboat landing, paying them partly in money & the bal in Clothing & Provisions—[8]

Edward L. Pierce, a special agent for the Treasury Department, who arrived at Port Royal a few weeks after the cotton agents, found some of them practicing "a reign of terror over the Negroes." One of them, a carpenter from New York City, had the "profoundest contempt" for his laborers.[9] Others also wrote of the dubious practices of the cotton agents. "Mr. Whiting has not been a Government agent for two months," Miss Towne wrote indignantly in 1862, "and yet he lives in Government

---
[8] Port Royal Correspondence. Wm. H. Reynolds to S. P. Chase, Jan. 1, 1862.
[9] *Ibid.*, Edward L. Pierce to S. P. Chase, March 30, 1862.

property, making the negroes work without pay for him and living upon 'the fat of the lamb,'—selling too, the sugar, etc., at rates most wicked, such as brown sugar, twenty-five cents a pound; using Government horses and carriages, furniture, corn, garden vegetables, etc. It is too bad. The cotton agents, many of them, are doing this."[10]

While the cotton agents promised wages to the laborers, they were slow to pay, for the Department expected the fund arising from the sale of cotton to take care of the expense of picking it. The difficulty in getting the Negroes to work, together with the difficulty in getting the cotton ginned and to the New York market, added to the delay. The agents had expected to bale the cotton on the plantations, but the Negroes had quite generally broken up the gins so that most of it had to be sent to New York for this purpose. Consequently, it was April, 1862, before the Negroes received any pay for their labor, and then some of it was in orders on the agents' stores where prices were high. Consequently, the Government was facing general discontent and uneasiness among the Negroes only a few months after having taken them under its protection.

At the time that the Treasury Department was assigned the task of marketing the cotton, it was also given jurisdiction over the operation of the plantations and, consequently, the general welfare of the laborers on them. As early as January 15, 1862, General Sherman had applied to headquarters for authority to put into operation

[10] *Letters and Diary of Laura M. Towne*, pp. 55, 61. See also pp. 16, 17, 66, 67.

a plan for the superintendence of agriculture and education within his department. He wrote to the adjutant-general on this date:

> For the future maintenance of these people some system must be established, and one which will permit them to sustain themselves; but before they can be left entirely to their own government they must be trained and instructed into a knowledge of personal responsibility—which will be a matter of time. I have, therefore, the honor to recommend that suitable instructors be sent to them, to teach them all the necessary rudiments of civilization and secondly, and in the meantime, that agents, properly qualified, be employed and sent here to take charge of plantations and superintend the work of the blacks until they are sufficiently enlightened to think and provide for themselves. They should receive wages, and the profits of the plantations, after all expenses are paid, should go to the Government. I can see no other way to lay a groundwork for future usefulness with this unfortunate class of people.[11]

The next month General Sherman issued an order appealing to the benevolent people of the land "in behalf of the helpless blacks of South Carolina within the limits of his command."[12]

When the Treasury assumed the responsibility of the Negro, Secretary Chase had in mind some such plan as Sherman had already suggested. It occurred to Chase that here was an opportunity to test the ability of the Negro to exercise freedom in case it were eventually given him. Under a fostering benevolence, the Negro was to be given the chance of revealing his capabilities. Out of the battle of Port Royal there gradually arose in the minds of those in the North the scheme for a great social experi-

---

[11] *Official Records*, ser. I, vol. VI, serial no. 6, p. 218.
[12] *House Ex. Doc. No. 142*, 41st Cong. 2d Sess.

ment which would form some basis for a decision concerning the status which the Negro should be given after the war.

To put some such scheme in operation the Department chose Edward L. Pierce, a young abolitionist of Boston who had studied in Chase's law office. He had been at Hampton, Virginia, and after he was mustered out of military service in July, 1861, went to Washington where he had occasion to relate some of his recent experiences with the Negroes to Secretary Chase. This fact together with their personal friendship was perhaps responsible for the Secretary's sending Pierce, then practicing law in Boston, a wire December 21, 1861: "If you incline to visit Beaufort in connection with contrabands and cotton, come to Washington at once."[13] On the twenty-fifth Pierce conferred with Chase and, on January 13, 1862, left New York City for Beaufort to make an investigation of social conditions among the Negroes under the temporary appointment as special agent for the Treasury Department.

Pierce found the "contrabands" discontented with the treatment they had received at the hands of the cotton agents and the Army. They were suspicious and reticent. When asked if they desired to be free, they would often answer, "De vite man do w'at he pleases wit' us. We yunnah niggers now, Massa."[14] But, concluded Pierce, "in spite of their condition, reputed to be worse here than in many other parts of the rebellious region, there are such features in their life and character, that the opportunity is now offered to us to make of them, partially in

[13] Pierce, *Addresses and Papers*, p. 54.
[14] Pierce, "Report," *Rebellion Record*, sup., I, 308.

this generation, and fully in the next, a happy, industrious law-abiding, free and Christian people, if we have but the courage and patience to accept it."[15] Whereupon he outlined a plan to the Secretary by which he thought this ideal might be realized.

He was much opposed to the plan of leasing the plantations with the people upon them to the highest bidder, as the cotton agents had recommended. Instead, he would propose a system of superintendents of plantations whereby certain men, carefully chosen for the position, should be appointed to manage the cultivation of the plantations, their chief object being "to promote the moral and intellectual culture of the wards" and "to prepare them for useful and worthy citizenship." The superintendents, who were to be selected "as carefully as one would choose a guardian for his children," were to have complete authority on their respective plantations subject only to a director-general. The superintendents were to be compensated by a good salary, say $1,000, and the laborers by a standard wage graduated by the wants of the laborers and the ability of the Government to pay, this ability to be determined by the profits arising from the cultivation of the plantations. He thought, however, that the Government should be able to allow rations and 40 cents a day.

As a part of the plan, Pierce advised the Government to send missionaries "to address the religious element of a race so emotional in their nature" and teachers to instruct the laborers in reading, writing, and arithmetic. For the

[15] *Ibid.*, p. 310.

salaries of these persons, Pierce thought that the Government could rely upon private benevolence.[16]

While Pierce's "Report to the Secretary of the Treasury," of February 3, 1862, which at once received wide publication, was for the most part enthusiastically received in the North, there were some who thought that he went too far in presuming upon the Negro's ultimate citizenship. Even his personal friends in Congress refused to support the plan, and President Lincoln did not wish to be troubled with "such details"; for, so Pierce thought, he approached the great question of the status of the Negro "slowly and reluctantly."[17] Chase seems to have been well pleased with the report and at once put it in operation.[18] In looking about for the proper person to put this difficult and important experiment into effect, it was natural that the Secretary should choose the father of the plan.

Although the Department had adopted the plan of superintendents, it had no funds with which to pay them. At this critical stage the Educational Commission, organized in Boston February 7, 1862, and the Freedman's Relief Association, organized in New York on the twentieth of the same month, volunteered to pay both superintend-

[16] *Ibid.*, pp. 311, 312.
[17] Pierce, *Addresses and Papers*, p. 65.
[18] *Official Records*, ser. III, vol. II, serial no. 123, p. 55. The authority by which the Treasury Department assumed the responsibilities outlined in the report was based upon the Act of July 13, 1861, by which the President was authorized to permit commercial intercourse with any part of the country in a state of insurrection under such rules and regulations as might be prescribed by the Secretary of the Treasury. The act authorized the Secretary to appoint the officers needed to carry into effect such permits, rules, and regulations. President Lincoln sanctioned the enterprise in a note to Pierce, February 15, 1862, and the War Department approved the plans in an order to General Sherman which he made a part of General Orders, No. 17.

ents and teachers. These two societies, together with the Port Royal Relief Committee, organized in Philadelphia, March 3, paid all salaries for four months, when the Treasury Department, having derived $200,000 from the sale of confiscated cotton, assumed payment of superintendents' salaries on July 1, still leaving the salaries of the teachers, however, to the benevolent societies. In the meantime other societies for the relief of the freedmen had been organized in the North and West and even in Great Britain.[19]

THE SOCIAL EXPERIMENT

On the morning of March 3, 1862, Pierce sailed from New York with the first delegation of superintendents and teachers, forty-one men and twelve women, each approved either by Pierce or Secretary Chase, each with a certificate of appointment from the Department. On the ninth they arrived at Beaufort. A few returned North immediately after their arrival, while still others came to take their places or to increase the number in the field. The largest number duly commissioned and in actual service did not exceed at any time seventy men and sixteen women.[20]

Many of those who came had little knowledge of the Negro and none whatever of slave conditions, but they were, for the most part, young, enthusiastic, and well educated. Youths just out of Harvard and Yale, divinity students fresh from the seminary, medical students and doctors with years of experience, they came, risking their

---

[19] Friends of the freedmen in England maintained a school on St. Helena Island from 1862 to 1869. See J. W. Alvord, *Letters from the South Relating to Freedmen*.

[20] Pierce, "Second Report," *Rebellion Record*, sup. I, p. 315.

lives in this region of malaria and typhoid, to train the Negro for citizenship.[21] While some refused to accept any remuneration, others served at from $30 to $50 a month, only one receiving as high as $100, a doctor on North Edisto. All, however, took their quarters in the deserted houses of the planters and received soldiers' rations from the Government.

In two weeks after their arrival each superintendent and teacher had been assigned a post and was at work, but his task was overwhelming. Stirred up by the careless and conflicting talk of the soldiers, victimized by the cotton agents, the Negroes were unwilling pupils. "We found them a herd of suspicious savages," wrote Edward

[21] MS in Treasury Department on superintendents and teachers for Port Royal. Those first appointed to plantations on St. Helena Island were as follows: Edward W. Hooper, of Boston, 22 years old, graduate of Harvard, served without compensation, teacher and superintendent at Pope's plantation; Edward S. Philbrick, of Brookline, Mass., 34 years old, railroad engineer and architect, received no compensation, superintendent at Coffin's Point; William C. Gannett, of Boston, 22 years old, divinity student, no compensation the first month, superintendent and teacher with Philbrick at Coffin's Point; James H. Palmer, of Southampton, N. H., 25 years old, medical student, assistant superintendent and teacher at Coffin's Frogmore plantation, $30 a month; David F. Thorpe, of Providence, R. I., student at Brown University, 25 years old, superintendent at Oliver Fripp's plantation, $40 a month; Dr. Adoniram Judson Wakefield, of Boston, 38 years old, physician, located on Thomas B. Fripp's plantation, medical attendant of Negroes in that section, $50 a month; T. Edwin Ruggles, of Milton, Mass., 24 years old, graduate of Yale, farmer, superintendent at Rev. Richard Fuller's plantation, $50 a month; Richard Soule, Sr., 49 years old, civil engineer and teacher, superintendent at Coffin's Frogmore, $50 a month; Dr. Charles H. Brown, of Boston, 45 years old, physician, medical attendant for Negroes in vicinity of Pope's plantation, $40 a month; William E. Park, of Andover, Mass., 24 years old, graduate of Yale, superintendent at Capt. Oliver Fripp's plantation, compensation undetermined; James E. Taylor, of Andover, Mass., 23 years old, student, superintendent and teacher at Dr. Jenkin's plantation, compensation undetermined; Samuel D. Phillips, of Boston, 23 years old, medical student and graduate of Harvard, nephew of Wendell Phillips, superintendent at Dr. Pope's plantation, $30 a month; George M. Wells, of Providence, R. I., 20 years old, clerk, teacher, plantation undetermined, salary undetermined; Robert N. Smith, of New York, 46 years old, superintendent at one of Dr. Jenkins' plantations, salary undetermined.

S. Philbrick, a prosperous engineer and architect who had left his home in Brookline, Massachusetts, to serve without remuneration in this social experiment, contributing himself $1,000 to the cause.[22] The superintendents generally had five or six plantations in charge, and, sometimes, with the assistance of a teacher, had as many as 500 Negroes to supervise. The superintendents found their laborers in need of clothes and implements, for the battle of Port Royal had occurred a few weeks before the customary time to issue winter clothes, and hoes were never given out until February. Moreover, the planting season had already advanced six weeks before the superintendents assumed charge of their respective plantations. In addition to these handicaps, they had to learn something about the methods of agriculture which they were supposed to oversee.

In every case the superintendent found it necessary to lean heavily upon the plantation driver for information and assistance and to follow the system of plantation management already established by the former owners. The driver was instructed to go about his accustomed work, stake off each hand's task as before, and manage the details of planting. The Negroes had already begun putting their own patches into corn, but they were reluctant to plant cotton, and it took much artful persuasion to induce them to do so. Thus, while the provision crop on St. Helena for 1862 was about the same as in ante-bellum times, the cotton crop fell far short. The cotton crops from both St. Helena and Ladies islands amounted to only $40,000.[23]

[22] *Letters from Port Royal*, p. 181.   [23] *Ibid.*, p. 109.

The new system of labor differed from the plantation management of the ante-bellum regime in two important particulars. The lash, under no circumstance, was to be used in obtaining discipline, and the laborers were to be paid for their work. The money, however, was slow to come, and the hands worked for six weeks or more on short rations and promises. On some islands, which had been entirely stripped of provisions by the Army, the Negroes received Government rations, but St. Helena Island was considered to have ample provisions to feed the laborers. "They are crying loudly & and with some reason, that we don't treat them so well as their old masters," wrote Philbrick to Pierce. 'They have no *salt* [,] no molasses, sugar or fresh meat. They see the soldiers kill their cattle & sit in idleness (as it seems to them) while their masters gave them a beef once a month & an allowance of the other luxuries. They consider tobacco a necessity, but can't get it at any price."[24]

They were unmindful of the fact that the Treasury Department was spending money to equip the plantations with seeds, implements, and mules, for in slavery days the planters had done this and fed them too. By the middle of May, the Department had forwarded Pierce $10,000 to pay for labor and had spent $15,000 for implements, seeds, and mules, having purchased and sent to Port Royal ninety mules and ten horses.[25] Early in May Pierce made the first payment to his laborers, $1 an acre

[24] Port Royal Correspondence, E. S. Philbrick to E. L. Pierce.
[25] *Official Records*, ser. III, vol. II, serial no. 123, p. 55. This was actually a very small amount for the purpose when it is considered that the Department was fostering the cultivation of some 13,795 acres. See Pierce, "Second Report," *Rebellion Record*, sup. I, 318.

for all cotton planted, distributed among them according to the amount done by each, a very small sum, they thought, for listing, planting, and hoeing. Pierce had planned to pay the Negroes for their work a little at a time, hoping to make them see that it was to their interest to tend the cotton after it was planted, but they were slow to grasp the significance of wages.[26]

Plantation work was further interrupted and the suspicion of the Negroes further aroused by an unexpected order from Major-General David Hunter, commanding the Department of the South, for the collection of all Negroes on the plantations between eighteen and forty-five able to bear arms, who were to be sent forthwith to the camp at Hilton Head. Pierce protested against the order as being contrary to the President's intentions and the instructions of the Treasury Department, and he was finally able to obtain the exemption of the drivers and a promise of the return of all those who were unwilling to bear arms. Nevertheless, he lost 600 laborers by this conscription and forfeited the confidence of many who were left behind.

The confusion resulting from the order disorganized the whole system, for it discouraged the superintendents and antagonized the Negroes. In most instances, the Negroes were taken from the fields without being permitted to go home for so much as a jacket, the soldiers, however, sometimes allowing wives and children to fetch a few necessary articles. On some plantations the wailing and screaming were loud and prolonged, and the women threw

---

[26] Pierce, "Second Report," p. 320; *Letters and Diary of Laura M. Towne,* p. 18.

themselves in despair upon the ground, while on other plantations where the news had leaked out, the men took to the woods and the marshes, and had to be hunted down by the soldiers.[27]

In June, 1862, the "experiment" was transferred from the Treasury to the War Department, and Brigadier-General Rufus Saxton placed in command with instructions to take possession of abandoned plantations and to make rules and regulations for the cultivation of the land.[28] Pierce was offered a place on his staff with the rank of colonel, but forseeing, no doubt, that the plan of the experiment was soon to be altered, he declined the appointment. General Saxton was, from the first, sympathetic with the Negro and honestly attempted to carry out the spirit of Pierce's plan, but he was constantly annoyed and prevented from doing so by those who were not.

General Saxton inherited the confusion which Pierce had found harmful to the successful cultivation of the plantations and which in his brief command he was unable to overcome. The superintendents at once besieged him with requests to make some change in the plan of management before another planting season, but he was slow to take up the matter. In the autumn Charles P. Ware, in despair, wrote to a friend, "We need people at headquarters who understand the details of plantation work. . . . There is a general want of concerted system on all the places. Each superintendent has to do as he thinks best in all cases himself. General plans are usually determined on just too late."[29] It was more imperative than

[27] *Official Records*, ser. III, vol. II, serial no. 123, pp. 52-60.
[28] *Ibid.*, pp. 27, 152, 153.
[29] *Letters from Port Royal*, p. 93.

ever that some scheme of management be hit upon which would make the plantations pay for themselves, for Congress showed no disposition to help the experiment along by an appropriation and the cotton fund, the amount realized from the sale of the crop of 1861, was getting low.[30]

Early in November General Saxton called a meeting of superintendents to consider plans for the coming year. Edward S. Philbrick, superintendent of Coffin's Point plantation, advocated an almost complete overthrow of the old plantation system. He would divide the plantations among the people, allotting the Negro families as much land as they could cultivate, paying them upon the basis of what they raised. This plan the government finally accepted for the crop of 1863. The plantations still under Government supervision were divided into plots and rented without charge to the plantation families, the land being apportioned at the rate of two acres for every working hand and five-sixteenths of an acre for every child. If they refused to raise cotton, they were compelled to pay a rent of not more than $2 a month. In addition, the Government supplied the implements and seeds and paid 25 cents for a day's work, usually the amount of work performed by task under the master.[31]

Saxton now divided the territory under his supervision into three areas and appointed a general superintendent over each. The local superintendents in charge of plantations were answerable to their respective general superintendents.[32]

---

[30] *Letters from Port Royal*, p. 115.

[31] Pierce, *Addresses and Papers*, p. 116. Pierce had approved of this plan in his "Second Report," p. 319.

[32] *Official Records*, ser. III, vol. IV, serial 125, pp. 1023, 1024.

In February, 1863, the Government began to sell the conquered territory at auction for the Federal direct tax levied by the Act of August 5, 1861. Some of the land was sold to private individuals and some was bid in by the United States for naval and military purposes and some for "school farms," the profits from which were to be applied to the education of the Negro, now declared free by Act of Congress, July 17, 1862,[33] and by virtue of the President's proclamation of January 1, 1863.

In 1864 all Government plantations were leased to white superintendents. After rejecting in 1862 the plan of the cotton agents to rent out the plantations, the Government had come two years later to accept it. But General Saxton, still the director of "freedmen's affairs," did not propose to stand by and see the Negro abused. In April, 1864, he issued a circular requiring all superintendents of plantations, whether of government or private ownership, to file a signed statement with their general superintendents setting forth the terms of the agreement existing between themselves and their laborers. The general superintendent was then ordered to visit the plantation, explain the contract to the Negroes, and affix to it the names of all who agreed to the terms. Any laborer who objected to them was warned to leave his employer or to stay at his own risk.[34]

In many instances, the general superintendents encouraged the teachers to lease the school farms and permitted them to do so free of rent, provided that they live on the plantation and teach the children of their "dis-

[33] *U. S. Statutes at Large*, XII, 591. Congress declared free all slaves of rebel masters on places occupied by the United States forces, or escaping thereto.
[34] *Letters from Port Royal*, p. 262n.

tricts." Arthur Sumner who had been the teacher for Chisolm's plantation on St. Helena Island since 1862 outlined in a letter to a friend some of the difficulties of planting under the system arising out of the sale of plantations:

> I think I have not told you that I have become a cotton-planter—or, as we style each other a speculator? I have been forced to this, most reluctantly, by the fact that this plantation has been made one of the School Farms. . . . If I did not lease the farm, it would be given to some one else, who might choose to remove me and employ some one else as the teacher of my school. And besides, the privileges which Government has hitherto allowed the teachers, and which are equivalent to a much larger sum of money than our salaries amount to, will probably be withdrawn before long so that I am obliged to make some money in order to support myself. I have therefore been obliged to borrow capital at the North, and before the crop is matured shall have to get a good deal more. The expenses are very large—including the purchase of mules, carts, grain, and before long, horses, furniture, cow harness, plows & so on. Carpentering, too, is to be no small item. And when the aforesaid privileges are disallowed, my expenses will reach a formidable figure. Add to this, that the young man who has undertaken to manage the farm for me, is to have one third of the profits, and there will remain to me after the sale of the crop no more than $1200 or $1500 net profit, with which to begin the ensuing year.[35]

The Government thus gave up the paternalistic idea of government-operated plantations and was content until the passage of the Freedman's Bureau Act[36] in 1865, to exercise only a general supervision over the Negro, permitting someone else, into whose qualifications it did not

---

[35] MS in Sumner Papers. St. Helena Island, March 1, 1864.
[36] *U. S. Statutes at Large*, XIII, 507-509.

inquire too closely, to cultivate the plantations, employ the Negroes, and teach them the ways of civilization. For one thing, this system was far more economical than that pursued in 1862 and 1863. The social experiment which had been started so enthusiastically had been an expensive enterprise,[37] and the Government, now more interested in winning the war than in "civilizing" ten thousand coastal Negroes, turned the responsibility over to someone else. Saxton's powers were now very much limited, but he still retained supervision of "regulations for the sanitary condition and police of the department and for the protection of the freedmen in their industry and its products." With the Port Royal experiment the Government began the policy of protection which later it was to apply to the Negro throughout the South during the period of Reconstruction.

TRAINING FOR CITIZENSHIP

The men and women led by Edward L. Pierce who reached Beaufort March 9, 1862, took seriously their charge to train the "contrabands" for citizenship. A few failed in this arduous undertaking because of their incapacity to govern men, but none failed from lack of purpose or unwillingness to endure hardships. Some even died at their posts, victims of smallpox and of the fevers from which the former masters had annually fled to the health-resort towns.

[37] *Letters from Port Royal*, p. 118n. "Taking the plantations as a whole, the Government lost in 1862 the whole $200,000 which it had cleared from the planter's big cotton crop of 1861." But see also *House Ex. Doc. no. 72*, 37th Cong. 3d Sess. in which Secretary Chase outlined on Feb. 18, 1863, the expenses of the Port Royal experiment. The receipts were $726,984.10 and the expenditures $225,705.34, giving a balance on hand of $501,278.76. The majority of the receipts arose from the sale of the confiscated cotton.

A superintendent's work kept him busy early and late. It was the duty of each to visit as often as possible all the plantations under him, some of which were as far as four miles from his quarters, equip them with implements from the Government storehouses, protect the cattle and other property upon them, urge the laborers to work the Government land as well as their own private patches, explain to them their own new condition and the purposes of the Government toward them, procure and distribute clothing and food whenever the army issued rations or the benevolent associations sent supplies,[38] draw pay rolls for labor on cotton, pay the amounts and settle the disputes which inevitably arose on such occasions. In addition to these duties which were essential to the cultivation of the land the superintendent was expected to attend the praise meetings whenever convenient, read the Bible to the people, instruct on Sundays and other days those wishing to learn to read, protect the laborers from injuries, settle disputes which arose among them, and endeavor "to elevate them, and prepare them to become worthy and self-supporting citizens."[39]

One of the most serious problems which the superintendents had to face was the discipline of their laborers. They were not permitted under any circumstance to whip insubordinate Negroes; they did not like to withhold rations; they had no place to imprison offenders except in the storehouses or in the closets of their own apartments. As a result, a wilful laborer had the upper hand of his

---

[38] *House Ex. Doc. no. 142*, 41st Cong., 2d sess. Pierce and his helpers distributed the first year of the experiment 91,834 garments, 35,829 books and pamphlets, 5,895 yards of cloth, and $3,000 of farming implements and seeds.

[39] Pierce, "Second Report," p. 317.

employer and he knew it. General Saxton attempted to meet this situation by the establishment in July, 1863, of plantation commissions, or courts for the administration of justice, composed of Government superintendents and certain superintendents of privately owned plantations. The commissions were allowed to make arrests whenever in their opinion it was necessary, but they were held liable for abuse of power. Having made an arrest, the commission proceeded to hear the trial.[40] Miss Harriet Ware, a teacher on St. Helena Island, after attending a meeting of court in 1864, thought it a very interesting but very sad experience. "Men and boys took the oath one after the other and then lied as if they had sworn to do so," she wrote. "Their ingenuity was wonderful, and we had to come to the conclusion that if those who we supposed spoke the truth had been on the other side they would have lied as badly as the others."[41]

Later in 1863 General Saxton obtained still further relief for the harassed superintendents. In the autumn the Government built a large number of houses near St. Helenaville for refugees brought to St. Helena from other places. These surplus houses permitted the superintendents to dispose of the turbulent and unruly on their plantations "without the scandal and excitement" which otherwise would have accompanied their removal.[42]

While the superintendents were busy with the crops, the women missionaries were visiting the cabins attempting to teach the mothers simple rules of health, cleanliness, and order. The presence of the women seemed to allay

[40] *Letters from Port Royal*, p. 201n.
[41] *Ibid.*, pp. 269, 270.
[42] *Ibid.*, p. 223.

the fears of the plantation people, making them "satisfy" with the new order. Miss Towne soon found the women appearing at her back door, shyly offering baskets of eggs in appreciation for the services she had rendered them.

Most of the Negroes Miss Towne thought to be "decidedly unhealthy" with bad teeth and general debility.[43] Their bedding and sleeping apartments were "unsuitable," and they often slept on the floor at night without a change of clothing. They did not take proper care of themselves after exposure to the weather and made little effort to prevent disease. Their medical knowledge was a combination of folk-wisdom, superstition, and facts gleaned from ante-bellum days. They insisted on bathing a patient when the tide was going out so that it might take the fever with it. In 1864 Miss Towne complained, "They keep their rooms so dark I cannot see the patients, and if I order a window opened, I find it nailed up the next time I come. The people are beginning to follow a practice which I dislike. They *will* wash the patients with strong pokeroot, and vinegar and salt."[44]

To the superintendents the family life of the people was one of the most distressing phases of the Negro community. Among the first orders which Pierce issued was one requiring that all marriages among the people be regularly performed by a minister according to law, and he strictly forbade a couple's living together until the ceremony had been pronounced. Charles Ware, assistant superintendent on Coffin's Point plantation, had to deal with several cases arising under this order. In 1862 he wrote to a friend at the North:

[43] *Letters and Diary of Laura M. Towne*, p. 22.   [44] *Ibid.*, p. 122.

I learned that old Nat's boy, Antony, who wanted to marry Phillis, had given her up and taken Mary Ann, July's daughter, without saying a word to me or any other white man. I called him up to me one afternoon when I was there and told him he must go to church and be married by the minister according to law. He flatly refused, with a good deal of impertinence, using some profane language learned at camp. I thereupon told him he must go home with me, showing him I had a pistol, which I put in my outside pocket. He came along, swearing all the way and muttering his determination not to comply. I gave him lodging in the dark hole under the stairs, with nothing to eat. Next morning old Nat came and expostulated with him, joined by old Ben and Uncle Sam, all of whom pitched into him and told him he was very foolish and ought to be proud of such a chance. He finally gave up and promised to go. So I let him off with an apology. Next Sunday he appeared and was married before a whole church full of people.[45]

But the missionaries found to their sorrow that the Negroes did not always have the proper respect for "a marriage according to law." Limus, a driver, had a wife and grown children on his own plantation and another wife on a plantation nearby. Nevertheless, the missionaries tried to settle such cases with a due regard for the parties concerned and attempted to build up among the people a feeling of family loyalty and pride. They urged the Negroes to buy a table whenever possible and to have regular times for the family meal when all should assemble for the occasion.

Pierce at once opened the two white churches on St. Helena Island which had been closed since "gun shoot." Among the superintendents there were several divinity students and ministers who preached to the Negroes on

---

[45] *Letters from Port Royal,* p. 95.

Sundays and helped conduct their praise meetings and funerals, but the Negroes were jealous of their praise meetings and did not want any of the whites to attend communion except those who were Baptists. The superintendents organized Sabbath schools so that those who did not attend the regular schools might have an opportunity of learning to read the Bible. It was not uncommon for as many as three hundred to gather at Brick Church on Sunday mornings for instruction.

The "contrabands" took readily to the schools which Pierce established. He attempted to place one teacher on every plantation who should conduct classes several hours a day in the praise house, but there was a great scarcity of teachers, so that on some plantations the people received only such instruction as the superintendents had time to give. Nevertheless, the schools were perhaps the best agents for obtaining the good will of the people. The books and slates which the benevolent societies supplied seemed a proof to them of the Yankees' interest in their welfare. By June, 1863, there were twelve schools in the department attended by 2,500 persons, some of whom were adults who received instruction after their work was done. By the next year there were thirty schools conducted by forty or forty-five teachers, with an average attendance of 2,000 pupils.[46]

The thought of the black folk within the Federal lines at Port Royal eagerly grasping for the crumbs of knowledge so long denied them inspired Whittier to write the following song for the schools of St. Helena Island:

---

[46] Pierce, *Addresses and Papers*, pp. 107, 108.

> "The very oaks are greener clad,
> The waters brighter smile;
> Oh, never shone a day so glad
> On sweet Saint Helen's Isle!
>
> "For none in all the world before
> Were ever glad as we,
> We're free on Carolina's shore,
> We're all at home and free!"[47]

Among the first group of teachers to reach Port Royal was Miss Laura M. Towne of Philadelphia. Instead of beginning at once to teach, she acted as secretary to Pierce and greatly assisted him in his work. She was soon joined by her friend, Miss Ellen Murray, who at once began a school at The Oaks, where she and Miss Towne were stationed. Later in the year Miss Towne assisted her in the work. In August, 1862, she wrote, "We snatch a lunch and begin school. I have the middle class, Ellen the oldest and youngest. At four, school is out for the children. Ellen then takes the adults while I go doctoring down to the 'nigger houses.'"[48] Later Miss Towne obtained permission to hold her school in Brick Church and still later the Philadelphia Society, by whom she was employed, sent her a schoolhouse ready to be erected. This was the genesis of the school which Miss Towne and her associates in Pennsylvania came finally to call Penn School. Year after year she and Miss Murray labored against great odds to maintain the school, teaching without salary when the funds of the benevolent societies ran low, meeting many of the expenses with personal funds.

[47] *Atlantic Monthly*, XII (September, 1863), 304.
[48] *Letters and Diary*, p. 87.

When the Government abandoned Pierce's plan of training the Negro for citizenship with the sale of plantations in 1863, it did not give up the idea of teaching them to read and write. Some plantations and parts of others were set aside as school farms, the profits of which were to be applied to the education of the people. Later when Congress ordered the sale of the school farms in 1866, it provided that the money arising from the sale should be invested in United States bonds and be appropriated to "the support of schools, without distinction of color or race, on the islands in the parishes of Saint Helena and Saint Luke."[49]

Pierce, in his "Second Report to the Secretary of the Treasury," declared that the movement which he had inaugurated had exceeded his "most sanguine expectations." "Industrial results have been reached, which put at rest the often reiterated assumption that this territory and its products can only be cultivated by slaves. A social problem which has vexed the wisest approaches a solution."[50] The superintendents, however, were by no means willing to concede as much. Philbrick wrote in 1862, "I don't believe much can be made out of this generation by free labor, nor out of the next without teaching them to read."[51] In 1863 W. C. Gannett thought their state of morals "decidedly better than it was under slavery—less of licentiousness, lying, and stealing,—and more general manliness and self-respect." "But," he added, "they are very far behind, in character as well as intelligence, and I

---

[49] *U. S. Statutes at Large*, XIV, chap. CC, sec. 8.
[50] "Second Report," *Rebellion Record*, sup., I, 323.
[51] *Letters from Port Royal*, p. 110.

suspect that most abolitionist views of their character are exaggerated in their favor."[52]

THE LAND SALES

Congress by Act of August 5, 1861, levied an annual tax of $20,000,000 on all the states and territories for the purpose of conducting the war, of which South Carolina's quota was $363,570.66.[53] To collect the tax in the eleven insurrectionary states, Congress passed an act, June 7, 1862, calling for the appointment of direct tax commissioners. Collections were made in all the southern states during the war and after its close either by voluntary payment or by sale of land. Commissioners sold land for the non-payment of taxes in Virginia, Florida, Arkansas, Tennessee, and South Carolina, but in every state except that of South Carolina the lands were bid in at the tax sales by the commissioners for the United States. The presence of the northern missionaries in the region of the tax sales altered the situation in South Carolina.

The commissioners for South Carolina, W. E. Wording, W. Henry Brisbane, and A. D. Smith, having been appointed, ordered the first sale of land to take place at Beaufort, February 11, 1863. The land to be sold was that in St. Helena's and St. Luke's parishes in Beaufort District, the area occupied by the Federal Army, and included the whole town of Beaufort. Many friends of the Negro both at Port Royal and at the North objected to a sale under the Act of June 7, for they wanted some special

---
[52] *Ibid.*, p. 241.
[53] By Act of Congress approved July 1, 1862, the operations of the Act of August 5, 1861, were suspended until April 1, 1865, except for the collection of the first annual tax, and by Act of June 30, 1864, it was further suspended until additional legislation.

provision whereby land might be reserved for the ownership of the Negroes. A. D. Smith, chairman of the commission, was himself eager for some such provision to be made. In his preliminary report to Secretary Chase of January 1, 1863, he wrote meaningfully:

The great object to be attained is the proper, permanent, and efficient organization of a system or systems of labor for the freed people. . . . The essential prerequisite . . . to this end is to obtain such a control of and title to the soil as will enable it to give a fixed and permanent character to whatever measures may be inaugurated for the organization of their industrial and social energies. All this, by the operation of the act of June 7, 1862, is placed within the grasp of the government. There can be no doubt that the government will be reimbursed many fold, even in a pecuniary point of view, for any appropriation it shall make, or outlay incur, in inaugurating this system.[54]

Miss Towne claims responsibility for the idea which made possible the establishment of such a scheme. "General Saxton is much opposed to the sale of the land to speculators," wrote Miss Towne, February 1, after a visit from him. "He thinks they ought to be preempted by the people, or else so divided and sold that the people can buy, and not be left a prey to greedy speculators and large landholders." Miss Towne suggested that General Hunter stop the February sale as a military necessity, and "General Saxton caught at the idea."[55] General Hunter immediately issued the order against the sale, and the commissioners, after striking off one lot in Beaufort, adjourned until further notice.

[54] *Senate Ex. Doc. no. 26*, 37th Cong., 3d sess.
[55] *Letters and Diary*, pp. 100, 101.

The commissioners took the matter to the War Department, and the order came back to proceed with the sales, leaving, however, Hunter, Saxton, and the commissioners to make restrictions as they saw fit. Accordingly, on March 9 plantations and lots in Beaufort were put up for sale and struck off, some to the United States and others to "speculators," for the most part, superintendents and teachers, at about $1 an acre.[56] About two-thirds of the land was bid in by the United States and the other third bought by fourteen "loyal citizens."

Eleven of the plantations sold to private citizens were bought by Philbrick. Like Pierce, Edward L. Philbrick thought that the social experiment of training slaves for future citizenship had not been given a fair trial. When he learned that the conquered territory was to be sold for taxes, he conceived the idea of carrying on the experiment privately. In setting forth his plan to friends at the North he explained, "I . . . don't undertake it for the sake of making money at all, but for the sake of carrying out to a more satisfactory issue the present short-lived and unfairly judged experiment of free labor, and for the sake of keeping the people out of the hands of bad men."[57] Accordingly, he interested fourteen men, all but

[56] MS, South Carolina Maps, 1866. In Archives of U. S. Treasury Department. The average price paid per acre for all the lands reserved by the United States was 34 cents. See speech of William Elliott in House of Representatives, Dec. 11, 1888, *Congressional Record*, XX, pt. III, Appendix, pp. 239-242.

[57] *Letters from Port Royal*, p. 135. See also pp. 140, 141. The agreement made on April 8, 1863, between Philbrick and his backers provided that the land be bought in his name and that he have complete responsibility for managing the estates. Philbrick, after paying the subscribers 6 per cent interest, should receive one-fourth the net profits, but he was to be liable for losses and did not have the right to call for further contributions. He was protected by the provision that no subscription could be withdrawn unless he ceased to superintend the enterprise. On closing the experiment, the net proceeds were to be divided *pro rata*.

one of Boston, in the project, and on March 9 bought 6,795 acres, valued by the commissioners at $24,120, for about $7,000, eleven plantations including Coffin's Point, Fripp's Point, Cherry Hill, Pine Grove, John Fripp's Big House, Mulberry Hill, Corner Farm, two plantations on Ladies Island, and Morgan Island.[58] For the most part he employed to help him in the experiment the superintendents and teachers who were already on the plantations. After conducting the enterprise for two years with many vexations and losses, he began to sell the land in 1865, some plantations to white men from the North, others in small tracts to Negroes. He got from $5 to $10 an acre for land for which he had paid a little more than a dollar.[59]

The land bid in for the United States had been bought with the idea of providing for military and naval purposes and with the hope eventually of placing land within the reach of the Negro. The President's instructions to the tax commissioners of September 16, 1863, outlined a plan whereby this hope might be realized. After listing the land to be reserved for military and naval purposes, providing for land to be sold to men serving in the army, navy, or marine corps, and setting apart thirty-six school farms of 160 acres each, he directed that all parts of certain tracts not otherwise appropriated be surveyed into twenty-acre plots and sold to "heads of families of the African race, only one to each, preferring such as by their good conduct, meritorious services, or exemplary character, will be examples of moral propriety and industry to

[58] MS, South Carolina Maps, 1866. But see *Letters from Port Royal*, p. 172.
[59] *Letters from Port Royal*, pp. 277, 296, 315, 324, 326.

those of the same race, for the charitable purpose of providing homes for such heads of families."[60] The land thus reserved was to be sold to Negroes at not less than $1.25 an acre. All other land the President authorized to be sold in parcels of not more than 320 acres at public auction.

On December 10, 1863, the sales to heads of families began and were continued at irregular intervals until 1870 when the board was dissolved. In 1863 General Saxton issued a circular to the freedmen of South Carolina, authorizing them to locate on the land set aside for them. They were then directed to deposit with the commissioners on days announced for this purpose the full purchase price of the land together with a description of it and the date of preemption.[61] Buildings on any of these tracts were to be sold at one-third the appraised value. By June, 1865, there had been 347 purchases made on St. Helena Island. Of this number, 243 bought ten acres, 166 paying $1.50 an acre and 72 paying $1.25, the other five paying from $2 to $6.50 an acre. The highest price paid for any tract was $350 for twenty acres. In only two instances did purchasers buy land as low as $1 an acre.[62]

[60] "Instructions Issued By President Lincoln . . . to the United States Direct Tax Commissioners for South Carolina," *Compilation of Direct Tax Laws*, pp. 61-66; *House Ex. Doc. no. 146*, 40th Cong., 2d sess. Parts of the following plantations on St. Helena Island were set aside: The Oaks, Oakland, Indian Hill, Eddings' Point, Tom Fripp's plantation, Cedar Grove, Hamilton Fripp's plantation, the McTureous lands, Hope plantation, Woodstock, Frogmore, Frank Pritchard's plantation, Jane Pritchard's plantation, Scott plantation, Oliver Fripp's plantation, Wallace plantation, and the Fendon tract.

[61] The right of preemption was later abandoned. See Saxton's report to Stanton, *Official Records*, ser. III, vol. IV, serial no. 125, pp. 1022-1031.

[62] See MSS, Heads of Families Certificate Books. In Archives of U. S. Treasury Department.

General Sherman, after having finally reached the sea in his famous march thereto, as a result of a conference with Secretary Stanton, issued Special Field Order No. 15 on January 16, 1865, setting aside "the islands from Charleston, south, the abandoned rice fields along the rivers for thirty miles back from the sea, and the country bordering the St. John's River, Florida," for the freedmen, and especially reserved the islands for "the sole and exclusive management" of the Negroes.[63] The order, however, specifically exempted from its operation those whites who had bought land at the tax sales. Saxton, who was authorized to put the terms of the order in operation, at once began to settle Negroes on the land. No Negro, however, acquired the title to the land by virtue of General Sherman's order. Later, Congress, for the relief of those who had been settled on abandoned plantations, ordered, in an amendment to the Freedman's Bureau Act of July 16, 1866, a sale of most of the public land at $1.50 an acre to "such persons and to such only as have acquired and are now occupying lands under and agreeably to the provisions of General Sherman's special field order." This same act called for a sale of the school farms in St. Helena's Parish at $10 an acre.[64]

Before the Government had sold all the land which it had taken over in 1863 for the non-payment of taxes, the possession of it had become an irksome problem, grievous alike to the Government and to the people who were trying to rehabilitate the region after the War. Money was scarce and the buyers few. It was not until 1876 that the Government finally disposed of all the land.

[63] *House Ex. Doc. no. 11*, 39th Cong., 1st sess.
[64] *U. S. Statutes at Large*, XIV, chap. CC, secs. 6-12.

The injustice of the tax sales[65] finally became apparent. The entire property-owning population of two parishes, except for a few free colored citizens in Beaufort and one loyal citizen on Ladies Island, had been deprived of their homes and all they possessed[66] to meet the tax apportioned to the entire state. In cases where the Government was still in possession of the property, former owners were permitted under the redemption act of 1872 to reclaim their lands upon the payment of the tax, costs, interest, and penalties, and under this provision a few plantations on St. Helena Island were redeemed. Through the ceaseless efforts of Congressman William Elliott, of Beaufort, Congress at last in 1891 passed an act providing a meager compensation of $1 an acre for woodland and $5 an acre for cultivated land, after the United States Supreme Court had declared the Direct Tax Act unconstitutional. The Government also refunded the amount of tax collected from each landholder. Sea-island planters, once the inhabitants of one of the wealthiest areas in the South, were now scattered throughout the United States, and the region which had been their homes for more than a century was left in the possession of their former slaves and the men and women from the North who had helped in the experiment of converting chattel into citizens.

[65] The history of the tax sales might well be a volume in itself, and can only be briefly summarized for the purposes of this study. For excellent summaries see *Compilation of Direct Tax Laws; House Ex. Doc. no. 11*, 39th Cong., 1st sess.; Speech of William Elliott in the House of Representatives, Dec. 11, 1888, *Congressional Record*, XX, pt. III, Appendix, pp. 239-242; and see *U. S. Statutes at Large*, XIV, ch. CC, secs. 6-12; DeTrevelle v. Smalls, 98 U. S., 513; Court of Claims Reports (1891-1892), XXVII, p. 27.

[66] MS, Record of Sale of Household and Plantation Equipment in South Carolina. In Archives of U. S. Treasury Department. The personal property on the plantations was sold at auction in 1864.

THE NEGRO AS A LANDOWNER

The opportunity to buy land of their own created the first real excitement among the Negroes which had occurred since "gun shoot." They were all astir trying to stake out claims and then trying to get their claims considered by the commissioners. They had the money which they had earned as plantation hands for the Government and as laborers at the camps with which to meet the purchase price. Besides, many of them had sold fish, chickens, and garden truck to the superintendents and the soldiers. W. C. Gannett estimated in 1863 that a driver on one of the St. Helena plantations had made four or five hundred dollars since the Federal occupation. "He is all ready to buy land," he wrote, "and I expect to see him in ten years a tolerably rich man."[67] Many Negroes who did not have sufficient funds to buy tracts of the size they desired organized clubs and bought land in this way.[68]

Whenever it was possible the Negroes chose to purchase land on the plantations where they had been born. In staking out their claims they invariably moved their cabin in the "street" to the new plots of land, and started life as landholding citizens on the very ground which they had cultivated as slaves. Thus the transition from slavery to freedom scarcely interrupted the daily routine. Now they had freedom of movement, but with it had come the responsibility of earning their own living, and the only method open to most of them was the cultivation of their little tracts after the manner learned in slavery.

[67] *Letters from Port Royal*, p. 37n.
[68] *Beaufort Republican*, May 30, 1872.

CHAPTER IX

THE AFTERMATH

A ST. HELENA PICTURE IN 1865

IT WAS SUNDAY in May, 1865. The sandy road, covered in the low places with a top dressing of oyster shells, led off among the cotton fields down the Island. On either side were sagging wire fences, reminders of plantation boundaries before the war, the wire sometimes propped by drooping posts, at other times deeply embedded in the trunks of fine trees forming magnificent avenues.

Here and there were small frame houses, with narrow porches and four or five rooms, the residences of former overseers. Rude pine-log cabins, newly built, and clap-boarded shanties leaning crazily in the mid-day sun dotted the fields. Gardens of growing vegetables separated the cabins from the rows of cotton that extended away as far as one could see. Little stakes occasionally marked off private holdings, sometimes the only boundaries in fields of a hundred or more acres of cotton. Just beyond was a large tract lying fallow, covered with a luxurious growth of cassina and dewberries, or perhaps a young forest of pines had sprung up among cotton furrows which, though idle for many years, were yet plainly visible.

The cotton was small, for it was not more than four weeks out of the ground, but the corn was knee high. Neat ridges were already piled up about the cabins waiting until the young sweet potato slips were large enough for transplanting. Here the fields were beautifully clean, carefully hilled up with the hoe by the women and old men, for the young men were still away in the army or at work in the camps for "cash money." Across the road the cotton was scarcely up, struggling bravely against wild phlox and grass, a picturesque battle bearing witness that the owner would beg for Government rations in the winter and perhaps stand by and see his land sold for taxes a few years later.

The freedmen, some of them now making their second crop on their own little "plantations," were on their way to "Brick Church" to hear "old Massa Richard,"[1] who had preached to them before "big gun shoot," speak in the open under the moss-hung live oaks. They crowded the road, a gaily-dressed throng of black folk, some on foot, some on horseback, some in wagons, others in the rude ox cart of plantation days, some even in northern trotting buggies drawn by Government-condemned horses which the proud owners had bought for perhaps as much as $300 cash. They were a colorful sight in their gaudy calicoes and crinolines. The younger women wore straw bonnets, stays, and cotton gloves, but the grannies clung to their many-colored handkerchiefs and their loose gowns cut after the fashion of slavery days.

Their loud laughter and gay chatter rang out as they passed through the gates which in plantation days had made a private road to the church. As a buggy containing a group of white teachers and superintendents approached, those on foot stopped and drew aside, out of respect, to let the vehicle pass. The old women gave the white party a droll bob of the head, the young ones made

---

[1] The Reverend Richard Fuller, former pastor of "Brick Church" and owner of a plantation on St. Helena Island.

curtseys, and the men touched their hats in a soldier's salute, or swept them quickly from their heads.

The Reverend Richard Fuller created a sensation when he arrived. Stares brightened and eyes grew moist. Amid shouts of "Bress de Lo'd, Bres de Lo'd!" "Hebenly Massa!" "Gra-a-ate King!" he mounted to the platform. When all were seated a quaint old man, clad in cotton checks, bowed from many years of cotton hoeing, stepped out on the platform and, leaning on his cane, gently swaying his body as if to keep time, struck up in a shrill, cracked voice the tune:

> "Ma-a-assa Fullah a sittin' on de tree ob life
> For to yeddy when Jordan roll,
> Roll, Jordan; roll, Jordan,
> Roll, Jordan, roll."

And then a plain, middle-aged black preacher came forward and commenced a prayer, which he pursued at great length with frequent interruptions from the congregation of "Amen," "Glory," and "Lo'd, do!" They had already been to their praise-house meetings twice during the week and some of them earlier that morning, but they were none the less eager for this Sunday-noon meeting when fellow freedmen from all over the Island gathered for worship and recreation.[2]

A few former planters, like the Reverend Richard Fuller, had returned to Beaufort to try to take up life again in the little town now overrun with freedmen, Fed-

---

[2] The foregoing description is based on Reid, *After the War: A Southern Tour;* "The South As It Is," *Nation,* Dec. 1865, pp. 746-747; J. W. Alvord, *Letters from the South,* pp. 8-10; Charles Nordoff, *The Freedmen of South Carolina;* S. G. W. Benjamin, "The Sea Islands," *Harper's Monthly,* LVII, 839-861.

eral officials, and northern speculators who hoped to make of Beaufort, or if not of Beaufort, of Hilton Head or Bay Point, a great seaport second only to New York. A few planters were able to redeem their land and begin planting under contracts with their former slaves made on terms approved by General Saxton, now assistant commissioner of the Freedman's Bureau.[3] Dr. Clarence Fripp, for instance, began to practice medicine on St. Helena Island shortly after the close of the war and by November, 1865, had obtained a surgeon's contract from General Saxton and was living at St. Helenaville next door to his former residence which was then occupied by Miss Towne.[4] Not more than three or four planters were able to redeem land on St. Helena. The heirs of Captain John Fripp redeemed a part of Corner Farm; Mrs. Eliza H. Chaplin, five acres of her Indian Hill plantation which originally contained 400 acres; and Edgar W. Fripp, 732 acres of

[3] Saxton was succeeded January 15, 1866, by General Robert K. Scott of Ohio. See Webster, "The Operation of the Freedmen's Bureau in South Carolina," *Smith College Studies*, I, 86-91.

[4] Dennett, special correspondent for the *Nation*, in the issue of Nov. 30, 1865, gives a picture of Clarence Fripp on his return to St. Helena. Among the northern soldiers and traders in the hotel at Hilton Head, Dennett discovered a "person who had the easily distinguishable appearance and manners of a South Carolinian." This gentleman, a person of some fifty years old, dressed tolerably well in a suit of grey clothes, with a large display of crumpled linen at the collar and cuffs of his coat, sat before the stove, smoking and talking very freely about his present poverty and his plans for the future. After saying that he had left St. Helena when DuPont captured Port Royal, leaving his plate and furniture behind, he told about the sale of his plantation for federal taxes. "Some Massachusetts man had bought it, and he didn't know when he would get it back. . . . Up in Greenville he soon spent all his money to support his family, but if he'd had money he couldn't have saved his property. How was he to come back inside the Yankee lines and pay the tax? The Commissioners knew very well it couldn't be done; the sale was a very unfair thing." By returning to Beaufort now, "he hoped to be able to pick up a little medical practice; but if his profession failed him, he supposed his son and himself could put up a cabin somewhere in the vicinity, and get fish and oysters enough to live on."

an estate which had numbered 1,284 acres.[5] All but Edgar W. Fripp after a few years sold their land in small plots to Negroes. Fripp, a minor at the time of the war, retained his holding until recently when he sold it for a hunting preserve.

The prosperity in which the freedmen of Port Royal found themselves in 1865 was largely delusive, for it was the prosperity of war times. The presence of the soldiers afforded a ready market for whatever the Negroes had to sell; the presence of the camps offered ready work at high wages for those who wanted it; the fostering care of the Freedman's Bureau kept them from starvation in time of necessity. The magnificent bounty of $300 which "Government" offered all volunteers led many a St. Helena youth to enter the army. The bounty money he used to buy ten acres of land and the equipment for his "plantation," keeping out $100, perhaps, to "pleasure" himself. Whenever it was possible to peddle chickens, fish, and garden truck to the soldiers, the freedmen never raised cotton, for they got high prices for their wares.

All who had bought land by the close of the war, had for the most part erected their own cabins and equipped them with a few pieces of cheap furniture, beds, tables, and chairs. They now must have plates and knives and forks. They must have both a work suit and a "Sunday best," and the cloth must be of the finest. They must have carts, buggies, and horses. Indeed, their purchases at the trade stores were so liberal that the military authorities several times interfered to prevent what they consid-

---

[5] Direct Tax Case, No. 17, 498 filed in Court of Claims March 25, 1892; No. 17, 366 filed Feb. 6, 1892.

ered extravagance. They lived better, clothed themselves better, and worked fewer hours than in slavery days, but they had not yet crystallized themselves into industrious and orderly communities.

WAS FREEDOM TOO EASY?

In 1865 Philbrick had not yet sold all of his eleven plantations. Besides his holdings, there were several other plantations on St. Helena owned and operated by men from the North. The Government, too, was still leasing the school farms to white overseers. Most of these men, employers of Negro labor, superintendents and teachers who had witnessed the transition from slavery to freedom, were of the opinion that freedom had been made too easy for the Negro.

Charles P. Ware, who had been an assistant superintendent under Philbrick for the Government and later remained on St. Helena to help Philbrick carry through his scheme of training the Negro for citizenship with private funds, wrote in despair at the beginning of the harvest season, the first year of emancipation, "The untrustworthiness of these people is more apparent and troublesome than ever. I feel as if it would not be safe to allow them to gin the cotton—it seems certain that a great deal of it would be stolen." He then set down the characteristics of the Negroes which made it so difficult to deal with them as laborers: "Their skill in lying, their great reticence, their habit of shielding one another (generally by silence), their invariable habit of taking a rod when you, after much persuasion, have been induced to grant an inch, their assumed innocence and ignorance of the simplest rules of *meum* and *tuum,* joined with amazing impudence in making claims,—these are the traits which try us continually in our dealings with them, and sometimes almost make us despair of their improvement—at least, in the present generation. It is certain that their freedom has been too easy for them,—they have not had a hard enough time of it. In many cases they have been 'fair spoiled.' "[6]

Arthur Sumner, who had come to St. Helena in 1862 as a teacher, seriously questioned the wisdom of the Government's policy toward the Negro in the early days of the Federal occupation of Port Royal and came finally in 1865 to believe that the Negroes' friends at the North had done the freedmen a grave injustice by protecting them against "natural economic laws." He wrote from St. Helena in February, 1865:

I am exasperated (and so is every other white man in this place) at the mischievous indulgence shown to the negro. It is a common remark here, that "a white man can get no justice." This inhumane leniency is doing a great deal of harm, in many ways. It is teaching them to despise the laws, and to believe that Liberty means License. It is creating in the minds of the white people a very bitter feeling against the blacks, which, of course, is mutual. If Justice had been shown to both parties, from the beginning there would, I believe, have been far less antagonism. There will always be, however, until the blacks are as intelligent and well-educated as the whites, a contempt felt by the latter, and dislike and distrust by the former. It is so here and must be so everywhere. The negro has always been oppressed by the white man, and knows that even now he has it in his power, from his superior intelligence and acquirements, to cheat him. Even the best of the young men sent down here by benevolent societies at the North, have failed to gain their confidence. . . . The Black has got a long struggle before

[6] *Letters from Port Royal,* p. 287.

him, ere he will gain all his rights; but I would rather, for his own sake, see him oppressed for generations, than be spoiled and petted as he has been here. He would come out of the struggle more manly and self-reliant.[7]

Philbrick had been opposed from the first to giving the Negroes anything except in payment for services actually performed. He observed in the autumn of 1862 that they were more economical of food than they had been in the spring when they thought that the Government would ration them as their masters had done. Philbrick would have followed the same rule in regard to tools, paying them wages enough to enable each person to buy his own hoe and spade. The superintendents were likewise opposed to the Government policy of selling land to the Negroes at a special price. After the sales had been effected and the Negroes had been in possession of their holdings for more than a year, Philbrick was of the opinion that "no race of men on God's earth ever acquired the right to the soil" with so little effort as the Negroes on St. Helena. He thought that they would have been better off had they paid the market value of the land, "because they would use the land for which they had paid full price more economically, would be likely to get more out of it, and would be taught a feeling of independence more readily than by being made the recipients of charity."[8]

Philbrick himself had acquired his land at a lower price than the Negroes had paid, but he overlooked this fact in evaluating the Government's policy toward the Negro because he was honestly attempting to put into

[7] MS in Arthur Sumner Papers. Feb., 1865.
[8] *Letters from Port Royal*, pp. 276, 277.

operation a system whereby he might train the Negro to ways of thrift and independence. Nor did the Government ever give the Negroes tools and farm equipment except as laborers on the government-operated plantations. When the Negro became a landowner he equipped his own farm from supplies at the trade stores for which he paid prices two or three times greater than those in the New York market;[9] or he bought equipment at the auction sales of confiscated property, paying the highest prices and often bidding against white men.

Nevertheless, it was a fact that the character of the Negro as a hired laborer had been injured by the inflated prices which the soldiers paid them for their wares and by the injudicious policy of their well-meaning friends of the North. White planters, for instance, were jealously watched by officials of the Freedmen's Bureau who were over-anxious lest the freedmen be victimized. Officials of the Freedmen's Bureau laid down the terms of the contract between planter and employee,[10] giving the employer practically no control over his laborers.

Under the system of labor thus established the Negro worked for his employer less than three months in the year.[11] He seldom worked more than five hours a day and half of that time he spent on his own crop of corn, potatoes, and peanuts so that the planter had the use of his services about one-fourth of each working day. In addition, the planter supplied each family of laborers with

[9] Reid, *After the War*, p. 114.
[10] See Webster, "The Operations of the Freedmen's Bureau in South Carolina," *Smith College Studies*, I, 93-104, 113-118.
[11] See "The South As It Is," *Nation*, Dec., 1865, p. 747. Dennett interviewed most of the planters on St. Helena. See also *Sen. Ex. Doc. no. 6*, 39th Cong., 2d sess., p. 123.

a house and fuel and all the land for their own use that they chose to cultivate, usually three or four acres. Upon the corn land, however, they paid a rent of a bushel to the acre and usually supplied all the sweet potatoes needed by the white family. But the planter also paid his laborers a money wage of about $15 an acre for listing, planting, and hoeing the cotton crop and 2½ cents a pound for picking it. The withdrawal of the army and a succession of crop failures were going, however, in a few years to change the situation.

THE STARVING TIME

The only good crop of sea-island cotton grown during the Federal occupation was that of 1863. After the war, sea-island cotton planters faced a series of failures and the freedmen began to feel the pinch of hard times. "The negroes' crops did not turn out very well, as a general rule," wrote Charles Ware from St. Helena in 1865, "want of manure and careless working being the principal causes; the caterpillar did a great deal of damage."[12] The crops of 1866, 1867, 1868, were likewise failures, and at the same time the price of cotton dropped. These conditions drove several of the northern planters from St. Helena; and, for the first time, large tracts of land lay idle. Miss Towne who had bought a part of Frogmore plantation wrote in 1868, "I don't believe a white man would run the place for love or what money he could make, because there are so few white men, and so much unleased land."[13]

Planters everywhere in the coastal region were laboring against great odds. Factors in Charleston and Savan-

---

[12] *Letters from Port Royal*, pp. 297, 298. [13] *Letters and Diary*, p. 189.

nah, who were trying to carry on their business as before the war, had but little money with which to do so, but they lent and borrowed to the limit, taking great risks and demanding high percentages. Northern capital in many instances came to the rescue both of factors and planters. But the series of crop failures coupled with the drop in the price of cotton and the continued high price of provisions brought disaster to all. Frequently planters deeded large tracts of land, sometimes all except a hundred or more acres of what was once a large plantation, to northern firms for the cancellation of debts. James Gregorie, of Greenwood plantation, located not far from Beaufort, after making a tragic struggle for ten years to carry on his planting, finally gave up his property to a Philadelphia firm which he had involved heavily in debt.[14] In many instances these northern houses, after holding the plantations for a few years, began to sell them in small plots to Negroes, thus giving rise to the numerous communities of Negro landowners, aside from those in old Beaufort District, which now dot the coast of South Carolina and Georgia.

The Government offered relief by issuing rations to the freedmen, now hard-pressed. Later when the Freedmen's Bureau had been abandoned and the Negroes could no longer turn to the Government for aid, Miss Towne came forward with provisions, supplied sometimes from her own funds, at other times by gifts from the North which she had solicited. In 1876 when there was considerable distress, the whites of Beaufort organized a society to obtain funds with which to issue provisions.

[14] See MSS in Gregorie Papers.

William Elliott, one of several natives who had returned to Beaufort to live, was appointed to look after the needy in Beaufort and on the islands. In this way, the Negroes were able to face "the starving times."

If the profits from the cultivation of sea-island cotton were low in ante-bellum days, they were far less during the uncertain days of reconstruction. While some Negro landowners worked their cotton well, fertilizing the land and hoeing the crops regularly, still others were careless and indifferent. As a rule the cotton grown after slavery was of a coarser quality than that produced by ante-bellum planters. The fine seed, the result of many years of selection, had deteriorated. In fact, much of it was lost when the crop of 1861 was ginned at the North. Nor did the Negroes take pains to manure their fields. Gathering marsh grass and mud were disagreeable tasks which most of them preferred to avoid. The Negro landowners were further handicapped by the fact that they had to sell their cotton in the seed to the island stores and could not hold it for higher prices. A correspondent for *Harper's Monthly*, S. G. W. Benjamin, who visited St. Helena Island in 1878, found most of the Negroes growing vegetables and only a small quantity of cotton. Nevertheless, cotton remained the Islanders' only money crop. When, therefore, the boll weevil destroyed the production of sea-island cotton in 1918, the Negro landowners of St. Helena were confronted with an economic readjustment as radical as their fathers had faced after slavery.

After the inflation of war times, the Negroes of St. Helena quite generally settled down to an economic regime of self-sufficiency. They raised sweet potatoes and enough corn to supply themselves with hominy and grits and their chickens, pig, and ox with a scanty meal a day pieced out with marsh grass and with moss which they pulled down from the live oaks with long poles. When they sold their cotton in the late fall, they had a little money. With this they paid their taxes and bought clothes, and during the rest of the year lived without money.

Sometimes their crops did not yield enough to meet the taxes. In May, 1872, the *Beaufort Republican* advertised 318 farms on St. Helena and Ladies islands for sale, the taxes on which had not been paid for three years.[15] The size of their holdings was not only reduced by sale for taxes but also by division among heirs, so that it was not long until the condition which Philbrick had predicted in 1864 actually occurred. He had thought of dividing his plantations among the Negroes by selling them life-leases in order to protect them in the ownership of their land. In explaining his unwillingness to sell the land in fee simple he wrote to his superintendent:

This occurred to me as a means of avoiding the terrible and disastrous confusion which it will be next to impossible to avoid after a term of years, if the fee should be conveyed, when the purchasers die and sell or change land as they will to a certain extent in time. It is bad enough to trace a title and find out whether it is good for anything here in systematic New England, . . . but it makes my orderly bones ache to think of a time when, after some men now purchasing land shall die, leaving two or three sets of children, some born under wedlock and some not, some not their own but their wives' children, some even of questionable parentage, and some who were never heard of before, all claiming a slice of the

---

[15] *Beaufort Republican*, May 29, 1872.

deceased man's land, and of course claiming the best. Suppose it was bounded by a 'stake and stone' as of old here, minus the stones which are absent; suppose some of the claimants think best to set up new stakes where one has gone to decay, and suppose, as is more likely, their neighbor thinks the new stake encroaches on him and pulls it up entirely, stamping on the hole and putting it in according to his own ideas, etc., etc., ad infinitum. Now, as you must admit that all this is likely to occur, and worse too, would such a state of things tend to bring about a healthy and rapid development?[16]

As Philbrick predicted, controversies over land and the rightful title thereto retarded the progress of the St. Helena people by reducing the acreage and profits of farming and by arousing disputes which sent some of the best blood from the Island.

Hard times drove many of the young men from the Island and led many a mother and father to permit even their young children to be sent away as servants so that they might have a better opportunity of making a living than farming on St. Helena afforded. Early in 1867 Miss Towne wrote to a relative in Philadelphia, "I wish you could have the comfort the Heacocks have in the little darkies they sent North. The two young girls are large and strong and able to do pretty much all the work of the house. They work without wages till they are of age, but are to have the privilege of schooling. The experiment has been a perfect success, and every few weeks some one sends to them for another girl or boy, and all have given satisfaction so far."[17] Most of the boys and girls who left the Island in their teens went only as far as the nearby

[16] *Letters from Port Royal*, pp. 273, 274.
[17] *Letters and Diary*, p. 182.

towns where they found employment as servants and day laborers. Miss Towne speaks of their flocking back to St. Helena once a year "from Savannah, Charleston, Bull River, and all about" to attend the "exhibition" of Penn School.[18] Robert Smalls, famous during the war as the Beaufort Negro who turned over a Confederate steamer to Union officers and later conspicuous as a Congressman from South Carolina, attempted in 1879 to lead a group of Negroes from St. Helena's Parish to Arizona.

The discovery and utilization of the phosphate beds along the coast of South Carolina came in 1870 as a godsend to black laborers as well as to the whites who organized the companies. Many a St. Helena black man left his farm for his wife and children to cultivate while he went to the "Rock," as the phosphate mines in the coastal counties were called, to get "cash money." When digging was commenced just off Eddings' Point on St. Helena, the news "set all the boys wild."[19] In 1871 the *Beaufort Republican*, after announcing the enlargement of one of the phosphate mines, added, "Our colored friends can look to the future with pleasure and know that they will not have to roam over the country next summer to look for work but will find it on Bull River at the Oak Point Mine."[20] When the phosphate beds were exhausted, oyster factories began to be erected at Beaufort, on Ladies Island, and on St. Helena so that the Negroes still had a means of earning a little ready money either as hands in the factories or as laborers on the oyster boats. There were, also, still five or six white families on St. Helena

[18] *Ibid.*, p. 286.
[19] *Ibid.*, p. 273.
[20] *Beaufort Republican*, Nov. 23, 1871.

who owned and operated plantations and drew their labor from the Island.

Despite the fact that the majority of the inhabitants of St. Helena never made more than enough to carry them through the year, there were some who prospered. At the close of the Reconstruction period, small two-story houses with porches, window panes, and a neat coat of paint had begun to appear.[21] There were some who still rode to church, as in the days just after the war, in northern buggies drawn by trotting horses, and poverty-stricken, indeed, was the man who did not have a Sunday suit.

Just as St. Helena was beginning again to be a little prosperous, the disastrous storm of 1893 in a day and night of fearful wind and rain spread destruction everywhere. The crops had not been so promising in many years, but the tidal wave which swept over the Island in August destroyed the greater part of them. Houses were carried away and there was scarcely a family which did not suffer the loss of some member. Juliana, nurse in the family of James Ross Macdonald, white landowner and part owner of the chief store of the Island, described the storm to her mistress who was away at the time:

My fren,' the win' blow dat day fer true, but I ain't t'ink much about um, fer I see de win' blow nuff times in ma life. 'Bout four o'clock Sunday evenin' I lock de do' an' walk to Cousin Richard's house. . . . De house ben full ob people, an' I just get dere in time fer de win' bruck a-loose fer true, an' make sich a noise an' rock de house so, eberybody start to cry an' pray one time. Well, sir! 'stead ob growin' better he grow wuss, an' bime-bye de wing

---

[21] Benjamin, "The Sea Islands," *Harper's Monthly*, LVII, 858.

THE AFTERMATH 207

ob de house blow 'way an' seem like ebery minute de house go too; so we hab to get out.

He ben da'k now, an' where to go, dat's de trouble. To make de misery wuss, de rain seem like he bus' de sky open to fall top we-uns. We get on de side ob de house where de win' can't lick we so rash, an' dere we stan' de lib-long night, jus' like a passel ob turkeys wid dey head down. De watuh get higher an' higher. We ain't know den dat de tide keep a risin' all night an' nebber go down a-tall. Fus' it ben to ma knees, den cum up to ma wais' . . . I hold on to de window sill tell ma arms seem like dey drap off. When de blessed daylight cum at las,' sich a weepin' an' wailin' in de lan'! I wish I ben dead, for all los' something: some dere house, some dere animals, an' some dere wife an' chillun. So much sorrow an' misery I nebber want to see agen!²²

In 1911 a similar tidal wave, less disastrous than that of 1893, again swept away crops, homes, and live stock. In both instances Penn School, in 1893 under the guidance of Miss Towne with the assistance of the Red Cross and in 1911 under that of Miss Rossa B. Cooley and Miss Grace B. House, carried out the relief work and greatly aided the stricken people in beginning life anew.²³

THE NEGRO AS A CITIZEN

A gaunt woman of uncertain age leaned dejectedly against the door of her little cabin, two small children pulling at her skirts, airing herself in the hot sun of the summer of 1865 as though trying to rid her soul of misery. Her story was mournful enough. She had been sick. She had hired a woman to do her work. Her husband, Tony, had taken a fancy to the other woman, and after a while

---

²² Claire I. Macdonald, *Recollections of Juliana*, pp. 16-17.
²³ See annual *Report of Penn Normal, Industrial and Agricultural School for 1912* and MS, "Storm of 1911" in files of Penn School.

had gone away with her and "married." She had begged him to return and so he did, but after a few months he had gone off again to live with the other wife down the road a few tasks away. He was in the meeting-house yonder, a prayin' now.[24]

After Reconstruction, one heard fewer of such stories on St. Helena, for the church officials attempted to discipline all offenders. Although there were fewer cases of desertion, illegitimacy was none the less frequent despite the "churching." The significant change in family life was the elevated status of the husband. In attempting to stabilize family life, the superintendents and teachers had appealed to the man as the head of the family and had urged him to assume his rightful responsibilities. Black men who had been accustomed to the dominance of women during slavery came now to warn their wives to keep their places. The land which they bought from the Government was in their own names and they came to look upon the house as theirs, not that of their wives as in slavery days.

Freedom brought few changes in the religious life of the people. They still clung to their plantation praise houses, but instead of one praise house to a plantation they occasionally had as many as two or three. Besides this they built a few new churches, for "Brick Church" was too near Ladies Island to be within convenient reach of all the Islanders. But their church forms they changed very little except to make the praise house leaders subject to the Negro preachers of their churches whereas during antebellum days they had been subject to the white ministers.

[24] See Reid, *After the War*, p. 106n.

When a person wished to become a member of the church, he must go into seclusion for two or three weeks until he had received a vision that his sins had been forgiven. During this time of seclusion, he was said to be "seeking." Upon the genuineness of his vision the praise leader must pass judgment. Then the candidate must go through the catechism, thoroughly memorizing every sentence, and pass two examinations in the praise house and one in the church before being admitted to baptism. Once admitted, he wore the head cloth of the candidate until the day of baptism which was usually on communion Sunday. Dressed in white robes, the candidates came to the river at high tide to receive the ordinance of baptism. Miss Towne described a baptism in January, 1876, as being lengthy but impressive. Before communion, which preceded the baptismal service, the minister told the church members "that they were not to take a long drink of wine, but a sip only—that he had been told that 'some of they said they meant to get their two cents' worth.' (That is the amount generally subscribed by each to buy the wine.) He told them that was very naughty conduct in church members." The elders, Miss Towne explained, "used to take the first filled cup, throw back their heads, and drain it with gusto. That was their idea of partaking of the Lord's Supper." Communion over, the members filed outside to the river bank and amid prayer and song the candidates were immersed.

As in slavery days, the praise leaders attempted to regulate the affairs of the praise members, so in freedom the officers of the praise houses and the churches sought to regulate all the private and public disputes arising on the Island. As one of the preachers explained, "when one member gets wrong and the case cannot be settled at home it is taken to the church and sometimes the member is subjected [to] little embarrassment." [25]

It was many years, however, before the praise houses and churches obtained the prestige in settling disputes that they exercise today. In the first days of freedom, the cases going up to the "unjust law," as the people term legal processes, were numerous. Miss Towne's brother, William Edward Towne, was appointed a magistrate for St. Helena in 1869. "Some days half a dozen cases are brought before him," wrote Miss Towne, "and one day in the week, Tuesday, he and the other two selectmen have a meeting and make out jury lists, and do all sorts of township business. . . . I think a constable or two are here every day, to get orders or bring culprits." [26]

In 1866, as it has already been pointed out, the school farms were sold and the plantation schools abandoned, but the fund arising from the sale of the land was set aside for the establishment of schools in St. Helena's and St. Luke's parishes "without distinction of race or color." By 1871 this fund had amounted to something more than $68,000. [27] The benevolent associations, such as the Pennsylvania Freedmen's Relief Association, the Germantown Associ-

[25] MS, "St. Helena." In possession of Penn School.
[26] *Letters and Diary*, pp. 210, 211.
[27] *Senate Mis. Doc. no. 79*, 41st Cong., 3d sess. In response to an inquiry from Congress as to "the total amount of funds in the hands of any officer of the Government, set apart for the purposes of education in the parishes of St. Helena and St. Luke, in Beaufort County, South Carolina," Commissioner A. Pleasanton replied: " . . . there is invested in United States bonds . . . about $57,000; and there is in the hands of Collector Cloutman, of the second district, South Carolina, between three and four thousand dollars, and in the hands of Hon. W. E. Wording, not yet turned over to Collector Cloutman, between eight and nine thousand dollars."

THE AFTERMATH 211

ation, and the Benezet Association, all of Pennsylvania, continued to keep teachers in the field until about 1872,[28] and Philbrick employed teachers for the people on his plantations until he sold the land. State schools were not started on St. Helena Island until 1874, and then conducted for three months in "small rooms of dwelling houses, or rough cotton houses—out of repair and without glass windows."[29] The three trustees for St. Helena, of whom Miss Towne was one, hoped to build a schoolhouse each year until every part of the Island was accommodated. With the aid of the Federal fund, they were able to erect small buildings and keep them in repair.

The public schools, however, were always inadequate, for there were never sufficient funds to equip them properly and no money whatever to provide the pupils with books and slates, and the pupils themselves had no ready money with which to buy them. "The State schools," wrote Miss Towne in 1874, "are now taught by colored teachers of small attainment and experience, mostly from our Penn Schools[30] in this district, or by the returned 'old owners,' who also have little experience."[31]

Miss Towne, with the assistance of Miss Murray and sometimes with that of her graduates, enlarged the curriculum of Penn School and gradually extended the school's influence over the Island. The school offered its pupils the orthodox classical education in the elementary

---

[28] The Benezet Association gave some aid to Penn School until about 1879.

[29] MS, Letters of Laura M. Towne. Laura M. Towne to F. R. Cope, Nov. 13, 1873.

[30] There were several schools in the region around Beaufort during the periods of occupation and reconstruction supported by Pennsylvania benevolent societies.

[31] MS, Letters of Laura M. Towne. Laura M. Towne to F. R. Cope, April 11, 1874.

grades. The school was equipped with blackboards, charts, and maps, and in most cases provided the pupils with books and slates. After Miss Towne's death in 1901, Miss Murray carried on the work of the school until 1904 when Miss Rossa B. Cooley and Miss Grace B. House, teachers at Hampton Institute in Virginia, took over the work, and the curriculum was enlarged to include industrial and agricultural training similar to that offered by Hampton.

As in slavery the laborer had stopped work at noon Saturday and declared a holiday until Monday morning, so did the freedman. Saturday afternoon saw the island roads lined with pedestrians and carts, for each head of the family, regardless of where he lived, felt that he must pay a visit to "Corner Store" or even go to Beaufort. Saturday night was the time for general merriment, a dance for non-church members, a sing or a shout for those who were. Miss Towne complained in 1876 that on Frogmore plantation where she lived the people were beginning to have parties on other nights of the week as well. "Last night," she wrote, "our boys went to a party again, and to-day they are sleeping it out. We have issued the edict, 'No more parties this winter,' for there is arising among the Frogmore young men a constant desire for gayety,—suppers, etc., that we intend to begin to frown upon. They are flush just now, and are spending too much. They are all temperance parties, which is one good thing."[32]

Although there were occasions when people from all parts of the Island assembled together, as on Saturday afternoons at Corner Store, at church on Sunday mornings,

---

[32] *Letters and Diary*, p. 257.

or at funerals, social life on St. Helena, as Miss Towne suggested in her complaint against the Frogmore people, was still by plantations. Distances on the Island were too great to enable any considerable amount of inter-plantation visiting. The old plantation names were retained, therefore, and though a man owned his little plot of the old master's land, he still regarded himself as belonging to the old plantation. He was a Tom Fripp Negro, a Frogmore Negro, or an Indian Hill Negro as the case might be, and he usually "pleasured himself" with his "own people."

To the customary holidays of slavery times, the freedmen added three others, the Fourth of July, Decoration Day, and Emancipation Day, celebrations introduced under northern influence. Dr. J. M. Hawks, who was stationed in the conquered territory during the early days of the occupation of Port Royal, wrote to his wife, "Where I live, we [sic] the negroes had a great celebration on the fourth, first at 6 A. M. raised a big flag to the top of the cupalo, . . . Then they had a regular barbecue—a beef was killed and roasted a la mode Southern. P. M. dancing commenced and was kept up all the rest of the day. Our Supts. and Schoolmaster and an officer joined in the dance."[33]

The people of St. Helena modified the celebration until it came to be an occasion centering chiefly about Corner Store. There in the grove of trees opposite the store, people from all over the Island erected their stands until the string of tables reached out to a task's length. There were so many trying to sell that there was scarcely any one left to buy.

[33] MS in Hawks Letters. J. M. Hawks to Esther Hawks, July 6, 1862.

Decoration Day was the one occasion of the year when all of St. Helena paid a visit to Beaufort, where there was always a ceremony at National Cemetery. "The Thirtieth of May," said a native of St. Helena, born in the early days of freedom, "was a day that I looked for [*sic*] tc happiness. Early in the morning work was suspended and nearly all the people on the Island went to Beaufort. I can now recall how I used to watch with interest the great crowd that used to pass by our house from the other end of the Island on the eve of Decoration in order to be over in town before the rush. We had to cross a ferry then and the accommodation was not very good."[34]

The people of St. Helena celebrated the First of January not so much as New Year's Day as the anniversary of their freedom, for it was January 1, 1863, that President Lincoln issued his Emancipation Proclamation. Here again the celebration was at Corner Store. Brass bands, perhaps one hired for the occasion and another composed of members of one of the fraternal orders, furnished music for the day. On a platform erected in a grove of trees, speakers, usually chosen from among their own people, addressed an attentive audience upon the benefits arising from freedom.

The freedmen had no sports as did the whites in the rural districts. They still fished as in slavery days and could now hunt when they chose, but they did not know how to play together in combative sports. Yet they were a good-natured, contented people, happy in their freedom, ignorant in their isolation, suspicious of all "foreigners," but gentle and courteous when once this suspicion had been

[34] MS, "St. Helena." In files of Penn School.

allayed. Their folk-ways were the outgrowth of slavery; their songs, the ones they sang in bondage; their speech, the English their ancestors had learned when they were "tamed." But their home was one of the proudest of the Sea Islands, about whose history there is a glamour scarcely equalled in the new world. The object of French colonization, a Spanish presidio, a Scotch settlement, the home of the lone Indian trader and frontiersman, a center of indigo culture, the heart of sea-island cotton production, the scene of southern culture at its height, and one of the densest black belts in the South, this region had finally become suddenly and dramatically the home of the black people who had tilled the land and whose labor had made many of these things possible.

BIBLIOGRAPHY
A. PRIMARY SOURCES
I. MANUSCRIPTS

Army and Navy Sales [in St. Helena's and St. Luke's Parishes, South Carolina]. In archives of the United States Treasury Department.

Beaufort College, Minutes of, 1796-1860. In possession of William Elliott, Columbia, S. C.

Couper, James Hamilton, Agricultural Notes. In possession of Mrs. W. S. Lovell, Birmingham, Ala.

    Hopeton Plantation Book, 1818-1831. In possession of Mrs. W. S. Lovell, Birmingham, Ala.

    Journal No. 2, 1839-1854. In possession Library University of North Carolina.

    Ledger, 1826-1850. In possession Library University of North Carolina.

Couper-Wylly Papers. In possession of Mrs. W. S. Lovell, Birmingham, Ala.

Edwards, Morgan, Materials Toward a History of the Baptists in South Carolina. In Bucknell Library, Crozer Theological Seminary, Chester, Pa.

Elliott, Mary B., Account Book. In possession of William Elliott, Columbia, S. C.

Elliott, Congressman William, Papers. In possession of William Elliott, Columbia, S. C.

Ellis, Mrs. S. W., Papers. In possession of Mrs. R. L. Fripp, Burton, S. C.

Fripp, Papers. In possession of Miss Alice Fripp, Ridgeland, S. C.

Fripp, John E., Plantation Book. In possession of Miss Alice Fripp, Ridgeland, S. C.

Gregorie, A. F., Account Book, 1836-1845. In possession of Dr. M. G. Elliott, Beaufort, S. C.

Guerard, B. E., "Beaufort." In possession of Yates Snowden, Columbia, S. C. Autobiography of a Confederate soldier at the close of the war.

Heads of Families Certificate Books. In archives of the United State Treasury Department.

Land Grant Books, 1694-1739. In office of the Secretary of State, Columbia, S. C.

Land Plats, 1680-1776. In office of the Secretary of State, Columbia, S. C.

Land Warrants, 1672-1711. In office of the Historical Commission of South Carolina, Columbia, S. C.

McPherson and Gregorie Papers. In possession of Dr. M. G. Elliott, Beaufort, S. C.

Memorial Books, 14 vols. In office of the Historical Commission of South Carolina, Columbia, S. C. Abstracts of titles to lands in South Carolina prior to 1776.

Merchant's Account Book, Beaufort, S. C., 1785-1791. In office of Secretary of South Carolina Historical Society, Charleston, S. C.

Middleton, Henry A., Jr., Plantation Book. In possession of Langdon Cheves, Charleston, S. C.

Miscellaneous Papers concerning sale of land for direct taxes in South Carolina. In archives of United States Treasury Department.

Penn Normal, Industrial, and Agricultural School, Miscellaneous Papers. In possession of Penn School, St. Helena Island, S. C.

Port Royal Correspondence. In archives of United States Treasury Department.

Public Records of South Carolina: Transcripts of South Carolina Documents in the Public Record Office (1663-1734), I-XVI.

Return of Tax Collected by John M. Baker in the Parish of St. Helena for the Year Commencing Oct. 1, 1860. Duplicate of original in possession of William Elliott, Columbia, S. C.

Sale of Household and Plantation Equipment in South Carolina. In archives of United States Treasury Department.

South Carolina Maps. In archives of United States Treasury Department.

Stuart, Henry M., Receipt Book. In possession of William Elliott, Columbia, S. C.

Sumner, Arthur, Papers. Typescripts in possession of Penn School, St. Helena Island, S. C.
Towne, Laura M., Letters. Typescripts in possession of Penn School, St. Helena Island, S. C.
Whaley Papers. In possession of J. Swinton Whaley, Little Edisto Island, S. C.

II. PRINTED SOURCES

A. OFFICIAL DOCUMENTS

1. South Carolina

Salley, A. S., Jr. (ed.), *Commissions and Instructions from the Lords Proprietors of Carolina to Public Officials of South Carolina, 1685-1715.* Columbia, S. C., 1916.
Journal of the Commons House of Assembly of South Carolina for the Session Beginning September 20, 1692, and Ending October 15, 1692. Columbia, S. C., 1907.
Journals of the Commons House of Assembly of South Carolina for the Four Sessions of 1693. Columbia, S. C., 1907.
Journal of the Commons House of Assembly of South Carolina for the Session Beginning January 30, 1696, and Ending March 17, 1696. Columbia, S. C., 1908.
Journal of the Commons House of Assembly of South Carolina for the Session Beginning November 24, 1696, and Ending December 5, 1696. Columbia, S. C., 1912.
Journals of the Commons House of Assembly of South Carolina for the Two Sessions of 1697. Columbia, S. C., 1913.
Journals of the Commons House of Assembly of South Carolina for the Two Sessions of 1698. Columbia, S. C., 1914.
Journal of the Commissioners of the Indian Trade of South Carolina, September 20, 1710-April 12, 1715. Columbia, S. C., 1926.
Journal of the General Assembly of South Carolina, September 17, 1776-October 20, 1776. Columbia, S. C., 1909.

BIBLIOGRAPHY 219

Journal of the House of Representatives of South Carolina, January 8, 1782-February 26, 1782. Columbia, S. C., 1916.
Records in the British Public Record Office Relating to South Carolina, 1685-1690, 2 vols. Atlanta, Ga., 1928-1929.
Warrants for Lands in South Carolina, 1672-1679. Columbia, S. C., 1910.
Warrants for Lands in South Carolina, 1680-1692. Columbia, S. C., 1911.
Warrants for Lands in South Carolina, 1692-1711. Columbia, S. C., 1915.
Statutes at Large of South Carolina.

2. United States

Alvord, J. W., *Freedmen's Bureau: Semi-Annual Reports on Schools and Finances of Freedmen.* Washington, 1866-1870.
Census Reports, 1790-1880.
Congressional Globe, 36th Cong.-38th Cong.
Congressional Record, 38th Cong.-51st Cong.
A Compilation of the Direct Tax Laws of the United States from August 5, 1861: with the regulations and instructions; . . . giving a history of direct tax legislation up to that time, and the proceedings under the same. Washington, 1874.
Court of Claims Reports, XXVII (1892).
Heads of Families at the First Census of the United States, 1790: State of South Carolina. Washington, 1908.
Letter from the Secretary of the Treasury in regard to work on the Sea Islands. *House Ex. Doc. no. 72,* 37th Cong., 3d sess.
President Lincoln's Instructions to the Tax Commissioners of South Carolina. *House Ex. Doc. no. 146,* 40th Cong., 2d sess.
Reports of Assistant Commissioners of Bureau of Refugees and Abandoned Lands. *Senate Ex. Doc. no. 27,* 39th Cong., 1st sess.; *Senate Ex. Doc. no. 6,* 39th Cong., 2d sess.
Report of the Commissioner of the Bureau of Refugees, Freedmen and Abandoned Lands, 1865-1870.

Reports of Committees on the Affairs in the Late Insurrectionary States: South Carolina, 3 vols., 42d Cong., 2d sess.

Reports of Committees on Direct Taxes in the Southern States. *House Reports, Doc. no. 46,* 44th Cong., 1st sess.; *Senate Ex. Doc. no. 82,* 47th Cong., 1st sess.; *House Ex. Doc. no. 159,* 49th Cong., 2d sess.; *House Reports, Doc. no.* 552, 50th Cong., 1st sess.; *House Reports, Doc. no. 683,* 51st Cong., 1st sess.

Report of the Joint Committee on Reconstruction, 1866. 39th Cong., 1st sess.

Reports of Tax Commissioners. *Senate Ex. Doc. no. 26,* 37th Cong., 3d sess.; *House Ex. Doc. no. 133,* 39th Cong., 1st sess.; *House Ex. Doc. no. 312,* 41st Cong., 2d sess.; *House Misc. Doc. no. 101,* 41st Cong., 3d sess.; *Senate Misc. Doc. no. 79,* 41st Cong., 3d sess.; *Senate Ex. Doc. no. 46,* 42d Cong., 2d sess.; *House Ex. Doc. no. 101,* 45th Cong., 3d sess.

Richardson, James D. (comp.), *Messages and Papers of the Presidents, 1789-1897,* 10 vols. Washington, 1896-1899.

United States Reports.

United States Statutes at Large, vols. 12-28.

War of the Rebellion: A Compilation of the Official Records of the Union and Confederate Armies, 70 vols. in 128. Washington, 1880-1901.

B. COLLECTED DOCUMENTS

Barnwell, Joseph W. and Mabel L. Webber (eds.), "St. Helena's Parish Register," *South Carolina Historical and Genealogical Magazine,* XXIII, 8-33, 46-71, 102-151, 171-204.

Calendar of State Papers, Colonial Series, 21 vols. London, 1860-1922.

Carroll, B. R., *Historical Collections of South Carolina,* 2 vols. New York, 1836.

Collections of the South Carolina Historical Society, 5 vols. Charleston, 1857-1897.

Fleming, Walter L. (ed.), *Documentary History of Reconstruction,* 2 vols. Cleveland, O., 1906-1907.

Moore, Frank (comp.), *Rebellion Record*, 11 vols. and supplement vol. New York, 1861-1868.
Phillips, Ulrich Bonnell (ed.), *Plantation and Frontier Documents*, 2 vols. Cleveland, 1910.
Salley, A. S., Jr. (ed.), *Minutes of the Vestry of St. Helena's Parish, South Carolina, 1726-1812.* Columbia, S. C., 1919. *Narratives of Early Carolina.* New York, 1911.
Saunders, W. L. (ed.), *Colonial Records of North Carolina*, 10 vols. Raleigh, 1886-1890.
Turner, J. A. (ed.), *The Cotton Planters Manual.* New York, 1857.

c. Autobiographies, Diaries, Letters

Botume, Elizabeth Hyde, *First Days Amongst the Contrabands.* Boston, 1893.
Bryan, Hugh, and Mary Hutson, *Living Christianity Delineated in the Letters and Diaries.* London, 1760.
Holland, Rupert S. (ed.), *Letters and Diary of Laura M. Towne.* Cambridge, 1912.
Howard, Oliver Otis, *Autobiography*, 2 vols. New York, 1907.
Hughes, Sarah Forbes (ed.), *Letters and Recollections of John Murray Forbes.* Boston and New York, 1899.
Kemble, Frances Anne, *Journal of a Residence on a Georgian Plantation in 1838-1839.* New York, 1863.
Pearson, Elizabeth Ware (ed.), *Letters From Port Royal Written at the Time of the Civil War.* Boston, 1906.
Perry, Bliss (ed.), *Life and Letters of Henry Lee Higginson.* Boston, 1921.
Pierce, Edward L., *Addresses and Papers.* Boston, 1896.
Pringle, Elizabeth Waties, *Chronicles of Chicora Wood.* New York, 1922.
[Pringle, Elizabeth Waties], *A Woman Rice Planter.* New York, 1913.
Towne, Laura M., "Pioneer Work on the Sea Islands," *Southern Workman.* (July, 1901).
Wylly, Charles Spalding, *The Seed That Was Sown in the Colony of Georgia.* New York, 1910.

D. Travelers' Accounts

Benjamin, S. G. W., "The Sea Islands," *Harper's New Monthly Magazine*, LVII, 839-861 (1878).
Bremer, Fredrika, *The Homes of the New World; Impressions of America*, 2 vols. New York, 1854.
Hall, Basil, *Travels in North America in the Years 1827 and 1828*, 2 vols. Philadelphia, 1829.
Lyell, Sir Charles, *A Second Visit to the United States of North America*, 2 vols. New York, 1849.
Murray, Hon. Amelia M., *Letters from the United States, Cuba and Canada*, 2 vols. New York, 1856.
Nordoff, Charles, *The Freedmen of South Carolina*. New York, 1863.
"Two Weeks at Port Royal, S. C.," *Harper's New Monthly Magazine*, XXVII, 110-118 (1863).
Olmsted, Frederick Law, *A Journey in the Seaboard Slave States*. New York, 1856.
Pike, J. S., *The Prostrate State; South Carolina Under Negro Government*. New York, 1874.
Reid, Whitelaw, *After the War; a Southern Tour, May 1, 1865 to May 1, 1866*. New York, 1866.
Russell, W. H., *My Diary North and South*. London, 1863.
"The South As It Is," *Nation*, I, *passim* (1865).
Trowbridge, J. T., *The South, a Tour of Its Battle-Fields and Ruined Cities*. Hartford, Conn., 1866.

E. Miscellaneous Printed Documents

Allen, W. F., and Others, *Slave Songs of the United States*. New York, 1867 and 1929.
Allston, R. F., *Essay on Sea Coast Crops; read before the Agricultural Association of the Planting States*. Charleston, 1854.
Alvord, J. W., *Letters from the South Relating to the Condition of Freedmen*. Washington, 1870.
Charleston Year Book, 1883. Charleston, 1883.
Connor, Jeannette Thurber (ed.), *Jean Ribaut, the Whole & True Discouerye of Terra Florida*. Publications of the Florida State Historical Society, no. 7. De Land, Fla., 1927.

BIBLIOGRAPHY 223

DeBow, J. D. B., *The Industrial Resources, Statistics, Etc., of the United States, and More Particularly of the Southern and Western States*, 3 vols. New York, 1854.

Elliott, William, *Carolina Sports by Land and Water*. 2d ed. Columbia, S. C., 1918.

[Gannett, W. C.], "The Freedmen at Port Royal," *North American Review*, CI, 1-28.

Howard, O. O., *Statement Before the Committee on Education and Labor in Defense Against the Charges Presented by Hon. Fernando Wood*. New York, 1870.

Mills, Robert, *Statistical Atlas of South Carolina*. Charleston, 1825.

Mills, Robert, *Statistics of South Carolina, including a view of its natural, civil, and military history, general and particular*. Charleston, 1826.

[Nairne, Thomas ?], *A Letter from South Carolina; giving an Account of the Soil, Air, Product, Trade, Government, Laws, Religion, People, Military Strength, &c. of that Province*. London, 1710.

New England Freedmen's Aid Society, *Annual Report*. Boston, 1863-1864.

Second Series of Extracts from Letters Received by the Educational Commission of Boston, from Teachers Employed at Port Royal and its Vicinity. Boston, 1862.

Pierce, Edward L., "Freedmen at Port Royal," *Atlantic Monthly*, XII, 291 (1863).

The Negroes at Port Royal. Report to Salmon P. Chase, Secretary of the Treasury. Boston, 1862.

Reynolds, W. S., *The Agricultural Prospects of South-Carolina; Her Resources and Her True Policy*. Charleston, 1845.

Ruffin, Edmund, *Report of the Commencement and Progress of the Agricultural Survey of South-Carolina for 1843*. Columbia, S. C., 1843.

Seabrook, Whitemarsh B., *An Essay on the Agricultural Capabilities of South Carolina*. Columbia, S. C., 1848.

A Memoir on the Origin, Cultivation, and Uses of Cotton at the Present Time, with Special Reference to the Sea-Island Cotton Plant. Charleston, 1844.

A Report Accompanied with Sundry Letters on the Causes Which Contribute to the Production of Fine Sea-Island Cotton. Charleston, 1827.

Simons, J. Hume, *The Planter's Guide and Family Book of Medicine.* 2d ed. Charleston, 1848.

Tuomey, M., *Report on the Geology of South Carolina.* Columbia, S. C., 1848.

F. Newspapers and Magazines

The Beaufort Republican, Oct. 12, 1871-Oct. 16, 1873.

Charleston Courier, 1803-1873. Became *The Charleston Daily Courier* in 1852.

Charleston Mercury, 1823-Feb., 1865; Nov., 1866-1868.

DeBow's Review, vols. I-XXXI. New Orleans, 1846-1861.

New York Times, 1860-1874.

Port Royal Commercial and Beaufort County Republican, Oct. 30, 1873-April 30, 1874. Formerly the *Beaufort Republican.*

South Carolina Gazette, 1732-1802. Appears under various names.

South Carolina Historical and Genealogical Magazine, vols. I-XXVIII. Charleston, 1900-1927.

The Southern Agriculturist, vols. I-XVII. Charleston, 1828-1846.

B. SECONDARY SOURCES

Bolton, Herbert E. (ed.), *Arredondo's Historical Proof of Spain's Title to Georgia: A Contribution to the History of One of the Spanish Borderlands.* Berkeley, Cal., 1925.

Christensen, Niels, "Fifty Years of Freedom: Conditions in the Sea Coast Regions," *The Negro's Progress in Fifty Years.* Annals of the American Academy of Political and Social Sciences, XLIX, 58-66 (Sept., 1913).

Cooley, Rossa B., *Homes of the Freed.* New York, 1926.

"Liberty and Literacy," *Survey*, LIX, 443-445, 572-578; LX, 293-297, 470-474. (Jan. 1, Feb. 1, June 1, August 1, 1928).

Crane, Verner W., *The Southern Frontier, 1670-1732*. Durham, N. C., 1929.

Cutler, H. G., *History of South Carolina*, 5 vols. Chicago and New York, 1920.

Dalcho, Frederic, *Historical Account of the Protestant Episcopal Church in South Carolina*. Charleston, 1820.

[Dargan, John O. B.?], *Christian Fellowship: or the Solemn Covenant of the Baptist Church of Christ in Beaufort, S. C.* Charleston, 1834.

Davis, J. E., "A Unique People's School," *Southern Workman*, XLIII, 217-330 (April, 1914).

Donnan, Elizabeth, "The Slave Trade into South Carolina before the Revolution," *American Historical Review*, XXIII, 804-828 (1928).

Donnel, E. J., *Chronological and Statistical History of Cotton*, New York, 1872.

"Education of the Freedmen," *North American Review*, CI, 528-549 (Oct., 1865).

Elzas, Barnett A., *The Jews of South Carolina*. Philadelphia, 1905.

Foote, Henry Wilder, "The Penn School on St. Helena Island," *Southern Workman*, XXXIII (1904).

Grimké, Sara M., *American Slavery as It Is*. New York, 1839.

Henry, H. M., *The Police Control of the Slave in South Carolina*. Emory, Va., 1914.

Hollis, John Porter, "Early Period of Reconstruction in South Carolina," *John Hopkins University Studies*, ser. 23, nos. 1-2. Baltimore, 1905.

Insh, G. P., *Scottish Colonial Schemes, 1620-1686*. Glasgow, 1922.

Jones, Charles Colcock, *The Religious Instruction of the Negroes*. Savannah, 1842.

McGrady, Edward, *History of South Carolina under the Proprietary Government, 1670-1719.* New York, 1897.
History of South Carolina Under the Royal Government, 1719-1776. New York, 1889.
"Slavery in the Province of South Carolina (1670-1770)." *Annual Report* American Historical Association, 1895, pp. 631-673. Washington, 1896.
Macdonald, Clare I., *Recollections of Juliana.* Columbia, S. C., 1924.
McMahon, John R., "Growing Wings for Airplanes: Sea Island Cotton Will Swoop Down on Kaiser Bill," *Country Gentleman,* Dec. 29, 1917.
"The Long Cotton Belt Broadens," *Country Gentleman,* Feb. 2, 1918.
Phillips, Ulrich Bonnell, *American Negro Slavery.* New York, 1918.
Life and Labor in the Old South. Boston, 1929.
Pierce, Paul Sheels, "The Freedmen's Bureau," *State University of Iowa Studies in Sociology, Economics, Politics and History,* III, no. 1 (1904).
Ramsay, David, *The History of South-Carolina, from Its First Settlement in 1670, to the Year 1808,* 2 vols. Charleston, 1809.
"The Religious Life of the Negro Slave," *Harper's Monthly Magazine,* XXVII, 479-485; 676-682; 816-825. (1863).
Reynolds, John S., *Reconstruction in South Carolina, 1865-1877.* Columbia, S. C., 1905.
[Rivers, William James], *A Sketch of the History of South Carolina to the Close of the Proprietary Government by the Revolution of 1719.* Charleston, 1856.
Ross, Mary, "The Spanish Settlement of Santa Elena (Port Royal) in 1578," *Georgia Historical Quarterly,* IX, 352-379 (Dec., 1925).
Salley, A. S., Jr., "The Introduction of Rice Culture into South Carolina." *Bulletins of the Historical Commission of South Carolina,* no. 6. Columbia, S. C., 1919.

"The Origin of Carolina," *Bulletins of the Historical Commission of South Carolina*, no. 8. Columbia, S. C., 1926.

"Parris Island, the Site of the First Attempt at a Settlement of White People Within the Bounds of What Is Now South Carolina." *Bulletins of the Historical Commission of South Carolina*, no. 5. Columbia, S. C., 1919.

Smith, Henry A. M., "Beaufort," *South Carolina Historical and Genealogical Magazine*, IX, 141-160 (July, 1908).

A South Carolinian, "Political Condition of South Carolina," *Atlantic Monthly*, XXXIX, 177-194 (February, 1877). "South Carolina Morals," *ibid.*, pp. 467-475 (April, 1877). "South Carolina Society," *ibid.*, pp. 670-684 (June, 1877).

Stevens, Hazard, *Life of Isaac Ingalls Stevens*, 2 vols. Boston, 1900.

Stuart, Benjamin R., *Magnolia Cemetery, an Interpretation of Some of its Monuments and Inscriptions*. Charleston, 1896.

Taylor, A. A., *The Negro in South Carolina during the Reconstruction*. Washington, 1924.

Tremain, Henry Edwin, *Two Days of War, a Gettysburg Narrative and Other Excursions*. New York, 1905.

Trescot, Wm. Henry, *Gen. Stephen Elliott*. Address in House of Representatives of South Carolina, Sept. 8, 1866. Reprint Columbia, S. C., 1926.

Webster, Laura Josephine, "The Operations of the Freedmen's Bureau in South Carolina," *Smith College Studies in History*, I, nos. 2-3. Northampton, 1916.

Whaley, J. Swinton, "A History of Sea-Island Cotton." In manuscript.

Wilson, Henry, *Rise and Fall of the Slave Power in America*, 3 vols. Boston, 1872.

INDEX

AFRICANS, 77, 131. *See also* Negroes, Slave Trade, Slaves.
Agriculture, majority small planters in Beaufort District, 38; sea-island cotton produces system of, 48; planting routine on sea-island cotton plantation, 46-48; farm implements used on sea-island plantation, 48-50; beginning of experimental, 50-55; improved methods, 53, 64; use of marsh mud, 55-58; use of compost, 56-57; rotation of crops, 60-64; an annual lottery, 64. *See also* Plantation Management, Planters, Slaves.
Agricultural Societies, 50, 59, 87.
Albemarle, 8.
Albemarle Point, 9.
Allston, R. F. W., on compost, 56.
Altamaha delta, 61.
Altamaha River, 62n, 144.
American Agriculturist, 59.
Anabaptists, 117. *See also* Baptist Denomination.
Anglo-Spanish Conflict, 7-10.
Angola, 33.
Ante-bellum Period, 59, 168, 169, 202, 208; clearing virgin land, 54; use of marsh mud, 55-58; use of oyster shells, 58-59; price of slave rations, 87; comparison of death rate of whites and Negroes, 99; whites and blacks in Beaufort District, 106; education in St. Helena's Parish, 113-114; religion among slaves, 146. *See also* Agriculture, Negroes, Plantation Management, Planters, St. Helena Island, Slaves.
Antigua, 31.
Archdale, Governor John, 10.
Argyle Island, 94.
Arkansas, 183.
Ashe, Thomas, 17.
Ashley, Lord, 8n, 15.
Ashley River, 8, 9.
Asiatic Cholera, 91.
Atlantic Monthly, 127.

Atlantic Ocean, 5, 129.
Avilés, Pedro Menendez de, 6.
Ayllon, Lucas Vasques de, 3, 5.

BAHAMA Islands, 23, 24.
Bailey, John, 103.
Bakers, settle on St. Helena Island, 103.
Bance Island, 33.
Baptism, on St. Helena Island, 209.
Baptist denomination, 117, 118, 147; preachers and missionaries, 150; communicants, 180.
Barbadians, 7, 8.
Barbados, 8; planters go to Carolina, 14, 15, 31; import pitch from Carolina, 17.
Barnwell, Colonel Edward, 24, 57.
Barnwell Island, 80; slave quarters, 90; Mrs. Trescot on slave health, 92.
Barnwell, John G., 118.
Barnwell, Robert, 115.
Bassa, on Windward Coast, 33.
Battery, the plantation, 71, 76.
Bay Point, 154, 156n, 194.
Baynard, William Grimbal, 109n.
Beaufort Benevolent Society, 122.
Beaufort Bible Society, 122.
Beaufort College, 113.
Beaufort County, 115n.
Beaufort District, indigo grown in, 21; extent of slaveholdings, 36-38, 39; one of densest black belts in South, 38; county seats, 38n; price of slaves, 40; price of land, 44; whites and blacks in, 106-107; schools in, 113-114; religion in, 117; sketch of, 118; parishes in, 115n; land sale in, 183; Negro communities in, 201.
Beaufort Republican, 203, 205.
Beaufort River, 5n.
Beaufort Society, 113. *See also* Education.
Beaufort Tract Society, 122.
Beaufort, town, 5, 11-12, 24, 80, 86, 107, 108, 110, 130, 158, 163, 175,

194, 201, 212, 213; charter, 12, 17; grants to lots, 13; fort, 13; growth, 14; Sir Charles Lyell's visit in 1845, 36, 111; county seat of Beaufort District, 38n; as cotton market, 72; slave quarters, 89; description, 111-112; college, 113; culture, 114-115; library, 114, 122; parish church, 116; societies, 122; difficult for St. Helena Negroes to reach, 129; health resort; 109, 110, 112, 131; capture in 1861, 154-155; looting of, 157; northern missionaries arrive, 166; sold for direct taxes, 183, 184, 185, 189; planters return, 193; aids Negroes, 201, 202; oyster factories, 205; Decoration Day in, 214.
Benezet Association, 211.
Benjamin, S. G. W., 202.
Bermuda, 15.
"Big house," 108-112, 121, 133, 158.
Bisset, Alexander, 23.
Bluff, Chechessee, plantation, routine of labor on, 47-48; equipment of, 49; John E. Fripp of, 71.
Board of Trade, 13.
Bombay, 144.
Boston, 163, 165, 167n, 186.
Bremer, Frederika, 61, 143.
"Brick Church" on St. Helena Island, 117, 118, 144, 147, 180, 181, 192, 208.
Brisbane, William, 25.
Brisbane, W. Henry, 183.
Bristol, 15.
Brookline, Mass., 167n, 168.
Brown, Dr. Charles H., 167n.
Brunswick Canal, 153.
Bryan, Hugh, 117, 146n.
"Buckra," 130.
Bull, General Stephen, 38.
Bull River, 205.
Bunder-boatmen, 144.
Burden, Kinsey, Sr., 25; cotton seed, 53.
Butler, General, 157.
Butler's Island, 76, 90.
Butler plantation, 76, 79, 126. *See* Butler's Island; St. Simon's Island.

CABIN, slave. *See* Quarters.
Calabars, "from Bight," 33.
Cambridge, Mass., 128.
Cannon's Point plantation, 60, 119.
Canterbury, 15.
Cape Fear, 7.
Cape Mount, on Grain Coast, 33.
Capers, Charles, 38.
Capers, Edward M., 118.
Capers, Mrs. Charles, 21, 105, 107.
Capers plantation, on St. Helena Island, 80.
Capers, Richard, 11n.
Capers, Will, slave cabinet maker, 153.
Capers, William, 11n, 38.
Caperses, settle on St. Helena Island, 103.
Cardross, Lord, 9.
"Caribbe" Islands, 17.
Caribbean Sea, 23.
Carolina, as province, 4, 10, 12, 31; charters to, 5, 8; type of settler desired, 15; occupation of settlers, 17-18. *See also* South Carolina.
Carr's Island, 67.
Cedar Grove plantation, 187n.
Chaplin, John, 36, 38.
Chaplin, Marion T., 42.
Chaplin, Mrs. Eliza H., 194.
Chaplin, Thomas, 38.
Chaplins, settle on St. Helena Island, 103.
Charles II of England, 5, 8.
Charlesfort, 5, 6.
Charleston, 3, 21, 24, 53, 68, 80, 93, 107, 118, 130, 188, 205; slave market, 34-35; price of slaves, 40; *Southern Agriculturist*, 21, 50, 57, 61; factors, 69, 70, 74, 200; cotton shipped to, 72; death rates, 1830-1835, 99; St. Helena planters entertain in, 120; planter on slave morals, 131-132; plantation near, 138; on capture of Port Royal, 154, 155n. *See also* Charles Town.
Charleston, College of, 113, 115.
Charleston Mercury, 114, 115.
"Charleston," the, 150.

INDEX

Charles Town, 9, 10, 12, 31, 68, 115; on Ashley River, 9; on Cape Fear River, 8n; type of settlers, 18; exports indigo, 19; credit system in slave trade, 32-33; slave-market, 32, 33. *See also* Charleston.

Chase, Salmon P., Secretary of Treasury, 163, 166; appoints cotton agents, 160; social experiment with Negroes, 162; Pierce proposes plan to, 164-165; report of tax commissioner to, 184. *See also* Treasury Department.

Cherry Hill plantation, 186.

Children, work of, 82; care of, 96-101, 138; names, 137; discipline, 138-139. *See also* Infant Welfare, Slaves, Negroes.

Chisolm's plantation, 174.

"Churching," 152, 208, 209-210.

Churches. *See* Religion.

Citizen, Negro, during Reconstruction, 207-208; after Reconstruction, 208-215.

Citizenship, training Negro for, 196; Sherman's plan, 162; Pierce's plan, 163-167; operation of plan, 175-183. *See also* Social Experiment, Superintendents of Plantations, Missionaries.

Civil War, 21, 80, 104, 109, 118, 137, 139, 150, 151, 188. *See also* Federal Government, Port Royal, Confederate Forces.

Clarendon, County of, 4.

Coachman, 81.

Coast, Atlantic, 3.

Cockran, James, 11n.

Coffin, Mrs. Mary, 42.

Coffin, Thomas Aston, 39, 49; answers to questionnaire, 52n-53n; rations issued slaves, 86; clothes issued slaves, 187; location of plantation, 108; library, 114; entertainments, 119-120; slaves report good treatment, 125. *See also* Coffin's Point Plantation, Coffins, Frogmore Plantation.

Coffin's Point plantation, 39, 52, 87, 89, 111, 131, 167n, 178, 186. *See also* Thomas Aston Coffin.

Coffins, the, planters, 44, 51, 52, 123; cotton seed, 53; settle on St. Helena Island, 103. *See also* Thomas Aston Coffin.

Coligny, Admiral, 5.

Colleton County, 12.

Colleton, Sir John, 8.

Colonies, settlers in Carolina from northern, 14; British allowed bounty on indigo to, 119; Sugar, 23.

Columbia, S. C., 87, 115n.

Combahee River, 14, 18, 158n.

Commissions, plantation, 177.

Compost, preparation and use, 56-57. *See* Fertilizers, Marsh Mud, Marsh Grass.

Confederate, officers, 154; scouts, 154; forces, 155; steamer, 205.

Congress, United States, 165, 172; Act of Aug. 5, 1861, 173, 183; Act of July 17, 1862, 173; orders sale of school farms, 182; Act of June 7, 1862, 183, 184; Freedman's Bureau Act, 174, 188.

Conjurer, 152. *See also* Witch Doctor, Superstitions.

Contraband of War, Butler declares slaves, 157, 159. *See also* Negroes, Freedmen.

"Contrabands," 163, 175, 180. *See also* Negroes, Freedmen, Contraband of War.

Cooley, Rossa B., 207, 212.

Corn, as sea-island crop, 17, 64; yield, 48; planting on Bluff plantation, 47, 48; raised on Hopeton plantation, 62; in slave diet, 85-87, 135, 136; as Negro farmer's crop, 202-203. *See also* Agriculture.

Corner Farm, 186, 194.

Corner Store, 212, 213, 214.

Coromantines, 33.

Cotton, *See* Sea-island Cotton.

Cotton agents, 160-161, 163.

Cotton fund, 172, 175n.

Cotton Planter's Manual, 49.

Couper, Hamilton, 124.

Couper, James, 95.

Couper, James Hamilton, 40n, 96; as scientific farmer, 60-61; rotation of crops, 62-63; on crop of 1818, 65; on crop of 1819, 67; general manager of Hopeton, 75-76; attitude toward slave tradesmen, 80-81; on slave diseases, 94; on malaria, 95; grieves over slave's death, 95-96; estimate of profit on sea-island plantation, 101-102; description of hospitality, 120; experiment with slaves, 141. See also Hopeton Plantation.

Couper, John, 58, 60, 68. See also Cannon's Point Plantation.

Cowan, John, 104; takes out land on St. Helena, 11n; slaves in 1790, 38.

Cowpen, "running" a, 57.

Crofts, on St. Helena Island, 103.

Crops, staple, 17-30, 32, 48; experimentation with, 60-64. See also Corn, Indigo, Naval Stores, Rice, Sea-Island Cotton, Rotation of Crops, Agriculture.

Cuba, 157.

Customs, African, 132, 133. See Folkways.

Dancing, Negro, 143, 144, 145, 150, 151. See also "Shout."

Decoration Day, 213, 214.

Department of the South, 170. See also General W. T. Sherman, General Rufus Saxton, General David Hunter.

Dialect, Negro, 127-128, 215.

Dicks, Arthur, 11n.

Dicks, Daniel, 11n.

Direct Tax, acts, 183, 184, 189; South Carolina's quota, 183; Commissioners for South Carolina, 183, 185; Lincoln's instructions to Commissioners, 186-187; refunded, 189.

Discipline, plantation, by masters, 124-126; by Federal superintendents, 169, 176-177. See also Negroes, Slaves.

Dissenters, 117.

Dorcas Society, 122.

Dorchester, 15.

Drivers, the, 77, 126; on St. Helena Island plantations, 75, 78, 79, 190; use in "taming" new Negroes, 77-78; "wand of office," 78; duties, 78-79, 145; clothes, 88; house, 108; social class of, 130; continue work after capture of Port Royal, 158; assist superintendents, 168; Limus, 79, 179; exempt from military service, 170.

Du Pont, Captain, 154, 156, 194n.

Eddingses, settle on St. Helena Island, 103.

Eddings' Island, 154.

Eddings, Joseph D., 122.

Eddings' Point, 205.

Eddings' Point plantation, 89, 187n.

Edisto Island, 10, 29, 103; slave smuggling traditions, 35; farm implements used, 48; Whaley plantation on, 55-56; soil analysis, 59, 60; planter, 70; Whitemarsh B. Seabrook of, 73; slave rations, 85; slave quarters, 90; Prospect Hill plantation, 92, 109n; Negroes of, 128, 129; "Old Jeff" of, 134-135; North Edisto, 167.

Education, of whites, 112-115; of slaves, 152-153; of Negroes within Federal lines, 173, 180-181; school farms, 173, 182, 186, 210; Penn School, 181, 207, 211-212; public schools, 211. See Teachers, Federal School Fund.

Educational Commission, 165.

Elliott, General Stephen, 118.

Elliott, George P., 114.

Elliott, Mary B., cost of marketing cotton, 71; grades of cotton sold, 72; price per bale of cotton, 73; salary paid overseers, 76; employs slave tradesmen, 80; plantation medical bill, 93; pays slaves for blades, 141.

Elliott, Stephen, 115.

Elliott, William, on indigo culture, 21-22; first successful grower of sea-island cotton in S. C., 24, 71; suggests improving cotton seed, 25; on cotton culture in St. Helena's Parish, 27-28;

INDEX 233

on cultivation of sea-island cotton, 50-52, 72.
Elliott, William, Congressman, 38n; estimate of land prices in 1860, 44; obtains compensation act, 189; looks after needy Negroes, 202.
Elliott, William, of Columbia, S. C., 149n.
Emancipation Day, 213, 214.
Emancipation Proclamation, 173, 214.
England, 5, 8, 14, 107, 113, 124, 166n; merchants go to Carolina, 15; indigo exported to, 18-19; market for sea-island cotton, 25; factorage in, 68; Church of, 115. See Anglo-Spanish Contest.
English, the, 5, 12, 25. See also Anglo-Spanish Contest, England.
Euhaws, the, 117.
Eustis plantation, 39, 148.
Eutaw Springs, 26.
Evans, Randolph, 11n.
Expeditionary Corps, 156.

FACTOR, statements show planters bought provisions, 48; and the planter, 68-73 and n; after Civil War, 200-201.
Family, Negro, better satisfied when sold by families, 35-36; record of sale, 35n-36n; garden patch, 86; slave family life, 135-140; Negro families fed by army, 158, 167, 169; superintendents try to improve, 178, 179; family life of freedmen, 208. See also Marriage, Children.
Fantees, 33.
Farm implements, furnished by factor, 70; used by St. Helena planters, 48-50; supplied by Federal Government, 169, 172. See also Agriculture.
Federal Army, 78, 90, 104, 112, 137; quarter Negroes on St. Helena, 128; capture of Port Royal, 155, 156, 159; raids Combahee River, 158; and the sea-island Negroes, 157-158, 159; confiscates plantation food, 159, 169; area occupied, 183. See also Federal Government, Port Royal, General W. T. Sherman.
Federal Government, 107, 108, 127; agents, 159, 160; Pierce's plan for social experiment, 163-165; missionaries, 164; rations, 158, 167, 169, 198, 201; operation of plantations in 1863, 172; land sales, 183-190; refunds direct tax, 189; bounty for volunteers, 195; leases school farms, 174, 196; policy toward Negro, 175, 197, 199; sale of school farms, 173, 174, 182, 186, 188, 196. See also Federal Army, Treasury Department, United States.
Fendon tract, 187n.
Ferry Point, 155.
Fertilizers, use, 53, 54, 64; marsh mud as, 55-58; compost, 56-57; commercial, 59; slave tasks in preparing, 84.
Field Hands, 130, 149, 153n, 158. See also Slaves.
First Regiment of Rhode Island Artillery, 160.
Fishing, 142, 214. See also Recreation.
Florida, 6, 26; cultural development of Negroes, 128-129; land sales, 183; land set aside for Negroes, 188. See also La Florida.
Florida, La, 3.
Folkways, 215. See Slaves, Negroes, Praise House, Shout, Seeking, Churching, Recreation, Marriage, Family life, Singing, Dancing.
Ford, Timothy, on slave quarters at Beaufort, 88-89.
Fort Beauregard, 154.
Fort San Marcos, 6.
Fort Walker, 154.
Fourth of July, 213.
France, 15.
Franciscans, 6.
Franco-Spanish Contest, 5-6.
Freedman's Bureau, 194, 195, 199, 201.
Freedman's Bureau Act, 174, 188.
Freedman's Relief Association, 165.
Freedmen, land preëmption, 187; transition from slavery, 190; houses, 191, 195; dress, 192, 196; overrun Beau-

234 INDEX

fort, 193; prosperity, 195; characteristics, 196-197; freedom too easy? 196-200; crop failures, 200; as farmers, 202-204; as landowners, 190, 191, 195, 196, 198, 201, 202, 203-204; family life, 207-208; religion, 208-210; adhere to plantation traditions, 213, 215. *See also* Negroes, Citizenship, Social Experiment.

French, expedition to Florida, 3.

French, the, 4.

Fripp, Captain John, 41, 42, 43, 44n, 74, 104, 118, 155n, 194.

Fripp, cotton seed, 53-54; family settles on St. Helena Island, 103, 104.

Fripp, Dr. Clarence, 194.

Fripp, Edgar, plantation, 89; member Southern Rights Association, 122.

Fripp, Edgar W., 194, 195.

Fripp, F. O. P., 122.

Fripp, Hamilton, plantation, 187n.

Fripp, John, 38, 104.

Fripp, John, Big House plantation, 186.

Fripp, John E., routine of work on plantation, 47-48; equipment for plantation, 49; account with factor, 69n-70n; child-bearing record of slaves, 101.

Fripp, John M., 122.

Fripp, Oliver, plantation, 167n, 187n.

Fripp, Paul, 38.

Fripp, Thomas, 38.

Fripp, Thomas B., plantation, 167n, 187n.

Fripp, William, 38.

Fripp, William, Sr., 42, 104, 122; estate, 44; houses, 111.

Fripp's Point plantation, 186.

Frogmore plantation, 167n, 187n, 200, 212.

Fuller, Dr. Thomas, 44.

Fuller, Rev. Richard, plantation, 167n, 192n; preaches to freedmen, 192, 193.

Fullers, on St. Helena Island, 103.

Gaillard, Peter, 25.

Gambia Negroes, 33, 35.

Gannett, William C., 167n; on praise houses, 148; on Negro morals, 182; on St. Helena driver, 190.

Gardiner, Rev. John S. I., 116.

General Assembly, of South Carolina, 12, 13, 14, 113.

General Orders, No. 17, 165n.

Georgetown County, S. C., 106.

Georgetown, S. C. 81, 84, 94.

Georgia, 23, 24, 26, 45, 61, 62, 68, 93, 104, 128; Liberty County, 72-73, 147; Glynn County, 62n, 75; Butler's Island, 76; Argyle Island, 94; seacoast, 101, 124; cultural development of Negroes, 128-129; Sea Islands, 151; Negro land owners, 201. *See also* St. Simon's Island, Hopeton Plantation.

Germantown Freedmen's Relief Association, 210.

Gillisonville, 38n, 112.

Gin, for sea-island cotton, 28, 49-50.

Glasgow, 60.

Glen, Governor, 19, 22.

Glover, Thomas W., 22.

Glynn County, Ga., 62n, 75.

Gold Coast, 33.

Gordillo, Francisco, 5.

Government, *See* Federal Government.

Grahamville, 112.

Granville County, 12, 17.

Great Britain, 13, 14, 166; importation of indigo, 19; pays bounty on indigo, 19, 22, 23.

Greenwood plantation, 40-41, 201.

Gregorie, James, 53; slaveholdings, 40-41; planting after Civil War, 201.

Grimball, Paul, 10.

Guale, Spanish province, 12.

Guiney Negroes, 33, 35.

"Gun shoot," 151, 158, 179.

Guy, Rev. Mr., 115, 116.

Hall, Captain Basil, 82, 86, 90, 131, 138, 144.

Hamilton, James, 101.

Hamilton plantation, receipts and disbursements on, 102.

INDEX

Hampton County, 115n.
Hampton Institute, 212.
Hampton Roads, 157.
Hampton, Va., 163.
Hands, slave laborers, 83. *See* Field Hands.
Harbor River, 118.
Harper, Chancellor, on slave marriages, 134.
Harper's Monthly, 202.
Harvard, 113, 166, 167n.
Hawks, Dr. J. M., 213.
Heads of Families. *See* Land Sales.
Health, "sickly season" on Sea Islands, 74-75, 108; resort, 75; medical care of slave, 88, 91-96; Asiatic cholera, 91; children's diseases, 96, 98; care of *enceinte* slave women, 96-97; plantation nurses, 96-97; children's diet, 98; comparison of death rates of whites and Negroes, 99; births and deaths on Weehaw plantation, 100-101; child-bearing record of Fripp slaves, 101; Negro health practices, 178.
Hext, Edward, 11n.
Hext, Hugh, 11n.
Heyward, Thomas, 38.
Heyward, Thomas, Jr., 115.
Heywardsville, 112.
Hilton, Captain William, 7.
Hilton Head Island, 24, 154, 158, 170, 194.
Holidays, for slaves, 144-146; observed by St. Helena Island people, 213-214.
Holland, 61.
Hooper, Edward W., 167n.
Hope plantation, 130, 187n.
Hopeton plantation, 40n, 60, 142; model plantation, 61; rotation of crops, 62; plan of crop, 1827, 63; book, 62, 65, 67; general manager's salary, 75-76; mechanics on, 81; slave quarters, 90-91; hospital, 92; cholera among slaves, 94; description of hospitality, 120; treatment of slaves, 124; slave children, 139; praise meeting, 151. *See also* James Hamilton Couper.

House, Grace B., 207, 212.
House, plantation. *See* Big House.
House servants, 75, 79, 81, 82, 87, 120, 129, 130, 153n, 155, 204, 205.
Hunter, Major-General David, 170, 184, 185.
Hunting Island, 104, 118.

INDENTURED servants, 15.
Indian Hill plantation, 187n, 194, 213.
Indians, 6, 8, 9, 10. *See also* Pocotaligoes, Westoes, Yamasee War.
Indigo, culture, 17, 18-23, 30; competition with sea-island cotton, 25; influence of price on slave trade, 32; heaps, 59.
Infant Welfare, 96-101.
Intermittent fevers. *See* Malaria.
Ireland, 13, 14, 15.
Islanders, St. Helena, 35, 208. *See also* St. Helena Island, Slaves, Negroes, Freedmen.

JAMAICA, 17, 31.
Jasper County, 115n.
Jenkins, Daniel, 122.
Jenkins, Dr. William J., 39, 41, 49, 74, 118; plantation, 89, 108, 116, 167n; "big house," 108; library, 114.
Jenkins, John, 38.
Jenkins, William, 99.
Jenkinses, settle on St. Helena Island, 103.
Jervey, William, 35.
Jesuits, 6.
Johnson, Rev. Mr., 115.
Jones, Donald B., 21.
Jones, Rev. Charles C., *The Catechism for Colored Persons*, 147; on religious life of slave, 152.
Jones, Rev. Lewis, 112, 116.
Joyner, Captain John, 24.

KIAWAH, 8, 9. *See also* Ashley River.
Kimball, William, 11n.
King, James, 24.
King, R. Jr., 76-77, 79, 126. *See also* Butler Plantation.

LABORERS, Negro, 212; characteristics, 196-197, 199; for Federal Government, 168, 169; as free laborers, 199-200; in phosphate mines, 205; in oyster factories, 205; for white planters, 206. *See also* Social Experiment, Negroes, Slaves, Freedmen.

Ladies Island, 5, 35, 39, 108, 189, 208; Eustis plantation, 39, 148; Marion Chaplin plantations, 42; abandonment by planters, 156; Federal Army takes corn, 159; cotton crop of 1862, 168; land sales, 186; farms sold for state taxes, 203; oyster factories, 205.

Landowners, Negro, 190, 191, 195, 196, 198, 201, 202, 203-204. *See also* Land Sales.

Landholding, on Sea Islands, 45; on St. Helena Island, 42, 44; in St. Helena's Parish, 43. *See* Landowners, Negro.

Land Sales, under Direct Tax Act, 183-190; prices received, 185; to heads of families, 186-187; army and navy sales, 186.

Land's End, St. Helena Island, 108, 116.

Laurel Hill plantation, 105.

Laurens, Henry, 31, 32.

Leake, Richard, 24.

Legare, J. D., 61.

Leisure time. *See* Recreation.

Liberty County, Ga., planter of, 72-73; religious revival among Negroes, 147.

Libraries, 114.

Limus, a St. Helena Island driver, 79, 179.

Lincoln, President, 165; Emancipation Proclamation, 173, 214; instructions to tax commissioners, 186-187.

Lindo, Moses, 19.

"List," 146.

Listing, process in cultivating sea-island cotton, 83, 170. *See* Agriculture.

Little Edisto Island, 66, 91, 93, 132n, 135n.

Liverpool, 15, 25.

London, 15.

Lords Proprietors, of Carolina, 4, 5, 7, 8, 12, 31; charter to Carolina, 5, 8; expedition to Port Royal, 8; encourage wealthy to settle, 15; urge settlers to grow tropical and semi-tropical plants, 17.

Louisiana, 128.

Lowndes, Thomas, 13.

Lucas, Eliza, 18.

Lyell, Sir Charles, 36, 96; on Hopeton plantation, 61; on sea-coast storms, 68; visits Hopeton plantation, 80-81; on slave quarters, 90-91; on medical care of slaves, 92; description of Beaufort, 111; visits Sea Islands, 120; on treatment of coastal slaves, 125; on cultural development of sea-island Negroes, 127; sea-island Negroes good natured, 153; on slave children, 139; on praise meeting, 151.

MACDONALD, James Ross, 206.

McPhersonville, 112.

McTureous, plantation, 89, 187n; family settles on St. Helena Island, 103.

Mainland, 151, 152. *See also* Coast, South Carolina, Georgia.

Malaria, 74, 95, 167. *See also* Health.

Manigault, Louis, and overseer, 77; combats cholera among slaves, 94.

Manure. *See* Fertilizers.

Marriages, slave, 131-135; Pierce requires legal marriage, 178-179; Negro's fidelity to, 207-208. *See also* Family, Negro.

Marsh grass, cutting for fodder and fertilizer, 48; as fertilizer, 57-58; slave tasks in gathering, 84; freedmen's use of, 202; as fodder, 203.

Marsh mud, digging, 48, 84; as fertilizer, 55-58; freedmen's use of, 202.

Marshes, 4, 112; drained for cotton fields, 54-55; Negroes hide in, 171.

Massachusetts, 109, 112, 130, 148, 194n.

"Masse-Congo," country, 33.

INDEX 237

Masters. *See* Planters.
Maum, slave title, 97.
May River, 24.
Meade, Bishop, *Sermons, Dialogues, and Narratives for Servants,* 146.
Meggett, William, 11n.
Merchants, commission. *See* Factor.
Merchants, dealing in slave trade, 31-32.
Methodist Church, 117, 118, 147; preachers and missionaries, 150, 151.
Middleton, Henry A., Jr., house servants on Weehaw, 81; combats dysentery among Negroes, 94-95; Weehaw Plantation Book, 95; care of slave women, 96; rewards for infants, 97; births and deaths on Weehaw, 100-101. *See also,* Weehaw Plantation.
Mills, Robert, *Statistics of South Carolina,* 44, 54, 118.
Minutes of the Vestry of St. Helena's Parish, 108.
Missionaries, 6, 127, 128, 131, 134, 151; on treatment of slave children, 139; planters encourage, 146, 147; Baptist, 150; Methodist, 150, 151; Government, 164; teachers, 164; instruct Negro women, 177, 178; try to improve Negro family life, 178-179; northern, 128, 183, 189. *See also* Missions, Teachers.
Missionary Society of South Carolina Conference, 147.
Missions, 6, 147. *See also* Spain, Missionaries.
Mistress, plantation, 120-121.
Monogamy, 132.
Morals, slave, 131-132, 133, 135, 152; Gannett on Negro morals, 182-183; Ware on Negro morals, 196-197; during Reconstruction, 207-208.
Morgan Island, 186.
Morris Town, N. J., 88-89.
Morton, Governor Joseph, 10, 103.
Moultrie, General William, 24.
Mulberry Hill plantation, St. Helena Island, 186.
Mules, use on plantation, 48, 49; Federal Army confiscates, 159; Federal Government supplies, 169.
Murray, Amelia M., 61, 124.
Murray, Ellen, begins school at The Oaks, 181; assists Miss Towne with Penn School, 211, 212.

NAIRNE, Thomas, 10, 11.
Naval Stores, as sea-island product, 17-18, 30.
Negro cloth. *See* Slave Clothes.
Negroes, 64; sale in Charles Town, 32-33; favorite tribes of planters, 33, 35; seasoned, 33, 77-78; planters try to sell by families, 35-36; broke gins quickly, 49; new, 33, 77-78; the driver, 75; change of overseer demoralizes, 76-77; free, 80; keep cattle, 86; provide master with poultry and eggs, 86-87; medical care, 91-96; 167n; missionaries to, 109, 110, 146, 147; comparison of Piedmont with Coastal Negroes, 126, 127; cultural development of sea-island Negroes, 126-130; social classes, 130-131; singing and dancing, 143-144; church service, 143, 193; religion, 146-152; accused of looting after battle, 156-157; attitude toward Federal Army, 157-158; remain on plantations, 158; Combahee River, 158n-159n; and cotton agents, 160; discontented, 161, 163, 167; training for citizenship, 162, 175-183; citizenship, 165, 182, 196; laborers for Federal Government, 168, 169; wages, 169-170, 172, 200; conscripted, 170-171; experiment with, 162-175; discipline, 169, 176-177; marriages, 178-179; jealous of praise meetings, 180; Congressional provision for education, 182; friends want land for, 183-184; Philbrick sells land to, 186; land sales to, 186-187; Sherman reserves land for, 188; landowners, 190, 191, 203-204; planters sell land to, 195; freedom too easy? 196-200; as free laborers, 199-200; as farmers, 202-

203, 205, 206; characteristics of St. Helena people, 214-215. *See also* Slaves, Plantation Management, Freedmen, Laborers, Landholders, Social Experiment, Drivers.
Netherlands, the, 15.
Nevis, 8.
New Englander, 79.
New Orleans, slave market, 40.
New York, 161, 165.
New York City, 160, 166, 194.
New York World, 114.
"Nigger street," 190. *See* Quarters.
North, the, 87, 107, 110, 122, 130, 178, 197, 201, 202; planters spend summer in, 109; missionaries from, 128, 183, 189; plan for Port Royal Negroes, 162-163; enthusiastic over Pierce's "Report," 165; organizes relief societies, 166; wants land sales stopped, 183; Philbrick sells land to men from, 186.
Norton, John, 11n.
Norton, Sarah, 11n.
Nurse, plantation, 96-97, 120. *See also* Health.

OAKATEE Creek, 24, 49, 71.
Oak Point Mine, 205.
Oak Point plantation, 76.
Oakland plantation, 187n.
Oaks, plantation on St. Helena Island, description of house, 109, 110; Miss Murray opens school, 181; reserved for Negroes, 187n.
Orangeburg District, 21, 22.
Overseers, 74-77, 107, 130; Weston's rule for, 91-92; house for, 108, 109; on Butler plantation, 140; and patrol system, 145; lease school farms, 196. *See also* Plantation Management.
Owens, George C., 53.
Oxen, use on plantation, 48, 49; Federal Army confiscates, 159; use by Negro farmer, 203.
Oyster factories, 205.
Oyster shells, as fertilizer, 58, 59.

PALMER, James H., 167n.
Palmetto, 54.
Park, William E., 167n.
Parris Island, 5, 6n, 7.
"Patch," Negro, 86, 136, 168.
Patrol system, 145.
Peas, "shinney," 47; crop rotation with, 62.
Penn School on St. Helena Island, 181, 207, 211-212.
Penn Schools, 211.
Pennsylvania, 181, 211.
Pennsylvania Freedmen's Relief Association, 210.
Perry, Peter, 36.
Philadelphia, 100, 101-102, 110, 166, 181, 201, 204.
Philadelphia Society, 181. *See* Port Royal Relief Committee.
Philbrick, Edward S., 167n, 167-168; reports slave rations on Coffin plantation, 85-86; description of Beaufort houses, 112; on social classes among Negroes, 131; on family affection, 140; on treatment of Negroes, 169; proposes new plan for plantations, 172; on Negroes' capacity for citizenship, 182; continues social experiment, 185-186, 194n, 196, 197-199; sale of land to Negroes, 196; opposed to giving Negroes anything, 198; on Negro landownership, 203-204; employs teachers for Negroes, 211.
Phillips, Samuel D., 167n.
Phillips, Wendell, 167n.
Phosphate mines, 205.
Pierce, Edward L., special agent for Treasury Department, 38, 39, 106n, 160, 163, 169, 175, 178, 185; "Report to Secretary of Treasury," 39, 165; classification of slave laborers on St. Helena, 81; on St. Helena slave rations, 85; on St. Helena slave quarters, 89; on plantation houses, 108-109; on cultural development of sea-island Negroes, 127; estimate of number slave church-members, 148; on praise meetings, 149; reports army

INDEX

took corn, 159; plan for social experiment with Negroes, 163-165, 171, 182; arrives in Beaufort, 166; protests conscription of Negroes, 170; opens churches, 179; establishes schools, 180; "Second Report to the Secretary of the Treasury," 182. *See also* Social Experiment.

Pine Grove plantation, 109n; praise house, 148; sold for direct taxes, 186.

Pitch, as sea-island product, 17.

Plantation books, 48. *See* Hopeton Plantation, Weehaw Plantation.

Plantation management, 61; overseer, 74-77; organization of slave labor, 77-81; task system, 82-85; food issued slaves, 85-87; clothes issued slaves, 87-88; slave quarters, 88-91; average cost of slave maintenance, 88; medical care of slave, 91-96; care of slave infants, 96-101; plantation profits and losses, 101-102; "big house," 108-112; superintendents follow established system, 168. *See also* Planters; Planters, St. Helena Island; Superintendents of Plantations.

Plantation regime, 61. *See* Plantation Management.

Plantations, natural increase of slave stock, 34; planting routine, 48-50; farm implements, 48-50; equipment for, 49; superintendents assume charge, 168; system of superintendents, 164, 165, 167, 168; Negroes taken from, 170-171; General Saxton assumes charge, 171; plan of cultivation for 1863, 172-173; plan of cultivation for 1864, 173; Government abandons, 174, 182; sale of, 173, 182, 185; reserved for Negroes on St. Helena, 187n; Sherman reserves for Negroes, 188; Negroes adhere to plantation traditions, 213, 215. *See also* Plantation Management, Planters, St. Helena Island, Sea-Island Cotton.

Planters, coming to S. C., 31; and slave trade, 31-33; favorite African tribes, 33, 35; keep slaves at financial sacrifice, 35, 36; try to sell slaves by families, 35-36; number slaves required for large scale production, 37-38; slaveholding in Beaufort District, 36-38; James Gregorie's slave investment, 40-41; bought provisions, 48; favoritism in sale of cotton, 51; method of applying marsh mud, 55-56; and factors, 68-73; mismanagement, 74; and overseers, 74-75; organization of slave labor, 77-81; medical care of slave, 91-96; need of medical knowledge, 93; recreation, 118-123; duties of wife, 120-121; "promotes" dancing, 143; and patrol system, 145; after Civil War, 200, 201. *See also* Planters of St. Helena Island; Plantation Management, Sea-Island Cotton.

Planter's Guide and Family Book of Medicine, The, 93.

Planters, of St. Helena Island, bought slaves in Charleston, 34-35; desire large slave possessions, 35; number of slaves, 38-39; size of plantations, 41-45; number of, 41; plantations elsewhere, 42; comparison of landholdings with those in the parish, 42-43; farm implements used, 48-50; raise fine cotton seed, 53-54; and overseers, 75; tradesmen on plantations, 80; division of labor among slaves, 81; slave rations, 85; infant death rate, 98; spend winter months on plantations, 108; "big house," 109-110, 111; entertain in Charleston, 120; societies, 122; withdraw from Southern Right's Association, 123; required slaves to marry, 132; flight upon fall of Port Royal, 154, 155; missionaries occupy houses of, 167; few redeem plantations, 194-195. *See also* Thomas Aston Coffin, Dr. William J. Jenkins, Captain John Fripp, Marion T. Chaplin, St. Helena Island.

"Pleasuring," 145, 153, 213.

Plow, use of on plantation, 48, 49, 54.

Plowmen, 81, 83.

240 INDEX

Pocotaligo, Indian town of, 12.
Pocotaligoes, 11. *See* Indians.
Polygamy, 132, 133.
Pope, George, 38.
Pope, James A., 98.
Pope, Joseph J., 114, 122.
Pope, J. J. T., 122.
Popes, the, planters, 51, 52; cotton seed, 53; plantations, 109, 167n; on St. Helena Island, 103.
Port Royal, region, 5, 8, 10, 11, 14; Scots Colony, 9-10; growth of settlement, 13; capture by Federal Army, 114, 125, 159, 180; Civil War area, 156, 157, 160, 169, 175, 183, 194n, 195, 197.
Port Royal, battle, 151, 154-155, 156, 158, 162, 168.
Port Royal Island, 12, 76, 108; abandonment by planters, 156.
Port Royal Relief Committee, 166, 181.
Port Royal River, 11, 12, 17.
Port Royal Sound, 3, 154, 155.
Potatoes, sweet, yield, 46; planting, 47, 48; use of fertilizer for, 54; raised on Hopeton plantation, 62; as freedmen's crop, 202.
Poultry minder, 81.
Praise houses, 147-149, 150, 151, 193, 208, 209, 210.
Praise leaders, 209. *See* Religious Leaders.
Preachers, Negro, 208. *See* Religious Leaders.
Presbyterian Church, 117.
Presidio, 6, 215.
Prince William's Parish, 115n.
Princeton, 113, 115.
Pritchard, Frank, plantation, 187n.
Pritchard, Jane, plantation, 187n.
Pritchards, settle on St. Helena Island, 103.
Prospect Hill plantation, 92, 109n.
Protestant Episcopal Church, 117, 146.
Public schools, for Negroes, 211.
Pumpkins, crop rotation with, 62.

Quarters, slave, 88-91, 133, 145, 150.

Quexos, Pedro de, 3, 5.

Ramsay, David, 64.
Rations, 85-87, 133, 136; plantation, 85-87, 133, 136; government, 158, 167, 169, 198, 201.
Reconstruction, 202, 211n; Port Royal experiment foreshadows, 175; condition of St. Helena farmers during, 206; condition after, 208.
Recreation, among whites, 118-123; among slaves, 142-146; among freedmen, 212-215.
Red Cross, 207.
Reid, Whitelaw, 144.
Religion, among whites, 115-118; Negro church service, 143; among slaves, 146-152; class meeting, 151; during Federal occupation, 179-180; among freedmen, 208-210. *See also* Praise House, "Shout," Missionaries.
Religious leaders, slave, 81; social class, 130; perform marriages, 132; duties, 151-152.
Report on the Geology of South Carolina, 22.
"Rest." *See* Rotation of Crops.
Revolution, American, 14, 19, 21, 23.
Rewards, to slaves, 124, 141, 145.
Reynolds, Lieut. Col. William H., 160.
Ribaut, Jean, 3, 4, 5.
Rice, culture, 18; influence of price on slave trade, 32; sea-island planters buy, 46; planting on Bluff plantation, 47, 48.
Richmond, 146.
Rojas, Hernando Maurique de, 6.
Roper, R. W., 87, 88.
Rose, John, 24.
Rotation of crops, 53, 60-63, 64.
Ruffin, Edmund, 59n, 60.
Ruggles, T. Edwin, 167n.
Russell, William Howard, on Barnwell Island quarters, 90.
Rutledge, John, 38.

Sabbath schools, 153, 180.
"St. Helena," on "saltmarsh," 57-58.

INDEX

St. Helena Agricultural Society, 50n.
St. Helena Island, 3, 8, 10, 12, 24, 159, 169, 174, 197; first white settlement near, 6; description, 3-5; warrants for land on, 10-11; former homes of settlers, 15-16; occupation of settlers, 16; staple crops, 17-30; naval stores and provision crops, 17-18, 22-23; rice culture, 18; indigo culture, 18-23; introduction of sea-island cotton, 23-26; early method of cultivating sea-island cotton, 26-30; favorite Negroes of planters, 34-35; slave smuggling tradition, 35; slaveholding, 38-39; capture by Federal Army, 39; price of slaves, 40; size of plantations, 41-45; number of plantations, 41; number of landholders, 41-42; size of landholdings, 42; comparison of landholdings with those in the parish, 42-43; working size of plantation, 44; farm implements used, 48-50; gin used, 49; Agricultural Society, 50n; Coffin's Point plantation, 39, 52; cotton seed, 53; John E. Fripp of, 71; planters ship cotton, 71-72; overseer, 74-75; driver, 75, 78, 79; capture by Federal Army, 78; missionaries to, 79, 80; slave tradesmen, 80; plantation tasks, 84; slave quarters, 89; doctors, 94; allowance for infants, 97; infant death rate, 98; child-bearing period of slaves, 101; first planters, 103-104; Fripp family settles on, 104; social life of planters, 104-106; number of slaves, 106; number of white families, 106; social classes among whites, 107-108; "big house," 108-110, 111; and Beaufort, 114; Chapel of Ease, 116; religion, 116-118; recreation of planters, 118-123; treatment of slaves, 125; cultural development of slaves, 127-130; Federal occupation, 128, 137; mulattoes, 134; dominance of slave women, 137-138; treatment of children, 139; tidal creeks, 142; songs, 144; slave holidays, 144; "Brick Church," 117, 118, 144, 147, 180, 181, 192, 208; "praise house," 147-149; Pine Grove plantation, 148; number slave church members, 148; praise meeting, 148-149; "shout," 149-150; cabinet maker, 153; abandonment by planters, 156; Negroes remain on plantations, 158; superintendents of plantations, 167n; crops of 1862, 168; teachers, 177; refugees quartered on, 177; white churches opened for Negroes, 179; Whittier's song for, 180-181; plantations bought by Philbrick, 186; Negroes purchase land, 187; few plantations redeemed, 189, 194; in 1865, 191; plantations owned by northerners, 196, 200, 205; Negro farmers, 202-203, 204; farms sold for state taxes, 203; Negro landowners, 203-204; Negro migration, 204-205; oyster factories, 205; storm of 1893, 206-207; storm of 1911, 207; recreation of freedmen, 212-215; characteristics of freedmen, 214-215. See also Thomas Aston Coffin, Dr. William J. Jenkins, Captain John Fripp, Marion T. Chaplin, Superintendents of Plantations, Laura M. Towne, Edward L. Pierce, Sea-Island Cotton.

St. Helena Mounted Riflemen, 155n, 156n.

St. Helena, region, 5; birth of first white child, 11. See Santa Elena, Port Royal.

St. Helena Society, 113. See also Education.

St. Helena Sound, 14.

St. Helena's Parish, 24, 50, 57, 76, 115n; act establishing, 12, 115; population in 1730, 13-14; size in 1730, 14; type of settlers, 14-16; register, 15, 16, 117; method of sea-island cotton culture, 27-28; price of land, 44; poor whites, 107-108; education, 112-113; religion, 115-118; Southern Rights Association, 122; Congressional provision for education of Negroes, 182; land sales, 183; sale of

school farms, 188, 210; school fund, 210.
St. Helenaville, 110n, 110-111, 112, 177, 194.
St. John's, Colleton, Agricultural Society, 59, 60.
St. John's Parish, Berkley, 24, 25, 26.
St. John's Parish, Colleton, 25.
St. John's River, 188.
St. Kitts, 31.
St. Luke's Parish, 24, 115n, 182, 183, 210.
St. Paul's Parish, 24, 25.
St. Peter's Parish, 115n.
St. Simon's Island, John Couper of, 58, 60; storm of 1756, 68; taskable hands on plantation, 82; price of slave produce, 86-87; St. Claire house, 118; Butler plantation, 126, 140; cultural development of Negroes, 127, 128.
Salt-marsh. *See* marsh. mud, marsh grass.
San Augustín, 7, 10, 12.
San Felipe, 6.
Sanford, Robert, 4, 7, 8.
Santa Elena, cassique, 7; region, 5, 6, 7; Anglo-Spanish contest for, 7.
Santa Elena, Punta de, 3.
Santa Elena, River, 3.
Santee River, 26.
Savannah, 3, 68, 118, 142, 147, 200-201, 205.
Savannah River, 14.
Saxton, Brigadier-General Rufus, 171, 172, 173, 177, 184, 185, 187, 188, 194.
Sayle, William, 8.
School farms, 173, 174, 182, 186, 188, 196.
School fund, 210, 211. *See also* Education.
Scientific farming, beginning of, 53-64.
Scotland, 15, 60, 91.
Scots, 9; colony, 9-10.
Scotts, settle on St. Helena Island, 103.
Screven, John, 24.
Sea-island cotton, 215; introduction, 23-26; competition with indigo, 25; prices, 25, 26, 50, 51, 53, 72-73, 201; area of cultivation, 26; early method of cultivation, 26-30; gins, 28, 49-50; preparation for market, 28-30; cost of ginning a bale, 30; number of slaves for large scale production, 37-38; yield, 48; planting routine, 46-48; farm implements used in cultivation, 48-50; seed selection, 53-54, 202; plant of small fruitage, 54; use of virgin land for, 54; fertilization of fields, 55-59; crop rotation, 60-64; uncertain crop, 64-65; diseases of, 65; destruction by leaf worm, 66; influence of weather on, 67-68; reaches market later than short-staple cotton, 71; cost of marketing bale, 71; grades of, 72; unsuccessfulness of growing, 74; tasks in cultivation, 83; profits and losses in cultivating plantation, 101-102; grown during Federal occupation, 200; Negroes' crops, 200, 202. *See also* Plantation Management, Planters.
Sea Islands, 3, 35, 215; description, 3-5; land taken up, 10-11; settlement, 12; indigo culture, 18-23; introduction of sea-island cotton, 23-26; early method of cultivating sea-island cotton, 26-30; slaveholding, 45; landholdings, 45; agricultural system, 48; farm implements used on, 48-50; advice to planters on, 51; oysters on, 58; rotation of crops on, 60-64; storms on, 68; "sickly season," 74-75; profits and losses in planting, 101-102; social life of planters, 104; hunting clubs, 118; Sir Charles Lyell visits, 120; cultural development of Negroes, 126-130; visitors to, 139, 143; of Georgia, 151; capture of Port Royal, 154-155; Sherman reserves for Negroes, 188; Planters scattered, 189. *See also* St. Helena Island, Edisto Island, Ladies Island, St. Simon's Island, Port Royal Island.
Seabrook, Whitemarsh B., 29, 55, 62, 64, 73, 74.

INDEX

Seabrook, William, 25.
Seabrooks, the, planters, 51.
Seed selection, 53, 202.
"Seeking," 209.
Shepard, Professor Charles U., 58-59, 60.
Sherman, General W. T., 156, 161, 165n; plan for Port Royal Negroes, 162; Special Field Order No. 15, 188.
"Shout," the, 149-151.
Shropshire, Bridgenorth, 15; Ludlow, 15.
"Sick house," 92.
"Sickly season." *See* Health.
Singing, Negro, 143-144.
Sinkler, Captain James, 25.
Slave market, African, 30, 33; for St. Helena, 34-36; Virginia, 40; New Orleans, 40; Charleston, 34-35, 40.
Slave trade, African market, 30; African, 31-34 and n; pre-revolutionary trade, 31-34; price of slaves, 32-33; credit system, 32-33; internal, 34.
Slaveholding, in Beaufort District in 1790 and 1860, 36-38; on St. Helena Island, 38-39; on Sea Islands, 45.
Slaves, Negro, pre-revolutionary price of, 32; in 1859, 39-40; in Beaufort District, 40; on Greenwood plantation, 40-41; seasoned, 33 and n; favorite tribes of planters, 33; number in S. C. in 1706, 33; in 1708, 34n; number at close of colonial period, 34; natural increase, 34; large possessions desired, 35; planters try to sell by families, 35-36; record of sale, 35n-36n; disgrace to be sold, 36; number in Beaufort District, 36, 39; number on St. Helena Island, 38-39; owned by James Gregorie, 40-41; names of, 41, 137; "taming," 77-78; organization of labor, 77-81; taskable hands, 82; tasks in cultivating cotton, 83; tasks on Weehaw plantation, 84; food, 85-87, 135, 136; clothes, 87-88, 168; quarters, 88-91, 133; average cost of maintenance, 88; price of produce, 86-87, 140; medical care of, 91-96; infant welfare, 96-101; work required, 83; 124-125; treatment, 124-126; cultural development, 126-130; marriages, 131-135; family life, 135-140; dominance of women, 135-138; superannuated, 82, 84n, 135; children, 96-101, 137, 138-139; leisure time, 140-146; personal property, 140-142; presents to, 124, 141, 145; singing and dancing, 143-144; holidays, 144-146; missionaries to, 146, 147; religion, 146-152; education, 152-153. *See also* Plantation Management, St. Helena Island, Negroes.
Slaves, white indentured, 15.
Smalls, Robert, 205.
Smith, A. D., 183, 184.
Smith, Robert N., 167n.
Social classes, among whites, 106-108; among slaves, 130-131.
Social experiment, Sherman's plan, 162; Chase considers, 162-163; Pierce's proposal, 163-165; plan in operation, 166-175; training for citizenship, 175-183. *See also* Superintendents of Plantations, Citizenship, Edward L. Pierce.
Societies, among planters, 122; for relief of freedmen, 165-166, 181, 197.
Society for Propagation of Gospel, 116.
Soil analysis, 53, 60.
Songs, Negro, 193. *See also* Singing.
Soule, Richard, Sr., 167n.
South, the, 38, 106, 126, 175, 215; destruction of cotton crop of 1847, 66; coastal slaves of, 128, 129; Hall's tour of, 138.
South Carolina, 25, 27, 45, 64, 103, 104, 107, 122, 146; as a province, 12; indigo culture in, 18-19; inspector general of indigo, 19; introduction of sea-island cotton, 23-26; price of sea-island cotton, 25; sea-island cotton area, 26; early method of cultivating sea-island cotton, 26-30; planters coming to, 31; pre-revolutionary slave trade, 31-34; number slaves in 1706, 33; in 1708, 34n; number at close of colonial period, 34; closed African slave trade, 34n;

reopens African slave trade, 34n; seaboard, 61, 123; wage of day laborer in 1860, 88; Weston's rice plantation, 91; proportion of whites to blacks, 106; Piedmont Negroes, 126; planter gives slaves fiddles, 143; religious revival on coast, 147; Sherman's appeal for Negroes, 162; land sales, 183; freedmen, 187; Negro landowners, 201; phosphate mines, 205. *See also* Sea Islands, Plantation Management.

South Carolina Agricultural Society, 87.

South Carolina College, 113.

South Carolina Gazette, 32.

Southern Agriculturist, 21, 50, 57, 61, 74, 76, 93.

Southern Review, 115.

Southern Rights Association of St. Helena's Parish, 122.

Spalding, Thomas, 23.

Spain, 3, 5, 6, 9; frontier policy, 6; missions, 6.

Spaniards, 10. *See* Spain, Spanish.

Spanish, the, 4, 5, 6.

Special Field Order No. 15, 188.

Spiritual, a, 148, 150, 193.

Stanton, Secretary of War, 188.

Steuart. *See* Stewart.

Stevens, Hazard, 156, 157.

Stewart, John, 10, 11.

Stock minder, 81.

Storms, Sir Charles Lyell on, 68; of 1893, 206-207; of 1911, 207.

Stuart, Henry M., salaries paid overseers, 76; employs slave tradesmen, 80.

Stuart, John A., 115.

Stuart's Town, 9.

Sugar cane, raised on Hopeton plantation, 62.

Sugar Islands, 14, 23.

Sully, Thomas, 111.

Sumner, Arthur, on Negro dialect, 128; on leasing school farms, 174; on Government policy toward Negroes, 197-198.

Superintendents of plantations, 167, 173, 178, 190, 196, 213; system proposed, 164; system adopted, 165; superintendents on St. Helena Island, 167n; begin work, 168; want plan changed, 171-180; duties, 176-177; character of, 175; ministers among, 179-180; on result of the "experiment," 182-183; opposed to making concessions to Negroes, 198.

Superstitions, 152, 178. *See* Folkways.

Swamps, drained for cotton fields, 54-55, 61; planters avoid in summer, 112; Negroes hide in, 158.

Switzerland, 15.

"Swonga," 130.

TASK, system of slave labor, 82-85; hours of work required, 124; after completion, 140.

Taxes, 203. *See* Direct Tax.

Taylor, James E., 167n.

Teachers, for Port Royal Negroes, 164, 181; assist superintendents, 168; lease school farms, 173-174; character of, 175; work among Negroes within Federal line, 180; sent by benevolent societies, 164, 166, 181, 211. *See* Education, Rossa B. Cooley, Grace B. House, Ellen Murray, Arthur Sumner, Laura M. Towne, Harriet Ware.

Tennessee, 183.

Thorpe, David F., 167n.

Ticket, 145-146.

Towne, Laura M., 194, 200, 205; missionary to St. Helena Island, 80, 110; on slave quarters, 89; on treatment of slaves, 125; on class feeling among Negroes, 131; on dominance of slave women, 137-138; on discipline of slave children, 139; on singing and dancing, 143, 144; on praise house, 147; on the "shout," 150; on Will Capers, 151; on cotton agents, 160-161; on Negro health, 178; reaches Port Royal, 181; and land sales, 184; aids Negroes, 201, 207; sends Negroes North, 204; description of baptism, 209; on administration of justice, 210; and public

schools, 211; death, 212; on Negro parties, 212.
Towne, William Edward, 210.
Townsend, John F., 48; plantation, 56.
Tradesmen, as settlers of Carolina, 15; slaves, 79-81, 82; social class of, 107; description of slave carpenter, 130, 153; slaves hire own time, 130.
Treasury Department, United States, 160, 161, 166, 170; jurisdiction over Port Royal plantations, 161, 162; sends Pierce to Port Royal, 163; adopts plan of superintendents, 165; fund from sale of cotton, 166, 175n; equips plantations, 169; "experiment" transferred, 171.
Treaty of 1763, 5.
Trescot, house built by slaves, 80; plantation, 90.
Trescot, Mrs. 92.
Tuomey, M., *Geological Survey of South Carolina*, 56, 60.

UNITED States, 68, 82, 90; first bag sea-island cotton grown in, 23; census, 1790, 38; best plantation in, 61; bids in land, 173, 183, 185, 186. *See also* Federal Government.
United States Supreme Court, 189.
"Unjust law," 210.

VANDERHORSTS, planters, 51.
Village, the, 119.
Virginia, 212; slave market, 40; land sales in, 183.

WAKEFIELD, Dr. Adoniram Judson, 167n.
Wallace plantation, 187n.
Wallaces, settle on St. Helena Island, 103.
Wales, 15.
War Department, United States, 160, 165n, 171, 185.
Ware, Charles P., on McTureous plantation quarters, 89; description of slave carpenter, 130; on system of superintendents, 171; on Negro marriage, 178-179; freedom too easy for Negro, 196-197; on Negroes' crops, 200.
Ware, Harriet, description of Limus, 79; description of plantation houses, 109-110, 111; on Edisto Negroes, 129; description of a "shout," 149-150; on Negro honesty, 177.
Warrants, for land, 10-11.
Washington, D. C., 163.
Watchmen, 81, 130, 151.
Watt, John, 11n.
Weehaw plantation, house servants on, 81; tasks, 84; dysentery among slaves, 94-95; Plantation Book, 95, 100; children's allowance, 98; infant death rate, 98; births and deaths on, 100-101. *See also* Henry A. Middleton, Jr.
Wells, George M., 167n.
West, the, organizes relief societies, 166.
West Indies, 19.
Westoes, 8.
Weston, P. C. J., on care of slaves, 91-92; on slave holidays, 144-145.
Whaley, E. M., 91, 93.
Whaley, J. Swinton, 66, 132n, 133n.
Whaley plantation, 55.
Whites, settle on St. Helena Island, 103.
Whittier, John Greenleaf, 180.
Wilson, Samuel, 31.
Witch doctor, 130, 152.
Witsell, Frederick, 38.
Woman, dominance in slave life, 118-123, 208.
Woodstock plantation, 187n.
Woodward, Dr. Henry, 7.
Wording, W. E., 183.
Wylly, Captain Charles S., 118, 119, 120.

YALE, 60, 113, 115, 124, 166, 167n.
Yamasee War, 12-13.
Yamasees, 12, 13.
Yankees, 180.
Yeamans, Sir John, 15.

www.ingramcontent.com/pod-product-compliance
Lightning Source LLC
Chambersburg PA
CBHW021121300426
44113CB00006B/242